THE
BLOODIEST
BATTLES

THE
BLOODIEST
BATTLES

TRUE STORIES OF THE FIERCEST FIREFIGHTS FROM THE AFGHAN WAR

DANNY COLLINS

JOHN BLAKE

Published by John Blake Publishing Ltd,
3 Bramber Court, 2 Bramber Road,
London W14 9PB, England

www.johnblakepublishing.co.uk

First published in hardback in 2009

ISBN 978 1 84454 693 0

British Library Cataloguing-in-Publication Data:
A catalogue record for this book is available from the British Library.

Design by www.envydesign.co.uk

Printed in the UK by CPI William Clowes Beccles NR34 7TL

1 3 5 7 9 10 8 6 4 2

Papers used by John Blake Publishing are natural, recyclable products made from wood
grown in sustainable forests. The manufacturing processes conform to the environmental
regulations of the country of origin.

Every attempt has been made to contact the relevant copyright-holders, but some were
unobtainable. We would be grateful if the appropriate people could contact us.

THE SOLDIER'S OATH

*'I swear by Almighty God that I will be faithful and
bear true allegiance to Her Majesty Queen Elizabeth II, her heirs
and successors and that I will, as in duty bound, honestly and
faithfully defend Her Majesty, her heirs and successors, in person,
crown and dignity against all enemies and will observe and obey
all orders of Her Majesty, her heirs and successors and of
the generals and officers set over me.'*

Dedicated to the memory of my maternal grandfather, Francis James Hill (1878–1945), who, as a 14-year-old drummer boy, beat British troops to their battle stations in the foothills of the Hindu Kush.

And to the courageous men and women who continue to guard our frontiers and daily put their lives on the line that our society may flourish. A salute to them all.

In peace there's nothing so becomes a man
As modest stillness and humility:
But when the blast of war blows in our ears,
Then imitate the action of the tiger...'

William Shakespeare, *Henry V*, Act III sc I

'*Fire-fight* – *1a: a usually brief intense exchange of fire between opposing military units; 1b: a hostile confrontation that involves gunfire; 2a: skirmish.'*

Merriam-Webster's Dictionary (1899 edition)

'*The drums begin to roll, my boys, the drums begin to roll,*
O it's "Thin red line of 'eroes" when the drums begin to roll.'

Rudyard Kipling, *Tommy*

'*The NATO International Security Assistance Force (ISAF) – including the UK forces – is in Afghanistan at the invitation of the democratically elected Afghan Government and with UN authorisation, to provide the secure environment necessary for reconstruction and development to take place.'*

Ministry of Defence, London

LEST WE FORGET

I am immensely proud to have been asked to write a book which honours the British soldier and his and her involvement in the war now raging in Afghanistan. I believe it to be a just war but, as in all wars, there is a tragic price that has to be paid. British servicemen and women are dying in a country far from home to preserve the basic freedoms that are the foundation stones of our Western society, so sadly lacking the further east one goes from our shores.

As with my last book, which dealt with a tragedy enacted much nearer to home, it is not my intention to profit from the tragedy of others, and what can be more tragic than the loss of a young life full of promise in a body that is left bereft and brutally bleeding upon the battlefield? As a result, a percentage of the royalties from this book will be donated to the Army Benevolent Fund, which has been operating for over 60 years, working tirelessly to support serving soldiers, former soldiers,

and their families in times of need. The people supported include those with disabilities or mental illness, people experiencing homelessness or unemployment, and older people. After reading this book, you may wish to contact the charity and make a donation on: www.armybenfund.org

Danny Collins
Sierra de Aitana
Spain
2007

ACKNOWLEDGEMENTS

For their help in the preparation of this book, I wish to thank those men and women of the British Army who took the time to answer my questions and give their views on service in Afghanistan. That goes especially to those who recounted their experiences under fire. I appreciate how painful it must have been to dredge up suppressed emotions and not to pretend they didn't exist. I hope I have repaid that debt in part by not revealing certain technical and operational information I was asked to withhold for reasons of operational security (OPSEC) given that Afghanistan is a continuing war zone.

I would also, at this point, beg the indulgence of the reader in the occasional (if not ubiquitous) use of equipment and unit acronyms. Such is the language of the British Army and I have followed it where I must. A glossary is provided in the early pages to assist those who may find themselves at times bewildered by the soldier's love of the acronym.

My thanks go to my commissioning editor at John Blake Publishing, Wensley Clarkson, for believing in the project and to my editor, the aptly named John Wordsworth, for being so gracious and helpful throughout. To all the rest of the team at John Blake Publishing who answer my emails, send me money, and generally make my day, thank you all.

My gratitude must extend to the staff at the Ministry of Defence for their unstinting assistance in providing information on recruitment into the British Army, its training programmes and equipment and for its no-quibble sharing of information sought under the Freedom of Information Act. We should thank our lucky stars that we live in a country where this is possible. Much of the information on Operation Veritas, army service and pay, and technical descriptions of weapons and transport is produced here under a Crown Copyright Waiver relating to Public Sector Information.

And last but never least, my love and thanks to my wife Nikki for her encouragement, patience and belief in what I do, as well as for those long hours reading countless pages of manuscript and telling me where I'd gone wrong again.

CONTENTS

GLOSSARY

203	M16 rifle with 40mm grenade launcher attached
66	Lightweight throwaway anti-tank rocket
AAA	Anti-aircraft artillery, sometimes referred to as 'Triple A'
ANA	Afghan National Army
APC	Armoured personnel carrier
ARRC	Allied Rapid Reaction Corps
ATGM	Anti-tank guided missile
AR15	Armalite version of the M16
CAS	Close air support
Camo up	Use camouflage paint
CBRN	Chemical, biological, radiological and nuclear (defence)
CIA	Central Intelligence Agency (USA)
C2	Command and control
Claymore	Anti-personnel area protection mine

CPV	Command post vehicle
CTR	Close target reconnoitre
DF	To find the direction of (by radio beam)
DOP	Drop-off point
DPM	Disruptive pattern material (camouflage)
EXINT	Extraction or insertion of troops and equipment
FAC	Forward air controller
Fast air	A pseudonym for rapid air support brought onto target in an emergency
FIBUA	Fighting in built-up areas
FISH	Fighting in somebody else's house (other ranks' version of above).
FLET	Forward line of enemy troops
FOB	Forward operating base
GPMG	General-purpose 7.62mm machine gun
GRIT	Group range indication target
HE	High explosive
HEAT	High explosive anti-tank
HESCO	Form of fabricated barricade
HMG	Heavy machine gun
Humvee	High mobility multipurpose wheeled vehicle
IED	Improvised explosive device (e.g. roadside bomb)
IFOR	International Force (UN)
IFR	Infra-red
ITT	Invitation to tender for MoD contract
JDAM	Joint direct attack munition

GLOSSARY

Klick	Soldiers' slang for a kilometre
LAW	Light anti-tank weapon
LMG	Light machine gun
LSW	Light support weapon
LSV	Light strike vehicle
LUP	Lying-up point
MANPADS	Man-portable air-defence system
M16	US standard 5.56mm combat rifle
NATO	North Atlantic Treaty Organisation
NBC	Nuclear, biological, chemical (in reference to warfare)
NVA	Night viewing aid
NVG	Night-vision goggles
NCO	Non-commissioned officer
OC	Officer commanding
OP	Observation post
OPV	Observation post vehicle
OPSEC	Operational security
OPTAG	Operational training advisory group
OR	Other ranks (any soldier below NCO rank)
Pak	A member of the Taliban (soldiers' slang)
PRR	Personal role radio
PRT	Provincial reconstruction team
RV	Rendezvous point
Rupert	An officer
SAM	Surface-to-air missile
SAS	Special Air Service
SAW	Squad assault weapon

SBS	Special Boat Service
SF	Special Forces
SFOR	Suppression Force (UN)
SOG	Special operations group
SOP	Standard operating procedure
TAB	Tactical advance to battle
TAC	Tactical air support
Tango	An enemy soldier as a target
Tommy	A British soldier
UAV	Unmanned air vehicle (drone)
UF	United Front
Squaddy	Soldier (other ranks)
Stand to	Go to battle stations
Syrette	One-time-use injector containing morphine
X-ray	Terrorist

FOREWORD

Although it was the Roman legions that first brought the discipline of arms to Europe, the origin of the Army in Britain was the Saxon *fyrd*, the part-time assembly of soldiers of the 9th century who were taken from their occupations on farms and other livelihoods and assembled by the *shire reeve* for his king in times of war and invasion. In Britain as it then was – aside from the enclaves of Cornwall and Wales where the Celts had retreated from the Roman and later Anglo-Saxon onslaughts – the kings of a divided Britain ruled over the four kingdoms of East Anglia, Mercia, Northumbria and Wessex. Other than the Danes and Norsemen – aka the Vikings – and, to a lesser degree, the more trade-conscious Swedish, very few nations had the urge for overseas conquests of rape and plunder, so the *fyrds* tended to fight either on their own soil or in an adjoining shire. Their weapons were scythes, reaping hooks, three-pronged eel spears and sharpened hoes, although

there were those who took time to ape their more professional comrades at arms and fashion themselves a warlike weapon for attack and defence when the need arose.

Throughout the following centuries, the custom continued of the landed gentry providing men at arms in times of war and civil unrest and many of the aristocracy maintained their own core armies, the numbers of which would be boosted by estate workers, foresters, labourers, tenant farmers and their sons when the call to arms came.

The British Army as the basis of what exists today came into being with the unification of England and Scotland into the Kingdom of Great Britain in 1707. Existing regiments from either country were incorporated into the new British Army which was administered by the War Office in London. In 1963, the responsibility of administration was taken up by the Ministry of Defence. As of April 2007, the British Army included roughly 101,310 regular personnel and 38,460 Territorial Army members.

The full-time element of the British Army has also been referred to as the 'Regular Army' since the creation of the reservist 'Territorial Army' in 1908. The British Army is deployed in many of the world's war zones as part of both Expeditionary Forces and in United Nations Peacekeeping forces. The British Army is currently deployed in Kosovo, Cyprus, Germany, Iraq, Afghanistan and in clandestine operations in many other places.

In contrast to the Royal Navy, Royal Marines and Royal Air Force, the British Army does not include 'Royal' in its title,

although many of its constituent regiments and co...

styled 'Royal'. The professional head of the British Army at t...

time of writing is the Chief of the General Staff Sir Richard

Dannatt, who replaced General (now Brigadier) Sir Michael

Jackson in 2006.

At the beginning of the 18th century, the standing of the

British Army was reduced after the Treaty of Ryswick, and

stood at 7,000 troops at home and 14,000 based overseas, with

recruits ranging from 17 to 50 years of age. The Army was kept

small by the Government during peacetime, mainly due to the

fear that the Army would be unduly influenced by the Crown

or used to depose the Government. For much of the 18th

century, the Army was recruited from various sources, and

many of its soldiers were mercenaries from continental Europe

including Danes, Hessians and Hanoverians. These mercenaries

were hired out by other rulers on contracted terms; other

regiments were formed of volunteers such as French

Huguenots. By 1709, during the War of the Spanish

Succession, the British Army totalled 150,000; of these, 81,000

were foreign mercenaries.

The rest of the Army consisted of conscripts, mainly

recruited from the poorest sections of society. Each regiment

was responsible for the recruitment of troops, and individual

colonels would lead recruiting parties on a tour of the towns

and villages. Other measures were introduced by the

Government forcibly to enlist vagrants and vagabonds. Some

of these powers were abused by recruiting officers desperate to

fill their quotas, although a legalised Navy press-gang system

kidnapped in the street and taken

otice to serve aboard a Royal Naval

emented until later. Even so, normal

d to supply the required annual influx

was not a popular profession, with low

r barbarous disciplinary measures.

ing methods and treatment of its soldiers

would remain the same for the rest of the 18th century but, as the 19th century unfolded, the next century would see the birth of the Victorian British Empire and witness such epic events as Isandhlwana, Rorke's Drift, the Boxer Rising, the Charge of the Light Brigade and the Great Indian Mutiny. The British Army would emerge at its most glorious and would inspire an illustrious clique of English writers such as Alfred Lord Tennyson, Henry Wadsworth Longfellow and Rudyard Kipling to document its exploits. Kipling, especially, was aware of the rigours of fighting on the north-west frontier, and his epic poem *Tommy* contains a verse that sums up the horror that still exists in warfare against a fanatical and savage enemy that gives no quarter:

> '*When you're lying out wounded on Afghanistan's plains,*
> *And the women come out to cut off what remains.*
> *You roll to your rifle and blow out your brains*
> *and go to your God like a soldier.*'

For the title of his poem, Kipling used a long-established nickname for a British soldier – 'Tommy' – from 'Tommy

Atkins', which derives from a specimen Army form circulated by the Adjutant-General Sir Harry Calvert to all units in 1815 where the blanks had been filled in with the particulars of a Private Thomas Atkins, No. 6 Company, 23rd Regiment of Foot. Present-day members of the Parachute Brigade are often referred to as 'Toms' or just 'Tom', and all British soldiers are referred to as 'squaddies' by the British popular press and the general public. The British Army magazine *Soldier* has a regular cartoon strip, *Tom*, featuring the everyday life of a British soldier.

Junior officers in the Army, as a residual acknowledgement of their more regular recruitment from the upper-middle classes and aristocracy rather than up through the ranks, are generally known as 'Ruperts' by other ranks, possibly derived from the tendency of the upper classes to name their children from a particular list – possibly Hector or Peregrine might have done just as well – or from the children's comic book character Rupert Bear who still epitomises traditional public school values.

Mandatory conscription was first introduced in the United Kingdom in 1916, and was in operation from 1916 to 1918 and from 1939 to 1960. After 1948, it became known as National Service and, during the two World Wars, was usually known as War Service, though the act reintroducing it in 1939 was entitled the National Service (Armed Forces) Act.

Conscription was introduced by the United Kingdom Government in January 1916, during the First World War, when Prime Minister Herbert Henry Asquith introduced the Military Service Act. Previous to this Act, the British

Government had relied on voluntary registration called the Derby Scheme. The act of January 1916 specified that men from the ages of 18 to 41 were liable to be called up for service unless they were married, widowed with children, or else served in one of a number of reserved professions, usually industrial, but which also included clergymen and teachers. Conscription in the UK lasted until termination of hostilities.

In 1939, as a result of the deteriorating international situation brought about by Adolf Hitler's increasingly aggressive stance towards Poland, the Minister of War, Leslie Hore-Belisha, persuaded the cabinet of Neville Chamberlain to reintroduce mandatory conscription in a limited form on 7 April 1939, with the British Military Training Act being passed the following month. Only single men in a restricted age group were liable to be 'called up', and they were to be known as 'militiamen' to distinguish them from the regular Army. To emphasise this distinction, each man was issued with a civilian suit in addition to a uniform. The intention was for the first intake to undergo six months' basic training before being discharged into an active reserve, being recalled for short training periods and an annual camp. This was overtaken by the outbreak of war in September and the passing of the National Service (Armed Forces) Act, when the first intake was absorbed into the Army.

As the war continued, conscription was progressively extended to all able-bodied men although, in addition to those rejected for medical reasons, exceptions were made in some cases. Those engaged in vital industries or occupations were

'reserved' at a particular age, beyond which no one in that job would be enlisted. (Lighthouse-keepers were 'reserved' at the age of 18.)

Later in the war, some conscripts were directed into the coal industry, the so-called 'Bevin Boys'. Provision was made for those with moral scruples, and those who were prepared to help the war effort but were not prepared to bear arms were enlisted into non-combatant roles or units. Quakers, for example, often served in the Medical Corps. Those who refused to help the war effort in any form had to justify their position to a tribunal. These individuals were grouped under the category of 'conscientious objectors', and were ostracised by a public who failed to see the viewpoint of an individual who would refuse to go to war to protect his nation and, ultimately, his family at a time when young men were dying all over Europe. In fairness, in the more enlightened 21st century it is realised that not every man can adapt to killing a fellow human being but the argument still continues in some quarters. Does conscientious objection, as well as being morally valid, also present an unethical avoidance of war service? The panel is still out.

By 1942, all male and female British subjects between 18 and 51 who were resident in Great Britain were liable to call-up. Only a few categories were exempt, including British subjects from outside Great Britain and the Isle of Man who had lived in Britain for less than two years or were students; persons employed by the government of any country of the British Empire except the United Kingdom; clergy of any

denomination; mental patients and the mentally defective; blind persons; married women; women who had living with them one or more children under the age of 14 including their own children, legitimate or illegitimate, stepchildren and adopted children, as long as the child was adopted before 18 December 1941. Oddly enough, pregnant women were liable to be called up, although in practice they were not. Britain was the only country in the Second World War to conscript single women.

Those under 20 were initially not liable to be sent overseas, but this exemption had been lifted by 1942. People called up before they were 51, but who passed their 51st birthday during their service, were liable to serve until the end of the war. People who had retired, resigned or been dismissed from the forces before the war were liable to be called back if they were under 51.

Britain never officially demobilised, as conscription continued after the war. Those already in the forces still had to satisfy a National Service engagement but were given a release class determined by length of service and age. In practice, releases began in June 1945, and the last of the wartime conscripts had been released by 1949. However, urgently needed men, particularly those in the building trades, were released in 1945, although some restrictions on their immediate employment were supposed to be enforced. All women were released at the end of the war.

The system of wartime conscription between 1939 and 1948 was called National Service, but is usually referred to as 'war service' in official documents relating to national insurance and state pensions.

FOREWORD

After the Second World War, peacetime conscription was used between 1949 and 1960, through the National Service Act passed in 1948. In the United Kingdom, it is this peacetime conscription that is usually referred to as 'National Service'. It remains the only peacetime conscription in UK history, apart from periods immediately before and after the Second World War. National Service as peacetime conscription was formalised by the National Service Act 1948. From 1 January 1949, every healthy man between 17 and 21 was expected to serve in the armed forces for 18 months and remain on the reserve list for four years. Men were exempt from National Service if they worked in three essential services – coal mining, farming and the merchant navy.

In October 1950, in response to the Korean War, the service period was extended to two years, although the reserve list period was reduced by six months to compensate. National Servicemen who showed promise could be commissioned as officers. To fulfil the reserve list requirement, men in the National Service joined reserve forces like the Territorial Army. Thus, such forces expanded considerably between 1949 and 1963. Almost every town had units, and many had full regiments or battalions. National Service personnel were used in full military operations, including the UK's colonial operations in Kenya, Malaya and Cyprus, where many lost their lives.

National Service formally ended on 31 December 1960. The last man called up for National Service, Private Fred Turner of the Army Catering Corps, was discharged on 7 May 1963. However, the last National Serviceman was Lieutenant Richard

Vaughan of the Royal Army Pay Corps, who was discharged six days later on 13 May 1963. When National Service ended, many National Servicemen continued serving voluntarily. The British Army, Royal Air Force and Royal Navy are now – once again – voluntary organisations. Those bewailing the current state of youth crime and vandalism in Britain can often be heard to call for a return to compulsory conscription.

Man is a warlike creature and combat, whether the tooth and nail of the street brawler or the measured armed contact of the professional soldier, is a form of self-defence. The soldier under fire is predominantly concerned with holding his line and defeating the enemy, but the underlying urge is self-preservation. Yet the idea that a human being could selflessly offer his or her life for sacrifice is a thing of credible legend. The Roman historian Titus Livius tells the story of the one-eyed Captain of Foot Caius Horatius Cocles and his gallant stand at Rome's Pons Sublicius bridge in 507bc with his comrades at arms Sporius Laritus and Julius Herminius holding back Lars Porsena's Etruscan horde of 50,000.

In 1879 – 1,300 years later – London would welcome home the heroes of Rorke's Drift, where 150 men of the 2nd Battalion, 24th (2nd Warwickshire) Regiment of Foot won seven VCs defending a supply station against an estimated 4,000 Zulu *impis* fresh from the victory at Isandhlwana, with four other awards of this highest medal for gallantry in the field going to serving members of the Army Medical Department, the Commisariat, the Native Natal Contingent and the Royal Engineers.

FOREWORD

Seventy-two years on, Britain would ring to the tale of the Glorious Gloucesters and their stubborn defence of Hill 235 at the Imjin River in late April 1951 until overrun by Chinese and North Korean forces.

That the hearts of English, Irish, Scots and Welshmen can rise to the demands of battle is without doubt – we have only to recall Churchill's Second World War exhortation to the people: 'If you're going through Hell, keep going', but what drives these extraordinary men and women who, on impulse, so readily 'imitate the visage of the tiger'? What is it that so invades their bodies and minds that the adrenalin surge will carry them beyond the pain of dreadful injury and imminent death to stand, bloodied and resolute, among their fallen comrades and fight on when the cause appears to be lost? In other words, what makes a hero? Are heroes born or do circumstances dictate?

Certainly, in the case of awards for bravery under fire, circumstances will dictate who gets the gong, for the heroic action must be witnessed and the recommendation made by an officer. 'Can't have other ranks dishing them out, be Gawd, or they'll all have one,' as the Duke of Wellington once famously, or perhaps infamously, said.

Equally, excluding cases in which the Victoria Cross was judged as merited, actions involving officers and other ranks will see the higher awards going to the officer class. But the purpose of this book is not primarily to list medals and awards but to record the lot of the fighting man and woman under fire in a modern-day theatre of war.

Afghanistan, the continuing fiefdom of Bin Laden, is undergoing an escalation of war not seen since the 1940s. The conflict began on 7 October 2001, when the United States, in alliance with the United Kingdom, launched Operation Enduring Freedom, the first decisive step in the George W Bush administration's promised 'war on terrorism' in answer to al-Qaeda's attack on the World Trade Center in New York on 11 September 2001 – an infamous assault by the organisation led by Osama bin Laden that claimed over 3,000 lives. The stated aims of the invasion by US and UK forces were to capture Osama bin Laden, who was enjoying the hospitality and protection of Afghanistan's Taliban-led Government, to destroy al-Qaeda, and to remove the Taliban regime as a supporter of terrorism against the West. It was no secret that bin Laden, a devout Islamist totally opposed to Western culture, had been living in Afghanistan and financing the operation of terrorist training camps condoned by the Taliban since the spring of 1996.

In 1999, the UN Security Council had issued Resolutions 1267 and 1333 in the wake of the 1998 US embassy bombings in Africa. The resolutions implemented financial and arms sanctions, including any machinery of war, against the Taliban to encourage the handing over of bin Laden and the closure of terrorist training camps. The strategy was unsuccessful.

In its first days, Operation Enduring Freedom swept all before it. Within a few days of the opening of the offensive, an aerial bombing campaign had caused massive infrastructural damage in Kabul and the military nerve centre of Kandahar,

and had laid waste many of the terrorist training camps surrounding the city of Jalalabad. This was followed by the deployment of American, British and Canadian ground troops supporting troops of the Afghan Northern Alliance, the ANA.

The initial attacks saw the Taliban reeling from power but the restriction of al-Qaeda has been much more difficult to achieve and has led to a renewal of Taliban strength as some Middle Eastern and Western Muslims have seen the war as an attack on Islam and have launched *jihad* in answer. No one in the West, so it seemed, had taken into account the waking of a sleeping tiger that an assault on an Islamic nation would cause among those still smarting at the old memories of the Crusaders and the Knights Templar of Jerusalem.

The remaining members of the Taliban Government and its troops began to regain confidence and, in the autumn of 2002, began preparations to launch a holy war fuelled by insurgents as had been promised by their leader, the Mullah Mohammed Omar, during the days before the collapse of the Government in the face of the US-led invasion. Driven from the north, the remnants of the Taliban established training camps in the south-east of the country. Al-Qaeda and Taliban instructors began forming fighting units out of the new recruits to *jihad* drawn from the *madrassas*, the religious schools of Pakistan from which the Taliban had emerged. These insurgents were the descendants of fierce tribal warriors against whom the professional soldiers of the West would test their military skills. British troops with an average age of 19, led by hard-bitten professional soldiers and career officers, would take part in

some of the fiercest fighting ever seen in modern combat. This is the story of just some of them, of the young men and women who make the world a safer place for us to go about our daily lives. This is the story of life on the front line.

Afghanistan is not new to conflict involving British troops. The gaudily dressed companies of artillery, infantry and the kilted highland regiments of Queen Victoria fought in the mountain passes surrounding Kabul in the middle and latter years of the 19th century. Lancers who would later charge the Russian guns at Balaklava rode into Kunduz years before the American Civil War saw the first cannon fired in Charleston Harbour and almost 50 years before the head of General George Gordon was paraded through the streets of Khartum by the forces of the Mahdi Mohamed Ahmed.

The early Afghan wars – there would be two before the 20th century dawned – were part of 'The Great Game', the 19th century battle for territory and influence between Great Britain and Imperial Russia. The first, 1838–42, under the unsteady hand of Lord Auckland in support of the dethroned Shah Shuja, was a disaster. The second, from 1843 to 1880, was an attempt to form a buffer state between Britain's interests in Europe and the territorially acquisitive Russia of Czar Nicholas II that ended in the Congress of Berlin. An uneasy peace then existed between the Bear of the North and the British Lion, until the traumas of cousinly rivalry were shattered by the Russian Revolution of 1917. Two years later, Amanullah Khan, a skilled and intelligent leader who had inherited the shaky throne of Afghanistan after the

assassination of his father Habibullah in 1919, had had enough
of the pair of them and declared full independence.

After several skirmishes with the newly independent forces,
a vengeful Britain – still at its military height of power despite
the losses of a generation on the fields of Belgium and France
– dictated the terms of the 1919 Rawalpindi Agreement, a
temporary armistice that grudgingly allowed for Afghan's self-
determination in foreign affairs. With not much to choose
between the two major powers, Afghanistan offered a cautious
handshake to the newly formed Soviet Union and went on to
form diplomatic relations with most major countries during
the 1920s.

Thus, even ignoring the in-house clashes of the Pashtun
tribes until unification under Afghanistan's founder Ahmad
Shah Durrani in 1747, the land of terrible beauty that is
Afghanistan has known war for centuries and has bred fierce
and unrelenting warriors as a result.

As a warrior state in which more than 35 languages are
spoken among a population half that of the UK, a system of
tribal rule and fiefdoms existed until a brief experiment in
democracy ended in a 1973 coup and a 1978 Communist
counter-coup. The Soviet Union, under the tired old pretence
of supporting an elected Government of the people – in this case
the tottering, war-beset Afghan Communist regime – invaded in
1979 and found its forces engaged in a bloody war of attrition
with the internationally supported *mujahedin* rebels until its
bloody-nosed withdrawal by Gorbachev in 1989. A succession
of civil wars among tribal factions saw Kabul finally fall in 1996

to the Pakistan-sponsored Taliban – who, despite the observer aid and weapons supplied by the Western allies during its fledgling incarnation in the war against the Russian invaders, would turn from a good servant to a bad master, eventually accused of supporting fundamentalist terrorism against the West.

This uneasy frontier watch came to an abrupt end on 11 September 2001 when terrorist attacks in New York City brought down the 110 floors of the World Trade Center's twin towers, killing more than 3,000. The result was the formation of the ongoing US, Allied, and anti-Taliban Northern Alliance military action to topple the Taliban on suspicion of sheltering the West's arch enemy, Osama Bin Laden, chief suspect in the New York bombing.

Despite the adoption of a new constitution and a presidential election in 2004 that saw Hamid Karzai become the first-ever democratically elected president of Afghanistan, that war – fuelled by the recruitment of foreign insurgents from surrounding Islamic states and home-grown Muslim sympathisers from Britain and the USA – continues.

During the early stages of the current war, the USA had national command of foreign forces in Afghanistan under the denominated Operation Enduring Freedom (OEF). This control was assumed by NATO with the creation of the International Security Assistance Force (ISAF), which now controls all combat and reconstruction operations by the provincial reconstruction teams.

The United States keeps its hand in through the ongoing command structure of Operation Enduring Freedom, through

which it controls some other coalition members, reporting through the NATO chain of command that took formal responsibility for the whole of Afghanistan in 2006.

British, Canadian and Dutch contingents in the south of the country are NATO ISAF forces, although some coalition units, such as ground-attack aircraft, support OEF as well as ISAF and the provisional reconstruction teams.

Most of the UK forces in Afghanistan are deployed in Helmand Province in the south of the country, an area of some of the fiercest fighting, but UK personnel are also deployed in support of both ISAF and OEF headquarters in the capital, Kabul. The Royal Air Force Joint Force Harrier detachment based at Kandahar provided close air support and reconnaissance to coalition and NATO forces operating in the south of the country before handing this responsibility over to the Fleet Air Arm's Harrier GR7 squadrons in October 2006. Deployments are constantly shifting with troop rotations, for reasons of operational security some information on troop movements are categorised as classified by the Ministry of Defence and cannot be reproduced here.

Following deployments in Helmand Province by 16 Air Assault Brigade and 3 Commando Brigade in mid-2007, UK forces in Afghanistan were drawn mainly from 12 Mechanised Brigade. In addition, following the UK handover of command of the ISAF in February 2007, some 150 personnel remain deployed with the ISAF Headquarters in Kabul. This meant that towards late summer 2007, the number of UK personnel in southern Afghanistan settled at around 5,800.

The UK MoD has also decided to maintain until April 2009 some capabilities already deployed in Afghanistan, including the Harrier GR7/GR9s, the Apache attack helicopters, Viking all-terrain vehicles, and Royal Engineers to support reconstruction activities. The principal units deployed under Operation Herrick in mid-2007 were:

HQ 12 Mechanised Brigade

Brigade Headquarters and Signal Squadron

The Light Dragoons

1st Battalion The Grenadier Guards

1st Battalion The Royal Anglian Regiment

1st Battalion The Worcestershire and Sherwood Foresters

26 Engineer Regiment Royal Engineers

19 Regiment Royal Artillery

2 Signal Regiment

4 Logistic Support Regiment

4 General Support Medical Regiment

Elements of other units were also deployed to provide niche capabilities. These included:

Armoured Support Group of the Royal Marines

2nd Royal Tank Regiment

3 Regiment, Army Air Corps

9 Regiment, Army Air Corps

RAF support is provided by:

1 (Fighter), IV (Army Co-Operation) Squadron

Elements of 18, 24, 27, 30, 47 and 70 Squadrons

Elements of 3, 5 and 7 Force Protection Wing
Headquarters
Elements of 2, 51 and 15 Squadrons of the Royal Air
Force Regiment

As with previous deployments to operational areas, there is a requirement to deploy reservists to Afghanistan. Early 2007 plans suggested that approximately 420 reservists would be required to support 12 Mechanised Brigade.

The ISAF is mandated under Chapter VII of the United Nations Charter (Peace Enforcing) by a number of UN Security Resolutions that carry the insistence that the ISAF exists to help the Afghan people, not to govern them. Additionally, under the UN mandate, the role of the ISAF is to assist in the maintenance of security to help the Islamic Republic of Afghanistan and the UN in those areas for which it is responsible. NATO assumed command and control of the ISAF mission on 11 August 2003. More than 35,000 troops make up the ISAF, with contributions from 37 nations with national contingent strengths changing on a regular basis.

With the uneasy realisation that the United States' headstrong invasion of Afghanistan that began on 7 October 2001 had awakened a slumbering tiger, Western Governments realised that a major war against fundamentalist world terrorism had begun. There were no sidelines. The USA was determined to crush terrorism at its source, within the fundamentalist communities of Africa and Asia. Afghanistan's crime was the suspicion that it harboured the West's arch

terrorist bogey man Osama bin Laden, suspected of having being the architect of the 9/11 atrocities.

The Saudi-born militant Islamist, reported to be the founder of the terrorist organisation al-Qaeda, is as picturesque a villain as ever to be seen playing the evil Grand Vizier in a pantomime at the Hackney Empire. The only problem here is that, in the real world production, there has been no happy ending and the curtain is still poised in the flies.

Osama bin Mohammed bin Awad bin Laden, to give him his full title, was born in Riyadh, Saudi Arabia on 10 March 1957 into a wealthy and prestigious Arab family. His father, Mohammed Awad, had close ties to the Saudi royal family, for whom he worked as a building contractor. But laying bricks held no attraction for his seventeenth son, Osama.

Soon after Osama's birth, his father divorced his mother, Hamida Alia Ghanem, by the simple process of renouncing her three times in public. Hamida soon remarried, choosing a former employee of her ex-husband's company to become stepfather to her son. The early family life of the young Osama, who was raised as a devout Sunni Muslim, was shared with three stepbrothers and a stepsister.

From the age of 9 until 20, Osama was educated into Muslim lore and religion at the élite, secular Al-Thager Model School, absorbing the writings of Sayyid Qutb, one of the most influential Islamic writers, whose tracts urge *jihad* against all that is un-Islamic in the world.

Mohammed Qutb, brother of the late Sayyid, was a regular lecturer at King Abdulaziz University in Jeddah, bin Laden's

next rung on the educational ladder, where he studied business administration and economics, falling under the revolutionary spell of Qutb and another charismatic Muslim brotherhood member, Abdallah Azzam. A Palestinian, Azzam was instrumental in building international Islamic support for *jihad* against the Soviets in Afghanistan and of recruiting zealous Middle Eastern Muslims like bin Laden to join the faithful in battle against the barbaric infidel hordes supporting the beleaguered and unpopular puppet Government of the so-called Democratic Republic in Kabul.

The Soviet invasion of Afghanistan took place in 1979, and bin Laden left college to join Azzam in the battle. It was in Afghanistan, fighting among the ranks of the *mujahedin*, that he and his group of warriors came together under the banner of al-Qaeda – which means 'the base' in Arabic. This new guerrilla force was financed by America's CIA under its Operation Cyclone programme, which aimed to support the Afghan 'freedom fighters' against the Soviet arch-enemy, aid that was later to be condemned by Robin Cook, former leader of the House of Commons and British Foreign Secretary from 1997 to 2001, as causing bin Laden to become 'a product of a monumental miscalculation by Western society agencies'. In Cook's opinion and that of many senior statesmen throughout the Western world, the *mujahedin* who were later to form the ranks of al-Qaeda were originally recruited and trained with the help of the CIA, although bin Laden's personal wealth and connections made a healthy contribution towards recruiting and arming the *mujahedin* who took on the Soviet Union during its occupation.

Whoever had been the paymaster, by 1988 bin Laden had fallen out with Azzam and had formed his own military wing of fierce *mujahedin* guerrillas led by carefully selected Arab field commanders, a force that was to win him acclaim as it took on and beat the Soviets in what Konstantin Chernenko's successor Gorbachev saw as a no-win situation that could only be saved by an orderly retreat or, as some Soviet apologists of that era insist, a tactical advance on a 180 degree axis.

With the departure of Soviet forces, bin Laden was able to move freely around the Middle East and decided to return to Saudi Arabia, where he offered Prince Sultan, the Minister of Defence, '10,000 fighters with good combat capability ready within three months' to defend Saudi interests in the region. Muslims could defend Muslim territory, he added, there was no need for Americans in the lands of the Prophet.

Bin Laden was rebuffed and angrily denounced Saudi Arabia's dependence on the US military, demanding an end to what he saw as 'an occupation' by infidel forces of the same peninsula as the holy cities of Mecca and Medina. More ominously, it was noted that foreign troop bases remained on the peninsula when the Gulf War had ended.

Unpopular with the authorities in his own country due to his harsh criticism of the regime's apparent alliance with the Great Satan, bin Laden left the country for Peshawar in 1992 to join in the Afghan Civil War, now raging in the wake of the Russian withdrawal as war lords and tribal chiefs battled for influence. From Sudan, he continued his verbal assault on Saudi King Fahd, who retaliated by revoking his citizenship

and removing his passport. Bin Laden's family were also persuaded to cut off his annual stipend, paid monthly, of around $7 million a year. Not the happiest of exiles, bin Laden associated himself with the Islamic Jihad (EIJ) against President Hosni Mubarak but a failed assassination attempt on Mubarak led to the expulsion of the EIJ from Sudan and bin Laden himself being shown the door.

His next land of refuge would be Afghanistan, where he joined Abdul Rasul Sayyaf, a member of the Afghan Northern Alliance and brother of the writer whose texts had so influenced the young bin Laden. He also forged firm alliances with some of Afghanistan's new leaders, the Taliban, whose Pakistan-backed forces were installing the Sharia Islamic values so dear to his heart, as they removed the old guard that had fought the Soviet forces so fiercely. In 1997, now supporting the Taliban regime with both paramilitary aid and hard cash, he moved to Kandahar, the Taliban stronghold. He was just four years away from the fall of the twin towers of the World Trade Center in New York and a new world order in the Middle East that would bring total, bloody war to his adopted country.

PROLOGUE

I – OPERATION DRAWN CLAW

Their belt kits and equipment had been muffled with strips of
material long before their incursion across the border into Iran
from Afghanistan. The valley formed a perfect route of entry
for the Iranian Revolutionary Guard Al-Quds squads
protecting the mixture of Iranian and Shi'ite militiamen
smuggling arms and fighters to the Taliban forces in-country.

The UK Special Forces team took up positions among the
rock- and boulder-strewn hillsides, and proceeded to mark out
fields of fire with line sticks, small insignificant markers that
would go unnoticed to opposition scouts but would warn the
support gunners on the .50 calibre Brownings or the 7.62
GPMGs not to encroach on a friendly forward position.

The men checked their weapons and magazines once more,
the magazines stowed in the webbing ammunition pouches
with the leading edge most easily accessible to their fingers for
quick extraction once the fire-fight erupted. There was no

manual-enforced rule of carrying kit, for these men were independent of the petty rules of warfare. In contacts with the enemy, each four-man patrol had its contact fire drills learned by long practice together in the field but, when it came to individual contact, each was his own man.

These men huddled against the cover of the hillside were members of the 22 SAS Regiment, known in British Army parlance as The Pilgrims after the extract from James Elroy Flecker's *Golden Journey to Samarkand*, which has become synonymous with the regiment since it was chosen to be inscribed on the base of the SAS memorial clock which stands in the regiment's new barracks at Credenhill, Herefordshire. The mission was to disrupt the supplies of arms and foreign volunteer insurgents crossing the border from Iran to support the guerrilla army of the Taliban.

The men watching for movement on the dark mountainside had been flown in from their Iraqi base in Basra. As much as the American commanders would have wished it, the regular 22 SAS seldom operate in Afghanistan, where Special Forces operations are more often left to the Parachute Regiment and the Special Boat Service.

Wireless earpieces crackled, weapons were already locked and loaded, for the sliding bolt of an American-built M16 rifle penetrates far in crisp night air. The waiting force did not carry the UK's newly issued SA80-A2 individual weapon, a modification of the ill-fated SA-80 that had become anathema to Special Forces operatives and serving soldiers in the field because of its capacity to jam in wet or dusty conditions and

its refusal to fire all but high-quality ammunition. Instead, men of the SAS favour the American M16, once christened the 'Jamming Jenny' because of its stoppages due to abuse by undertrained young conscripts in Vietnam, but restored to respect by careful maintenance which gave long and faithful service to its handler under battlefield conditions. Another advantage of the M16 assault rifle was its conversion to heavy firepower by the addition of the M203 40mm grenade-launcher slung under the barrel.

Finally, the word came: 'Tangos approaching from the east... Weapons free in five.' Each man mentally prepared for battle in his own way; some said a silent prayer and, perhaps for the less theologically minded, an unspoken invocation to their own private devils. A flare burst above the gunrunners' straggling column. A GPMG opened up from its position far up the hillside, a mule screamed, a man shouted, his words lost in the confusion of battle. A patrol leader of the SAS rose to one knee and sent a burst of rounds into a cluster of insurgent militiamen running towards his position in their haste to find cover. Others not immediately felled in the firestorm of lead and tracer flung themselves into cover or turned to race for the rear of the column as hissing rounds sent rock splintered by howling ricochets to tear at their heavy winter clothing. A sustained burst from a .50 calibre Browning machine gun picked up a fleeing militiaman and threw his corpse forward in accelerated flight amid a haze of blood and bone.

The firefight grew in howling fury as the insurgents fought back for their lives. These battle-hardened hill fighters had

well-equipped Iranian special forces in support and they knew no quarter would be given. A rocket-propelled grenade-launcher wrenched from its smashed box on the back of a dead mule sent a streak of smoke and a flash of intense green light across the lenses of the night-vision goggles now worn by some of the attacking SAS force. Some more independent souls preferred their own night vision to suffice rather than the sear of the NVGs caused by the exploding phosphorous grenades hurled by the enemy. The attacking British force, throats smarting from the intrusive bite of cordite, heightened their rate of fire until the entire hillside was alight with the glow of tracer rounds that ricocheted off the boulders with an echoing whine, flying skywards as fingers of light, and showering those taking cover with whirling rock shards that tore at exposed flesh.

The gunrunners began to fall back and seek the shelter of darkness, hoping to desert their besieged weapons train for an escape into the darkness of the surrounding hills, but the SAS were conducting no blocking operation but a war of attrition. They knew that those who escaped death tonight would be back within a week, hauling their complaining pack mules across the border, loaded once more with arms to supply the Taliban and its foreign insurgent fighters. A prearranged green flare rose high in the air and the forward SAS section began to force the gunrunners back into a previously designated killing zone. The Taliban fighters, who in any one crossing could include men from countries such as Pakistan, Chechnya, and even militant Muslims from the states of Europe, fought back for

their lives with a tremendous surge of fire but inexorably they were forced into the narrow wadi of the killing ground. Rounds from the unforgiving .50 calibre Browning machine guns and the high-cyclic-rate GPMGs tore into flesh, the heavy .50 calibre slugs capable of decapitation or the removal of a limb and leaving their victims to die in a welter of arterial blood.

Slowly, the surviving pockets of insurgents who had been unable to retreat into the hillsides were picked off and firing came to an end as the SAS troopers cautiously emerged from cover to move among the dead and dying. A mobile fighting force operating behind the lines in potentially dangerous territory has no facility for taking prisoners. The captured weapons considered of no use to the victorious troops or whose weight would delay a speedy withdrawal were heaped together and destroyed by explosive charges.

The patrol counted the dead, reported to base by radio and withdrew across the border into Afghanistan to a prearranged LZ where an RAF Chinook would ferry them back to the forward operating base at Camp Bastion and, from there, an aircraft would take them back to their base outside Basra.

The ambush, a result of intelligence gained by Farsi experts monitoring Iranian communications and shared in a reciprocal agreement with the USA, had achieved its aim. A cautiously worded communiqué, in which Britain was careful not to mention the connivance of the Iranian Government in the arms smuggling, was issued eight hours later. Operation Drawn Claw had been a success.

II – OPERATION VERITAS

Operation Veritas is the code word given to the UK's anti-terrorism programme in its relationship to the Islamic terror network of al-Qaeda. The four main goals of Veritas are to deny the network its base in Afghanistan, to deny it an alternative base outside Afghanistan, to attack the organisation internationally, and to support other states in their internal and external fight against the terrorist organisation. The UK was involved in Afghanistan alongside coalition forces, led by the USA, under Operation Enduring Freedom (OEF), from the first attacks in October 2001. Royal Navy submarines fired Tomahawk missiles against the Taliban and al-Qaeda bases, and RAF aircraft provided reconnaissance and air-to-air refuelling capabilities in support of US strike aircraft. The USA flew missions from Diego Garcia, part of the British Indian Ocean Territory.

UK troops were first involved in ground actions in the country in November 2001, when Royal Marines from 40 Commando helped to secure the airfield at Bagram. A 1,700-strong battle group based around Royal Marines from 45 Commando was subsequently deployed as Task Force Jacana. The role of the battle group was to destroy terrorist infrastructure and deny the movement of al-Qaeda in southern and eastern Afghanistan. In several major operations, Task Force Jacana destroyed a number of bunkers and caves in the Tora Bora region, strongly suspected of being the hiding place of Osama bin Laden. Humanitarian assistance is provided by medical teams and food air drops in areas previously dominated by the Taliban and al-Qaeda.

PROLOGUE

On 29 May 2002, troops from 45 Commando began patrols in the Kowst region of south-east Afghanistan under the codename of Operation Buzzard. The operation was conducted with the aim again of denying the area to terrorists and their support network and to continue to provide humanitarian aid to areas regained from the Taliban. One of the operation's early successes was the discovery by Royal Marines of a huge arms cache in a village. Operation Buzzard continued until 9 July, the same month that saw the final elements of Operation Jacana complete their tour of duty and return to their bases in the UK.

The Taliban administration and its forces had effectively collapsed by the end of 2001, melting back into the Pashtun populace in southern Afghanistan and the Pakistani tribal areas. The risk, however, was that once areas had been cleared of troops, Taliban elements would return to recruit fundamentalist opposition to the Western coalition in the ungoverned areas and set up their training camps in preparation for the ever-increasing calls from Taliban supporters such as Iran and Iraq for *jihad*. The West has put this forward as its prime reason for international forces to remain in Afghanistan to provide security and stability, to combat residual Taliban and al-Qaeda elements, and to support the development of Afghan security forces.

The International Security Assistance Force (ISAF), with the aim of assisting the country's transition into a stable democracy, was set up in December 2001, authorised by United Nations Security Council Resolution (UNSCR) 1386

and successive resolutions (the latest of which is UNSCR 1623). The UK led negotiations in December 2001 to create the ISAF, and Major General John McColl led the first mission with contributions from 16 nations. As well as providing the headquarters and much of the supporting forces for ISAF, the UK contributed the brigade headquarters and an infantry battalion. This contribution initially peaked at 2,100 troops, later decreasing to around 300 personnel after the transfer of ISAF leadership to Turkey in the summer of 2002.

It was accepted by the more foresighted members of the growing coalition that Afghanistan could not remain an occupied country without the very real risk of providing recruitment material for the Taliban. This syndrome had been well noted in other countries under occupation, with parallels being drawn with Northern Ireland where actions by the Crown forces to suppress terrorist incidents immediately led to a groundswell in recruitment for the Provisional Irish Republican Army (PIRA) and later the 'Real' IRA. The coalition was also aware that feudal Saudi Arabia, which had much to gain from the suppression of terrorist elements in the area, had avoided giving verbal support to the invasion of Afghanistan.

So it became an important part of the ISAF and OEF missions in Afghanistan to train and build the capacity of the Afghan National Security Forces to take on more responsibility for security in their own country. In March 2003, the UK began a programme to train Junior NCOs for the Afghan National Army. This has since been supplemented

by Sandhurst-inspired junior officer training in Kabul, and with Operational Mentoring and Liaison Teams in Helmand.

Following NATO's assumption of ISAF command in the autumn of 2003, expansion began in the north, with the Germans leading a Provincial Reconstruction Team (PRT) in Kunduz. NATO also transferred command of the UK-led PRTs in the north to ISAF in July 2004 and Germany and the Netherlands established PRTs in Feyzabad and Baghlan. The UK, meanwhile, was contributing the bulk of the troops needed for a Quick Reaction Force based in Mazar-e-Sharif, bringing the number of UK troops in the country to around 1,000. In September 2004, the UK also deployed six Harrier GR7s to Kandahar to support OEF and ISAF operations.

At the end of May 2005, NATO began to expand the ISAF into the west of Afghanistan. The process of Stage Two saw the ISAF take command of two Italian-led Provincial Reconstruction Teams in the provinces of Herat and Farah and of a Forward Support Base in Heart, also provided by Italy. Two further ISAF-led PRTs in the west became operational later that year, in Chagcharan, led by Lithuania, and Qal'eh-Now, led by Spain.

The staged NATO ISAF expansion had a positive role in extending the writ of the Kabul Government to the provinces, setting the conditions for reconstruction, and in helping the Afghan authorities provide security during the successful presidential elections in October 2004, which was sorely needed bearing in mind an assassination attempt on Afghanistan's then president-elect Hamid Karzai in Kandahar

in September 2002. Parliamentary elections, marking the successful culmination of the Bonn Process, followed in September 2005.

In May 2006 the UK deployed the HQ of the Allied Rapid Reaction Corps (ARRC) to Kabul for nine months to lead the ISAF, and oversee ISAF expansion into the more challenging south and east of Afghanistan. Stage Three of ISAF expansion, which came into effect in late July of 2006, took the NATO-led ISAF into southern Afghanistan. By now, eight nations are currently contributing a total of 10,000 forces to the south. The UK, USA, Canada and the Netherlands are leading PRTs in Helmand, Zabol, Kandahar and Oruzgan provinces, with Denmark, Estonia, Australia and Romania also contributing forces, and the UK making a substantial contribution.

In January 2006, the then Defence Secretary, John Reid, announced the deployment of another 3,300 UK military personnel to Helmand Province where they would be initially centred around 16 Air Assault Brigade. These forces were to be supplemented by 1,000 troops in addition to the UK's Harrier GR7s that support ISAF and OEF from Kandahar airbase.

Several small and medium-sized operations have taken place in Helmand Province since the UK deployment to clear the ground for the main ISAF mission, which is aimed at bringing order and governmental process to the area. Another important goal is the repair of infrastructure damaged in the fighting, for which the UK has deployed key personnel of the Royal Engineers (RE) and units of the Royal Electrical and Mechanical Engineers (REME).

PROLOGUE

The last stage of ISAF expansion, Stage Four, took place in October 2006 when the ISAF expanded into the east of the country, completing the circuit and meaning that ISAF forces were operating across all of Afghanistan for the first time. These also included contingents from the USA.

The official Ministry of Defence website, upon which many of the statistics and much of the information contained in these chapters is based, at times reflects a grand eloquence of purpose unheard even in Parliament at its most rhetorically effusive. One section reads:

'We, along with the rest of the international community, are determined never to allow Afghanistan to become a safe haven for terrorists again. We are working hard towards a common goal – to develop a self-sustaining, stable and democratic Afghanistan. Real progress has been made in the last five years, but clearly there will be many challenges and opportunities in the year ahead. Important to remember [is] that the institutions of a functioning democracy are being established from scratch. Children, including girls, are back in school. Women are participating in political life. The Afghan economy is picking up. Afghanistan has reclaimed its place in the community of nations. UK troops, as part of the 37-nation-strong NATO International Assistance Force (ISAF), are aiming to create a stable environment to enable the Afghan Government [to] extend its authority across the country and reconstruction and development to take place. We can and will succeed, but only if we all stand and work together, adopting a comprehensive approach that encompasses all our international partners and organisations.'

In the wake of Operation Veritas and its offshoot deployments, attention turned to how to bring about the creation of an Afghanistan nation that, once recovered from the gaping wounds of war, could become a durable democracy at peace with its neighbours and the West. With that goal in mind, the United Nations convened a meeting in Bonn in December 2001 between key Afghan figures and the international community. The result was the founding of an interim authority led by Hamid Karzai, effective from December 2001, and an emergency council (*loya jirga*) to legitimise a transitional administration led by Karzai in June 2002, together with a constitutional *jirga* to discuss and set out a new framework of government in December 2003; finally, democratic presidential elections would be held in October 2004, followed by parliamentary elections in September 2005.

Several G8 nations assumed responsibility for various sectors of Afghan development, reconstruction and reform of the security sector. The UK took leadership of the Counter-Narcotics (CN) effort as described elsewhere in this book. Taliban resurgence depends heavily on the profits of the Afghanistan opium industry. Other nations took on responsibility for other issues: the USA for Afghan National Army training and logistic development; Italy for judicial reform; Germany for police training and reform; and Japan for the disarmament, demobilisation and reintegration of the Afghanistan National Army.

Although the Bonn Process had now concluded, UK and international support for Afghanistan's ongoing stabilisation and

reconstruction remains as critical as ever. The UK and Afghanistan signed an Enduring Relationship declaration in July 2005, which stands as proof of the commitment to Afghanistan's long-term stability and development. The London Conference on 31 January–1 February 2006, jointly hosted by the UN, UK and Afghanistan, saw the launch of a new 'Afghanistan Compact', which sets out the framework for international engagement over the next five years. Aid to the value of $10.5 billion was pledged at the London Conference, including £500m of support committed by the UK up to 2009.

The NATO-led ISAF, created at the request of the Afghan Government and with the authorisation of the United Nations in 2001, expanded its support across the country. Stage 3 saw NATO taking command of international forces now building up in the south. The UK contribution to this, announced on 26 January 2006, was a Provincial Reconstruction Team in Lashkar Gah backed by the 3,300-strong Helmand Taskforce. In addition, in May 2006, the UK deployed the Headquarters Group of the Allied Rapid Reaction Corps to lead the entire ISAF for nine months.

The Afghan Security Forces are increasingly contributing to securing their own country, although much more needs to be done to help them achieve this. The Afghan National Army (ANA) has been reformed to be more professional, accountable and ethnically balanced. Approximately 30,000 ANA soldiers and close to 50,000 Afghan National Police officers have been recruited, trained and equipped. Work is under way to ensure greater co-ordination of the army and

police, with the development of command centres at provincial and regional levels.

Over 62,000 fighters have been disarmed under the UN and Afghan Government's Disarmament, Demobilisation and Rehabilitation (DDR) programme. The programme was succeeded in June 2005 by the Disbandment of Illegal Armed Groups (DIAG) process. More than 1,000 groups are engaged in this process, and over 22,000 weapons and over 200,000 items of ammunition have been collected to date. However, much remains to be done to ensure that these groups do not continue to jeopardise Afghanistan's stability. With increased security, over 4.6 million refugees have returned to their homes and form an essential part of the reconstruction process.

Afghanistan's fledgling democracy is also beginning to work. The Afghan people have enthusiastically embraced the opportunity to shape their country's future with 70 per cent of registered voters participating in the 2004 presidential elections, and 51.5 per cent in the 2005 Parliamentary and Provincial Council elections. It appears that the Afghan Government is working hard to strengthen its institutions and to extend its remit across the entire country.

A bonus for women's rights has been the change wrought by the overthrow of the Taliban and their harsh interpretation of the Koran's teachings. Although it will take time to secure the full participation of women in all sectors of the economy and society, and although serious problems remain, much progress has been made. Gender equality is now enshrined in the Afghan Constitution; women, once excluded from society by the

Taliban, are now in government and form a quarter of the total number of MPs sitting in the 351-member National Assembly.

Reconstruction of a country ravaged by over 25 years of conflict is a long-term endeavour. Since 2001, the UK has spent over £500 million on reconstruction and development in Afghanistan, making the UK Afghanistan's second-largest bilateral donor after the USA. While Afghanistan remains one of the poorest countries in the world, its legal economy has grown rapidly and is now around three times larger than it was in 2001. The IMF estimate that GDP grew by 14 per cent in 2005/06.

Provincial Reconstruction Teams (PRTs) are seen to be at the heart of the ISAF mission in that they embody a joint military and civilian approach to stabilising Afghanistan. A PRT is a combination of international military and civilian personnel based in provincial areas of Afghanistan. Its three core tasks are to support the extension of the authority of the Afghan central government, to support reform of the security sector and to facilitate development and reconstruction. Each is tailored to the prevailing security situation, socio-economic conditions, terrain and reach of the central government. Although a lead nation retains responsibility, the PRT may also contain military and civilian personnel from other nations.

The primary role of the military in a PRT is to provide an enabling security environment in which the authority of the Afghan Government can be extended, and development and reconstruction work carried out. Military personnel can help to do this by undertaking tasks such as patrolling, liaison with the

local population and by helping to develop the capacity of the Afghan security forces by training and operating alongside them.

Drugs are one of the gravest threats to the long-term security and prosperity of the Afghan people. Sustainable drug elimination strategies take time, and the Afghan Government has made clear its commitment to tackling the trade. The UK, as Afghanistan's partner nation in counter-narcotics, is working with the Afghan Government and the international community to bring about a sustainable reduction in the cultivation, production and trafficking of opium, helping the Afghan Government in its efforts to implement its National Drug Control Strategy (NDCS) and to turn international interest for counter-narcotics into support and resources.

The NDCS is well balanced and represents the right approach. It targets the trafficker and aims to strengthen legal livelihoods of the current crop growers, reduce demand and develop effective institutions. The international community has pledged $83.6 million to the UN-administered Counter-Narcotics Trust Fund to date, towards the implementation of the NDCS.

The Taliban derive economic benefits from the drug trade. It is in their interest and that of the traffickers to undermine the Afghan Government's efforts to establish stability. In the south, they encourage farmers to grow *papaver somniferum,* the opium-bearing poppies, and to resist eradication. Anti-narcotic operations by UK and US Special Forces actively support the Afghan Government's efforts to disrupt links between the Taliban and traffickers.

PROLOGUE

The drug trade cannot be treated in isolation and the coalition forces are working with the Afghan Government to ensure that counter-narcotics efforts are integrated across the Afghan rule of law sector. Progress is being made; the eighteen-month period throughout 2007 and into 2008 has seen the passage of vital counter-narcotics legislation resulting in the conviction of over 320 traffickers, and an increase in drug-related seizures. A high-security prison wing is now operational to accommodate those convicted of opium production and distribution but there is more to be done – despite coalition efforts, 2006 actually saw an increase in cultivation and reflected the challenging security situation and limited law enforcement capability in some parts of the country, particularly in the south. In areas of Afghanistan where access to government, security and development has improved, engineered cuts in narcotic production have been sustained. The result was that production in three of the four highest poppy-cultivating provinces was actually down in 2006 (Balkh – 33 per cent; Farah – 25 per cent; and Kandahar – 3 per cent). Cultivation also remained at manageable levels across much of Nangarhar and Laghman for the second consecutive year (the original heartland of Afghan cultivation and processing). This is a first in Afghanistan.

At the time of writing, figures are still not available for overall cultivation levels in 2007 although early indicators suggest a possible decrease in the north and increase in the south and east, including Helmand, Kandahar and Nangarhar. This appears to follow the previous year's pattern of cultivation

reductions being sustained in areas of improved access to government, security and development.

Opium poppy eradication is the responsibility of the Afghan Government, which sees it as an important means of deterrence in its crackdown on the drugs trade. However, it's hard to convince an Afghan scrub farmer to cease in the production of a profitable cash crop on political or moral grounds. Eradication, therefore, is targeted where the most opportunities for legal livelihoods exist.

UK military operations in Afghanistan were recently conducted under the name Operation Herrick. They have also been conducted under the names Operation Veritas and Operation Fingal (ISAF).

Operation Jacana, conducted by 45 Commando Group, included Operations Ptarmigan, Snipe, Condor and Buzzard.

The Ministry of Defence identifies the costs of military operations in terms of the net additional costs it has incurred, over and above planned expenditure on defence. The costs of UK operations in Afghanistan come from the Treasury Special Reserve; the overall cost of operations in Afghanistan in 2001–02 was £221 million and has risen steadily to £738 million for 2006–07.

1

A BLOODY COMBAT

Sangin, in the southern province of Helmand, is a hotbed of revolt against the Government of President Hamid Karzai. The town of approximately 14,000 inhabitants has traditionally supported the Taliban, perhaps more for the resurgent Taliban's economically provoked support of the opium trade, of which the town is a central location. It is also the home of the main bazaar for Sangin District.

Located in the valley of the Helmand River, and at an altitude of 888m, the town stands 95km south of the provincial capital Lashkar Gah, which is also the headquarters of UK forces deployed for Operation Herrick, the NATO-led operation employing British, Canadian and Dutch troops, whose goal is the pacification of Taliban rebels in the south of the country.

On 31 July 2005, it was the scene of a bloody engagement when a NATO convoy consisting of six vehicles came under a

ferocious attack by Taliban forces in an ambush set 2km south of the town. Aid for the beleaguered, retreating convoy and the international UN staff member on board one of the vehicles came from an American patrol of Humvees that responded with a characteristic surfeit of enthusiasm, driving off the Taliban but also wounding two Afghan personnel while shooting up the NATO vehicles, which its gunners mistook for part of the Taliban contingent. The retreating ambushers, meanwhile, were spotted crossing the nearby river and were summarily dispatched by a single 500lb bomb dropped by a USAF B-52 bomber in its role of air support.

In February 2006, Sangin saw the bloodiest fighting of the war when 200 Taliban ambushed a police patrol near the town and laid ambushes for arriving reinforcements, virtually placing the defenders under siege. British RAF Harriers joined battle with the Taliban ground forces, aided by US A10 tank busters and B-52 bombers. The battle lasted for two days and nights, with casualties mounting on both sides. The Taliban lost 18, including two influential commanders. The retreating rebels, having made their mark firmly on the occupying OEF forces, melted into the mountainous region of Ghorak in the neighbouring province of Kandahar, from where they would re-emerge to hold the town to siege until the early months of 2007.

Six months later, Sangin was under the command of NATO, defended by a garrison of A Company from 3 Battalion the Parachute Regiment. The Taliban attacks continued daily, with rocket and small arms fire with the accompanying thud of mortars raining 24 hours a day on the garrison's earth and

rock-walled platoon house in the district centre compound a mile and a half from the town centre.

On Sunday, 20 August, a decision was taken by battalion officers to clear a direct path through a nearby compound to allow troops leaving or returning on patrol rapid access to the compound to avoid enemy fire. Three sections of A Company were deployed around the compound in head-high corn and poppy fields, to protect the engineers laying explosive charges to demolish the intervening buildings. Unable to see through the tall corn stalks that moved sluggishly in the current of hot air rising from the baked soil, the young paras of A Company nervously fingered their L85 individual weapons and sweated in the hot, turgid air, all eyes fixed on their patrol leader, 29-year-old Para veteran Corporal Bryan Budd.

A month earlier, the Yorkshire-born father-of-two had won the admiration of his section when they came under fire from rooftop snipers while on a routine patrol in the centre of war-torn Sangin. Diving for nearby cover, the patrol sent a fierce burst of NATO 5.56mm lead hurtling towards its attackers and a massive firefight ensued with Taliban fighters opening up from other buildings around the perimeter as rounds burst holes the size of a man's fist in the earthen walls of the surrounding dwellings. Rounds were also creeping towards the still form of a colleague who had been struck down in the first burst of fire from the rooftop.

Undaunted by the bullets cracking around him, Budd shouted to his patrol to follow him in a desperate race to the heaviest-held building. The patrol charged, firing from the hip,

startling the Taliban within into an undisciplined and panicked retreat out of the rear of the building and across open fields. Having regained the initiative and rescued their fallen comrade, the triumphant and freshly blooded 'Toms' had rapidly mopped up the remaining opposition.

Today, their eyes turned once again to their battle-toughened corporal, who now raised a hand to indicate a group of Taliban – or 'Paks' – approaching through the corn. British troops in Afghanistan commonly refer to the Taliban insurgents, no doubt because of the movement's Pakistani origins, as 'Paks', hence an expression such as 'six-packs ahead' which might just confuse the enemy listening in on radio chatter and wondering at the British fighting man's obsession with beer.

Budd extended a hand, indicating a flanking movement to the right. As his patrol moved silently in that direction, another section's .50 calibre-armed Snatch 2 Land Rover patrolling on its left was spotted by the enemy, who immediately fell to cover and opened fire, the heavy 7.62mm bullets from their Kalashnikovs scything the corn heads like a manic reaper.

The patrol, now depleted by three more casualties, acted under the rules governing an ambushed force. It charged the enemy position. The withering fire from the besieged Taliban caused the advancing patrol members to hurl themselves to the ground, seeking the scant cover available. As they brought their arms to bear on the now hidden enemy, they heard the staccato thud of Bryan Budd's L85 firing on full automatic.

Fellow corporal Guy Roberts recalls 'a whole stream of

rapid fire' and shouting. Losing sight of Corporal Budd, he dropped to his knees among the ravaged corn and loosed off three bursts on automatic. He then rose to launch a grenade at the enemy's last seen position and was punched to the ground by the impact of a 7.62mm round slamming into his shoulder, fired by a Taliban fighter's AK-47.

As he lay bleeding among the corn, three members of the patrol crawled forward and began to drag him back to cover. Two of his rescuers also received gunshot wounds in the rescue but, despite the sustained fire from the enemy, managed to pull Corporal Roberts to safety. Firing continued ahead but there was still no sign of Corporal Budd.

Lieutenant Hugo Farmer, leading a squad to reinforce the trapped patrol, arrived to find three of his men injured. With the Para code that no one gets left behind uppermost in his mind – a code, incidentally, that exists throughout the entire British armed services – the officer reformed his troops before calling up more reinforcements and air support to harass the enemy, which he reported as 'all over the bloody area'.

Changing their magazines, as fast air support aircraft howled into action and released their death-dealing rockets at the Taliban positions, the paratroopers under their lieutenant surged forward with their rifles, firing from the hip on full automatic. Returning fire diminished in the face of relentless air support from circling Apache attack helicopters, whose M230 30mm chain-guns ripped into the fleeing enemy figures below. The Taliban bunched together in their scramble to escape the lethal chain guns despite being aware through

experience that the two-manned AH-64A Apache was also capable of letting fly with its own Hydra 70mm rockets fired by laser designator that were absolutely lethal in a ground-support role.

The discovery of Corporal Budd's lifeless body in an advance position surrounded by three dead Taliban fighters took the edge off the euphoria of a decisive enemy rout but there was no doubt that 3 Para had decisively won the day. There was some speculation that Corporal Budd may have been hit by a round from his own side fired in the confusion as he charged ahead of his section but the evidence of the dead Taliban scattered around him was sufficient to assume that he died in an unrelenting firefight with the enemy at close quarters.

Bryan Budd was later to receive a posthumous award of the Victoria Cross for his courageous action at Sangin that day and for his attack on the Taliban snipers' position a month earlier. But his unit's defence of army engineers at Sangin in that hot month of August in 2006 had given the Taliban a bloody nose they would not forget and a reminder that 3 PARA's motto 'Untrinque Paratus' meant just what it said – Ready for Anything.

2
HELMAND'S HELL
ON EARTH

Most British troops in Afghanistan are deployed in
Helmand Province, a desolate and largely lawless region
with a population of just over 1 million and a surface area of
23,058 square miles. The strategically located south-eastern
Afghan province has emerged as the centre of the neo-Taliban
and the broader Pashtun insurgency. A string of deadly
insurgent attacks in 2006 claimed the lives of several Helmand
officials. An attack on 3 March claimed the life of the Sangin
district governor, Amir Jan, who was killed while vacationing
in the Musa Qala district. Prior to this incident, at least 28
people, including the Musa Qala district chief, Abdul Quddus,
were killed on 2 February in intensive fighting with over 200
Taliban insurgents.

The battle – which lasted more than ten hours – took place
in the Sangin, Nawzad and Musa Qala districts, which are
located in the extreme south of Helmand. Fighting erupted

when militants attacked a government office in Musa Qala district, killing the local government district chief. Meanwhile, a spokesman for the Afghan Interior Ministry claimed that the battle in early February had been the most serious incident in 2005. It was also claimed that two Taliban leaders – Mullah Dadullah and Mullah Turjan – were killed in the fighting, although it was not made clear at the time if this referred to the notorious Mullah Dadullah, who was believed to be the leader of the resurgent Taliban movement in the south. If so, the ministry spokesman was mistaken. Mullah Dadullah was to die a year later, killed in a firefight with US troops.

Following the Helmand clashes, some of the representatives in parliament criticised the central government's strategies in counter-narcotics, anti-corruption campaigns and disarmament programmes. Helmand representative in the lower house of parliament, Nasima Niazi, blamed the formation of 200 Taliban militants as a result of the dissatisfaction felt by many distressed Afghan farmers. 'Now, when the farmers want to exploit the result of their plants, the Government has started destroying them,' said Niazi. 'Though I don't agree with planting opium, I still want the Government to have a definite strategy.' This attitude is generally true of most politicians in the emerging Afghanistan, many of whom have an interest in a profitable cash crop which is largely sold to the infidel West and is a boost to the fledgling democracy's economy.

Aside from agriculture and the opium trade, widespread unemployment is another major cause of unrest in Helmand. According to Mukhtar Pidram, an Afghan political analyst,

during the four years since 2002, the Government 'had not established even a small company to employ unskilled youths'. One might question, however, if that is a strategy to direct young men to join the Afghanistan National Army or the police force. If so, it is not working, since unemployment is one of the main factors driving dissatisfaction with the Hamid Karzai Government and is the main factor leading youths to embrace employment in the drug trade and subsequent recruitment to the ranks of the Taliban.

Moreover, heavy-handedness and perceived oppression by the police and the Afghan security forces is undermining efforts to bring stability to Helmand. A group of Helmand elders voiced their concerns about this issue in a February 2006 meeting with President Karzai in Kabul. Apparently, Karzai promised the Helmand elders that he would investigate their claims but little seems to have changed. It is a reality of conflict that heavy-handedness by the security forces goes hand in hand with the concept of civil unrest and the existence of an alternative authority, which in Afghanistan is the warlord, who constitutes a big challenge to the Government and the people. These elements are still strong and control most of the military and civilian institutions, especially in provinces such as Helmand.

Furthermore, Helmand, aside from being a largely Pashtun province, is from where many senior officials of the former Taliban regime originate. For instance, the culture and information minister of the former Taliban regime, Mullah Amir Khan Muttaqi, was from Helmand. Additionally, Helmand youths form some of the most effective and fearless units of the

Taliban military. When Kandahar fell in late 2001, it is believed that many Taliban leaders sought sanctuary in Helmand.

Given this long and deep-rooted association with the Taliban, it is not altogether surprising that former Taliban elements and sympathetic constituencies in broader Pashtun society are at the forefront of the insurgency in this war-torn province. If the Afghan Government and its Western allies are serious about tackling the problems in Helmand, they have to reach some sort of accommodation with aggrieved Pashtuns. If not, the Taliban will be able to count on their support indefinitely.

Disruptive foreign influence is another destabilising factor in the provinces bordering Pakistan, at which Afghan officials customarily point an accusing finger together with another at its notorious Inter-Services Intelligence Directorate (ISI) following every clash and suicide attack. For instance, following the ten-hour-long clashes in early February, Afghan Interior Minister Zarar Ahmad Muqbil, while speaking in the lower house of parliament, claimed that the 'eastern' neighbour to Afghanistan (Pakistan) 'has equipped and sent the Taliban to fight against the central government'. According to Muqbil, 'Helmand, Kandahar, Paktia, Paktika, Kunar and Nuristan are those provinces which are insecure and restive. I must say clearly that these are the provinces which have joint borders with Pakistan.'

Moreover, Afghan Defence Minister Abdul Rahim Wardak, while speaking at the lower house of parliament in 2006, implicitly accused Pakistan of causing unrest and chaos in Helmand. 'The terrorists who attack our young democracy

have been trained, equipped and sent from abroad,' Wardak stated, no doubt rolling his eyes towards the eastern border. National security chief, Amrullah Saleh, has also argued that the Afghan Government must put pressure on 'a specific country' which trains and co-operates with the terrorists and from where they have been sent to instigate terrorist attacks. It is believed by most Middle East observers that more than 60 countries with different strategies and policies are united in their stand against terrorism in Afghanistan. The only exception, apparently, is Pakistan.

Most of the insurgents and suicide bombers in Helmand Province are believed to be ideologically motivated and fully committed to the cause of *jihad*. Waheed Mujda, a senior former foreign ministry diplomat during the Taliban regime, has pointed out that the insurgents, mostly Taliban, are not fighting for power in Helmand or the rest of the provinces; they are fighting against foreigners because of the dictates of Sharia law. At the same time, Hezb-e-Islami Afghanistan leader, Gulbuddin Hekmatyar, claims he will 'never negotiate with the foreign-established Government in Afghanistan'. This is an important statement by the once all-powerful Hekmatyar, a former Afghan Prime Minister, whose current influence is perhaps underestimated. While Hekmatyar's influence in Helmand does not exceed that of the Taliban, his statement is seen as a clear sign by his followers in this region to engage in *jihad* against Government forces in Helmand and other south-western provinces. Despite having been militarily defeated by the Taliban in 1994, Hekmatyar is now co-operating with the neo-Taliban.

This development, coupled with Hekmatyar's statement of intent, is very bad news for the Kabul Government.

According to a Kabul daily published in early March 2006 and referring to a particularly bloody clash between US forces and insurgents, 'the bloodshed on Saturday underscored the challenge facing thousands of British and Canadian troops in coming months as they gradually relieve American forces in southern Afghanistan, a hotbed of insurgency and the drug trade'.

The consensus in Afghanistan is that the surge in violence was directly linked to the new mission of the British-led NATO ISAF in Helmand. This force was dominated by the British 16th Air Assault Brigade. It seemed likely that the insurgents, alongside al-Qaeda, were preparing to test the resolve of the British troops early, hoping to inflict serious losses on their forces.

The treacherous nature of the desolate and lawless region encompassed by Helmand Province, coupled with the complex factors driving the insurgency, made it unlikely to some of the more pessimistic observers that the British-led NATO force would be able to restore stability to Helmand in the foreseeable future. The more optimistic, however, have been proved correct in assuming that the British Army's reputation for the skilful handling of insurgencies and the local populations that sustain it would reduce the grievances of the Pashtuns of Helmand.

Nonetheless, the most intense and bloodiest fighting that the British Army had experienced for 50 years erupted in southern

Afghanistan in June of that same year of 2006, when Helmand Province, soon to become the Dante's Hell of the British forces, became the focal point for an upsurge of violence by the re-emerging Taliban. Two British soldiers, four Afghan soldiers and 29 Taliban insurgents were killed as fighting erupted between Taliban militants and forces of the US-led coalition and the Afghan Government. Caught by surprise in a scenario resembling the Panzers' of Sepp Dietrich and Hasso von Manteuffel desperate breakout in the Ardennes Forest in December 1944, British forces in the southern area reeled under a succession of hard hit-and-run attacks in 'days and days of intense fighting unseen since the Second World War', according to the NATO commander in Afghanistan, Lieutenant General David Richards, who reported that troops 'were under constant attack from persistent dirty fighting and hadn't slept for 24 hours'.

There was heavy fighting during June and July 2006 with the launch of Operation Mountain Thrust, a US-led operation employing British, Canadian and Afghan troops in a drive to rid southern Afghanistan of the insurgents, with the region seeing the bloodiest period since the fall of the Taliban regime. The Taliban showed great co-ordination in their attacks, even capturing two districts of Helmand Province at the end of July, which were retaken a few days later.

The Taliban suffered heavily during the fighting with more than 1,100 killed and close to 400 captured. Heavy aerial bombing was the main factor. The coalition forces had close to 150 killed and 40 Afghan policemen captured by the Taliban.

However, it is obvious to military observers that the reservoir of Taliban fighters is practically limitless and that, with the constant supply of young and angry Muslims from neighbouring countries anxious to join the holy war against the forces of the Great Satan, the movement will not be overcome by high casualty figures.

In the end, the operation did not manage to quell the Taliban insurgency, with the result that, after control of the region was transferred from the Americans to NATO forces, attacks continued and even intensified. On the first day that NATO took control, 1 August 2006, a British patrol was hit by enemy fire in Helmand Province; three soldiers were killed and one wounded. On the same day, 18 Taliban and one policeman were killed in an anti-Taliban coalition operation in the same province and 15 Afghan policemen were captured when they surrendered in Zabul Province while a Taliban force was preparing to attack their police post. Two days later, there were several incidents in and around Kandahar, including a suicide bombing which killed 21 civilians. In the other attacks in and around Kandahar, four Canadian soldiers were killed and ten were wounded. These sustained attacks, resulting in significant injuries and fatalities among coalition troops and innocent civilians, clearly demonstrated that the Taliban forces were still a threat.

There is no doubt that the province, which now came under the NATO mandate of British forces in Afghanistan, was the short straw drawn by the British. A major trouble spot was the town of Sangin, where ten British soldiers had been killed in

clashes with Taliban fighters in the previous two months. Sangin was the centre of the re-emerging cultivation of the opium poppy, a crop that had been the mainstay of agricultural economy before Taliban rule had banned the production, and was now returning in the chaos of war, its profits to be used to arm the insurgent armies flooding into Afghanistan in answer to the call for *jihad* against the occupying forces of the coalition.

The instability in the region had led British commanders to express concern at the vulnerability of British forward operating bases (FOBs) in the Sangin valley, many of them hill forts, now reinforced, originally built by the British Army in the 19th century, and the difficulty in resupplying them. Road transport was under constant threat from improvised explosive devices, the dreaded IEDs often made from the coalition's own unexploded artillery shells, with which the Taliban littered the roadsides. Resupply could only be effected by helicopter, with the aircraft vulnerable to rocket grenade attacks from compounds surrounding the Sangin FOB. Clearing these compounds in preparation for a resupply helicopter's approach was a bitter and taut mission against an elusive enemy.

Meanwhile, an Afghan Army patrol lost two of its number in an attack near Qalat, in the south-east of the country. General Rahmatullah Raufi, commanding ANA forces in the south, reported 11 Taliban killed in the encounter, including a local Taliban commander.

As summer approached, joint Afghan and coalition patrols were now coming under constant attack but were dealing out more punishment than they took in the bloody encounters –

with an attack on a joint patrol near Musa Qala in northern Helmand Province costing the insurgents eight killed for the cost of two ANA soldiers. A raid on a suspected Taliban compound in Uruzgan claimed another ten insurgents. Combined Forces Command later reported that the compound, located in the village of Saghayfu in the Shahidi Hass district of the province, belonged to a known weapons and IED manufacturer and supplier whose location had been identified through intelligence from British forces on reconnaissance missions in the area. The elation at the success of the mission was curbed by the news that two British soldiers had been killed overnight and another wounded in an engagement in the Sangin valley.

Further south, in the vicinity of Gereshk, a town located on the Helmand River that lies 120km north-west of Kandahar at 817m above sea level, USAF A-10 tank busters and RAF GR-7s were called in to provide close air support to coalition forces coming under incessant small arms and rocket-propelled grenade attack from Taliban militants.

Gereshk is the centre of a rich agricultural region with the Kajaki Dam upriver diverting water to the Boghra Irrigation Canal. Gereshk was originally built around a fort on the right bank of the river but was later rebuilt on the left. During the First Anglo–Afghan War (1839–42), the fort was captured by the British but it was conceded and returned in 1879. Gereshk has a population of about 48,546 and has a developed hospital and a school of engineering which was built back in 1957, but now the area was in turmoil.

Coalition and Afghan troops took cover as the A-10s carried out strafing passes over the marked enemy positions, alerted to the positions of British and other coalition troops by Firefly illuminators. The A-10 Thunderbolt is also known as the Warthog, the Flying Gun and the Tankbuster. The aircraft was used extensively during Operation Desert Storm, in support of NATO operations in response to the Kosovo crisis, in Operation Enduring Freedom in Afghanistan, and in Operation Iraqi Freedom. It is a high-survivability and versatile aircraft, popular with pilots for its 'get home' effectiveness. The mission of the aircraft is ground attack against tanks, armoured vehicles and installations, and close air support of ground forces. The A-10 is suitable for operation from forward airbases, with short take-off and landing capability. The aircraft has a range of 800 miles and the fuel endurance to loiter in the battle area. The manoeuvrability at low speed and at altitudes below 1,000ft allows accurate and effective targeting and weapon delivery over all types of terrain.

Now the troops below watched as the aircraft's nose-mounted 30mm cannon sent mud and bodies flying as its hail of depleted uranium armour-piercing ammunition, firing at a selected rate of 4,200 rounds per minute, chewed up the opposition. Arms and legs flew before the onslaught. Using the cannon, the A-10 is capable of disabling a main battle tank from a range of over 6,500m. The cannon can fire a range of ammunition including armour-piercing incendiary rounds (APIs) weighing up to 0.75kg, or uranium-depleted 0.43kg API rounds. The magazine can hold 1,350 rounds of

ammunition. The pilot can select a firing rate of 2,100 or 4,200 rounds per minute.

As a Warthog finished its run, an RAF GR-7 dropped down from where it had been circling above, relaying messages from the troops on the ground to command HQ. The Harrier dropped its right wing and screamed into its attacking run, releasing two Matra 155 rockets from its armament of six and strafing the ground with 25mm cannon shells. Air support is essential to coalition ground troops and gives weapon superiority in any daylight engagement against the hardy hill-fighters that make up the Taliban forces. As the aircraft flashed overhead in their grim aerial ballet, the exhausts of RGP7s, fired in frustration, rose from the Taliban positions.

In Ghazni, other coalition air forces were in action against the Taliban as French M2000s and F-1s provided close air support for coalition ground troops. The now gathering momentum of war throughout the four southern provinces was being fought by coalition troops without the support of the Americans, who had deployed to the east of the country following the takeover of the region by NATO on 1 August. More than 10,000 Afghan, British and Canadian troops were now deployed to crush the resurgent Taliban force in the largest military operation seen since the initial coalition invasion of 2001.

One of the main trouble spots now encountered was at Musa Qala, one of the centres of Taliban resistance to NATO ISAF control in Afghanistan. On 2 February 2006, intensive fighting had erupted there, leading to 28 deaths, including the

Musa Qala district chief, Abdul Quddus. On 3 March 2006, the Sangin district governor, Amir Jan, was killed there while on vacation. British forces were deployed to defend the district offices at Musa Qala, Sangin, Nowzad and Kajaki. Over several months, eight British soldiers died there.

Danish troops moved in to Musa Qala after the British; on 28 August, the Danish military pulled all of its troops out of Musa Qala and were replaced by the British. Currently, as I write in July 2008, a coalition push is concentrated around Arghandab, fighting to repel insurgents who have taken over villages in the area. The fighting is non-stop with little time for rest and British troops are in the thick of it. More than 5 million bullets have been fired in this savage war and hardly a week passes without a savage toll being paid in British and Afghan lives. There is no end in sight; there is no proverbial light at the end of the tunnel. What is now certain is that Helmand Province will live up to its name for many years to come, a veritable hell on earth for British forces in Afghanistan.

3

OPERATION PECHTAW

Keeping to tradition, they fried their chips in ammunition boxes, scrubbed out with sand until the interiors shone. The oil – which had been traded from the troops of the Afghan National Army whom they were supporting in exchange for empty brass cartridge cases collected from the range where they zeroed their weapons – hissed and bubbled and threatened to overflow as they tipped in the crudely chopped potatoes. The sizzling hot chips would be eaten with ravioli now heating on another fire in the monstrous NAAFI catering tin in which it was issued.

This was the Last Supper, the traditional feast of the troops of A (Grenadier) Company, the 2nd Battalion of the Mercian Regiment (Worcesters and Foresters) before they went into offensive action, this time against the Taliban occupying the southern Helmand region near the town of Garmsir. Tomorrow, A Company would fly north to the British Army

base of Camp Bastion; from there, another plane would take them back to the UK, marking the end of six months in the bandit country of southern Afghanistan, but tonight there was serious work afoot.

The aim of the operation, codenamed Operation Pechtaw, called for A Company under its commander Major Simon Boyle to confront and push back Taliban forces occupying buildings south of A Company's current station, FOB Delhi, forcing the insurgents newly arrived from across the borders with Pakistan and Iran to retreat in disorder and thus put an end to days and nights of sniping and rocket attacks. But the intention of Operation Pechtaw was not akin to throwing stones at yapping terriers but to give a decidedly bloody nose to the enemy and send him south at a run, clearing the area as a courtesy to the incoming Grenadier Guards who would be relieving the Company tomorrow, 8 September 2007.

The mood and morale among the troops was high; after weeks of ration packs, a mess tin piled high with ravioli and finger-scorching chips was a veritable feast. Days and nights of patrols, sleeping in full kit and body armour and always within hands' reach of their personal weapon, the revamped SA80 rifle now rechristened the L85A1 cocked and locked beside them, had welded the three platoons, each of 25 men, into a formidable fighting force. Such was the battlefield camaraderie that 1 Platoon had named itself 'The Spartans' in tribute to those hardened warriors of Greek legend and myth, some members even going so far as to brand an 'S' on some part of their body.

The high spirits continued as the last of the meal was washed down with fizzy cola. Some of the lads demonstrated their moves at break-dancing to the music of the ubiquitous iPods, much to the amusement and encouragement of spectators, which included their NCOs and officers. An enormous sense of brotherhood surrounded the group of young fighting men. Many had perhaps never heard of Rudyard Kipling, but all would empathise with the writer's sentiments of society's view of its fighting men. Coarse and rough as they may have been formed by life before entry into the Army, all felt they were now members of a vast family, with each man their brother. They would lay down their lives for each other's survival. Arms clasped around each other's shoulders, they sang their ribald soldiers' songs, and told jokes – and laughed too loudly.

Finally, the call came to move out and Platoon Sergeant Mike Lockett moved through his men of 1 Platoon as they camo'd up for the action that awaited them; the 27-year-old Notts-born sergeant encouraged his men with the odd word as he checked their kit for the forthcoming action. The sergeant, known as 'Locky' to his men, recalls, 'I checked the numbers and observed how each man settled into his battle discipline. It had been a great night but now we had serious business to attend to.' The three platoons of A Company left the base in patrol formation at last light. It was Saturday, 7 September 2007.

The battle plan called for deployment to the outskirts of the village of Darvisham, 1km from base. The three platoons

would then advance in a southerly line, clearing the mud-walled compounds and buildings as they went. 1 Platoon's ground was to the south-east, with 2 Platoon on its left flank. 3 Platoon held the south-westerly ground.

Lieutenant Simon Cupples led the six men of his point section to outflank a roofless walled compound, later that night to become a frail refuge against rockets and mortar attacks by the enemy. Privates Sam Cooper, the youngest of the group at 18, Luke Cole, Ben Johnson, Kyle Drury and Johan Botha, together with Corporal Ben Umney, advanced in line abreast with their officer towards a dimly perceived treeline about 30m ahead of the patrol. Also with the group was Second Lieutenant Rupert Bowers, fresh from officers' school in the UK and anxiously watching his platoon officer, Lieutenant Cupples, to see, in his own words, 'how it was done'. Behind their line in advancing battle order came two more sections of six men apiece. It was so dark, 25-year-old Simon Cupple recalls, 'If I had put my rifle on the ground, I wouldn't have been able to find it again.'

As they passed the compound that they would eventually christen the Three Walls and crossed a footpath in the darkness, an explosion of small arms fire, heavy machine guns and rockets erupted from behind the approaching treeline and four men were immediately hit. The others went down on to their knees on the hard, dusty ground, assuming fire positions in an attempt to pick out the form of their attackers in the staccato bursts of flame from the enemy's weapons. Through his night-sight, Second Lieutenant Rupert Bowers caught a glimpse of a

Taliban fighter aiming a Kalashnikov rifle. 'I put two rounds into him and heard him scream – he didn't fire again,' reported Bowers after the battle.

Lt Cupples lay in the exploding dust and darkness. Around him the rattle of small arms fire, the explosion of grenades and incoming RPG rounds rose to a crescendo. The air was thick with dust and earth thrown up by the solid impact of shrapnel. The point section was now organising itself into dealing out return fire and he called to them in order to place their positions in his mind in the brief lulls between firing. He knew his casualties were to his right but first he had to get the survivors of his platoon to cover.

To his left, he recalled from a sketch map of the ground, was an irrigation ditch, now separating his three sections from 2 Platoon. Calling to his men to follow him, he crawled the 30m to the ditch, aided by covering fire laid down by the following section under Sgt Lockett that had already withdrawn to cover. The ditch was marked by a solitary tree as the lieutenant's night vision kicked in.

Once in the scant cover of the ditch, Cupples went on the net to call in support from the artillery and mortars set up behind the attack line. Over his personal role radio (PRR) he heard 2 Platoon deploying to outflank the ambush force, which was still directing a furious fire across the killing ground where at least four casualties of 1 Platoon were lying close to the Taliban lines. Also chillingly over the PRR came the weakening Afrikaner accent of Private Botha, reporting his wounds – Botha had been hit in the upper arm and body and

was bleeding profusely from a ruptured major vessel in his chest – and pleading to be recovered before the Taliban found him. Every soldier fighting in Afghanistan knows of the torture and indignities that await them should they fall, alive, into enemy hands.

'Locky' Lockett at Lt Cupples' side was asking for volunteers to go forward into the withering fire and rescue their comrades-in-arms. 'Everyone was game to go,' he said later. 'It was just a case of picking the four blokes nearest me. If it meant going back into the face of enemy fire, I didn't care. I wanted my men back. Before we went to Afghanistan I promised them I'd bring them all back – if not alive, then their bodies would come home.'

The eventual rescue team was made up of Sgt Lockett, Lt Cupples, 2nd Lt Lieutenant Bowers and Lance Corporals McEwan and Chandler. They snaked over the ground in a leopard crawl, rising to their knees to scout the dark ground ahead and then moving forward once again through the choking dust kicked up by flying bullets and the whining ricochets when metal jacket met stone. Lance Corporal David Chandler described his feelings as he pushed forward into the night: 'I got called forward by Sergeant Lockett to go and get the boys out… went forward, round the tree – everyone knows where the tree is by now – and crawled forward under heavy fire that was quite accurate and landing just centimetres away from us as we were going forward. I don't know whether I felt it at the time to be honest, it was just like I was focused on getting the lads out. All you kept on thinking as you looked up

and considered the splash in the sand from the hit of a round in front of you, you got to thinking, "Fucking hell, that's where I'm moving to. Are they going to get me when I get there?" But you just kept on going and finally we got to them.'

Private Luke Cole, a Territorial Army soldier serving with the Mercian Regiment whose civilian job was driving a fork-lift truck, had gone down in the first burst of heavy machine gun fire from the Taliban position as a .50 calibre machine gun round struck his upper thigh, shattering five and a half inches of femur. Fighting the waves of agony, he saw movement from the ditch ahead as two insurgents crawled forward in a bid to grab the body of Johan Botha, who was lying between the Taliban and Cole. Cole sent them scattering back to cover with a sustained burst from his rifle. Now, as the rescue party closed on his position, he heard Sgt Lockett urging him to keep firing to ensure the enemy's heads stayed down. Lockett describes how Cole was hit again in the stomach but managed to crawl to a second wounded soldier, Private Cooper – who had sustained a fearsome head wound – and plunge a 10mm self-injecting syrette of morphine into the injured man's thigh. He then rolled away so as not to compromise his severely wounded companion, and again took up a rapid rate of fire against the enemy positions. His actions, which would earn him the Military Cross, were described by Lockett as 'fantastic'.

Cole's comments on hearing of the award were economical. 'I didn't think I was doing anything special. I was helping my mates out like they would do for me.' Of his crippling stomach wound, he recalled, 'I knew I'd been hit and my stomach was

open so I just tucked in my shirt to keep it all in place and kept firing.' He was rescued from the field by 2nd Lt Bowers who had just returned from carrying Cooper back to the shelter of the irrigation ditch on his back as rounds cracked around his head. With the assistance of other members of the rescue team, Bowers dragged Cole and another casualty, Private Umney, back to comparative safety. The platoon took another casualty as Weston was hit and fell, to be dragged to safety by his friend David Chandler.

Once in the irrigation ditch, Lt Cupples again called in artillery and mortar fire on the Taliban positions and the killing ground erupted in a cacophony of noise and confusion as the ground shook and trembled from the sheer weight of incoming friendly fire. Sgt Lockett meanwhile was calling on his platoon for volunteers to go out once again with him and Lt Cupples to bring in Johan Botha. Six attempts would be made to locate the big Afrikaner before the depleted platoon was ordered to withdraw from the field by A Company CO Major Boyle. Having overheard the contact, 2 Platoon was moving in to flank the enemy position and 3 Platoon had arrived at Three Walls with a heavy weapons team and a fire support team to direct air attacks. Two Viking armoured vehicles under the command of Sgt Major Peter Lewis were also arriving at the three-walled compound, carrying ammunition resupplies and company doctor Captain Henry Nwume with two assistant medics. But Johan Botha's body, lying just 5m from the Taliban positions amid the smoke from grenades, mortars and small arms fire was still out there, despite

Lieutenant Cupples and Sgt Lockett leading six forays into the killing ground in attempts to recover him. Meanwhile, 3 Platoon's fire support team had successfully co-ordinated the RAF to drop a 500lb Daisy Cutter bomb on the Taliban positions but the fire from the treeline, although lessened in volume, was still intense.

As his weary platoon members helped lift their wounded comrades into the Vikings for return to the FOB, Sgt Lockett sought out 3 Platoon sergeant Craig Brelsford. Lockett reports, 'I grabbed him and said, "Brellsie, I need you to go out and get the big man [Botha] for me." His last words to me were, "Mick, no dramas, don't worry about it, don't worry."'

The survivors of 1 Platoon fell in behind the laden Vikings to walk the 1km back to the base camp. The time was 03.30. Meanwhile, Sgt Craig Brelsford was preparing members of his platoon to cross the killing field in search of Johan Botha. As they approached the Taliban positions near to where Botha was lying, Sgt Brelsford was hit and fell mortally wounded; 3 Platoon was forced to retreat under sustained fire with its casualty. There was little doubt in anyone's mind that Johan Botha was dead, but the concept that men should risk their lives to bring back a corpse of a colleague is firmly embedded in the minds of troops fighting in Afghanistan. 'No one gets left behind' is the rallying cry – and no one does.

At 05.00 back at base camp, the survivors of 1 Platoon heard of Brelsford's death and a grim determination descended on the group. Sgt Lockett's face was set as he and his men rearmed and his call for volunteers to go once again into the killing

field hardly needed to be spoken. Sgt Lockett and five volunteers returned to the compound. Five Viking vehicles were now present at Three Walls and two, now carrying Sgt Lockett, Chandler, McEwan, Carlin, Drury, Lewis and Captain Henry Nwume, drove across the killing field until the body of Private Botha was located. The two vehicles then formed a V-shaped wedge between the rescuers and the depleted Taliban and Johan Botha's body was taken aboard. Henry Nwume examined the body as the grim-faced rescue team looked on and pronounced the big Afrikaner 'T4'. The British Army Medical Corps uses a four-point triage system for assessing battlefield casualties. T1 is minor, with T2 and T3 worsening in severity and in escalating need of urgent surgical intervention. T4, the least urgent of all, signifies death.

For their actions that day and night on the killing fields of Darvisham, on 7 and 8 September 2007, Lt Simon Cupples received the Conspicuous Gallantry Cross, Sgt Lockett the Military Cross, Private Luke Cole the Military Cross, and Sgt Brelsford a posthumous Military Cross. 2nd Lt Rupert Bowers was Mentioned in Dispatches. The action of that September night will remain forever in regimental lore.

4

FIT TO FIGHT

Following the fall of the Berlin Wall and the end of the Cold War in 1989, together with ever-changing operational commitments, there have been significant changes in the organisation and structure of Army training. The latest figures for the Personnel and Training Command show that, in 2005/2006, the available budget was £1.9 billion. Recruitment during that period for soldiers was 11,620; during the same period, 3,660 untrained personnel left the Army, together with 10,420 trained servicemen and women. The figures for 2006/2007 reveal that a combination of 14,910 trained and untrained personnel left the Army, against an influx of 12,400 recruits in the same timescale. These figures do not include officers seeking commission.

Calculation of the numbers that need to be enlisted to maintain the correct strength at contract level is made by the Standard Committee Army Manpower Forecasts (SCAMF),

which takes a six-monthly account of changing unit establishments, the natural wastage of servicemen and women leaving at the end of their service engagements, and those who choose to leave before their service is complete, categorised as 'Premature Voluntary Release' (PVR) or 'buying oneself out' in laymen's terms. All Army recruiting is run from an HQ in Upavon, Wiltshire, with recruiting activities taking place all over the country using a network of 125 Careers Offices, Schools Advisers, Army Youth Teams and Regimental Recruiting Teams.

Potential recruits interviewed for this book spoke of many reasons for opting for a career in the British Army. Many among these spoke of the attraction of an adventurous and sporting lifestyle, while others were drawn by the stability of Army life and the companionship involved. It's certainly true that, despite its inherent dangers, life in the today's Army offers a sense of job security unavailable to those currently employed in private industry or commerce.

The annual recruiting budget, including advertising – the overall spend for national marketing in 2006/2007 was £25.8 million for both Regular and TA advertising, including television and press, and the production of DVDs, leaflets, pamphlets and brochures – is approximately £700 million. With this, Upavon Army Recruiting and Training Directorate (ARTD) is charged with enlisting about 13,000 recruits and training a total of 100,000 officers and soldiers, involving almost 1,500 types of courses with over 6,000 actual courses run each year. At any one time in the year, an average of 12,000 officers and soldiers are undergoing training.

Across all training phases, the average annual unit cost of training a line infantry soldier is around £22,000. As a new entrant, he or she will receive £35.65 a day (£13,012 per annum) rising to £44.57 a day (£16,266 per annum) and again rising to £25,181 once established on the levels 1–7 pay scale. This led a veteran interviewed for this book to remark to me, 'Work it out, at 24 hours on call that comes to £1.50 an hour and it takes you less than a second to get shot. You actually earn less than a penny standing there like a numpty while some prat pulls the trigger,' thereby demonstrating that statistics can be used to prove anything. Although theoretically all servicemen and women are on call for duty 24 hours a day, the average day in a working unit is 08.30 to 17.00 including meal breaks.

As regular soldiers, the new entrants automatically become members of the non-contributory Armed Forces Pension Scheme. Healthcare and travel are free, with the Army charging the adult single soldier living on base £100 a month for food and £49 a month for accommodation, inclusive of council tax and all utility bills such as heating and lighting. Charges for food and accommodation are waived when field conditions are declared, i.e. when on exercises out of barracks. Married soldiers living in a one-bedroom, furnished army house pay £41.23 weekly rent. Two-bedroom houses are charged at £54.29, and a three-bedroom property costs £63.77, plus married soldiers or those with civil partners – the MoD has a liberal attitude towards unmarried relationships – are also responsible for their own electricity and gas costs.

There are also special allowances for serving overseas, such as the Northern Ireland Permanent Duty Payment, currently £6.11 per day, and a separation allowance for single and married personnel who have completed one year of service when serving away from their duty station for periods of 10 days or more. As one young servicewoman told me, 'I know whatever's in my bank account is mine to spend and I'll still have three meals a day and a roof over my head.'

After 18 years service and reaching the age of 40, soldiers are eligible for early departure payments and tax-free lump sums. If they choose to leave before this time, and provided they have served a minimum of two years, they will receive a preserved pension and tax-free lump sum at the age of 65. If, however, they serve up to the National Army's retirement age of 55, they receive this lump sum and the pension when they take retirement.

During service, the subsidised charges referred to earlier are made for accommodation and food and the new recruit signs on the dotted line for his or her kit for the loss of which he or she will be held financially responsible. The Army pay scale is far too complex to discuss fully here, but suffice to say that pay is enhanced by allowances covering most aspects of military life, including off-base lodging and subsistence allowance and scaled allowances for duty overseas, depending on the theatre of war served. The current pay scales are in any event subject to an annual revision by the Ministry of Defence, whose recommendations are passed on to the Treasury.

Bones of contention with all servicemen and women I

spoke to during research for this book were pay and life and injury insurance, the latter of which is paid out according to a standard MoD scale and can be bolstered by private-sector Government recommended policies whose premiums are paid by the individual. Recent comparisons have shown that the loss of an eye or limb in combat is compensated far below the civilian scale. There is no doubt that both Army pay and insurance scales need an urgent revision by Government and that compensation for injuries should be at least on a par with civilian awards. Certainly, remuneration against the tasks expected of a regular soldier has not escaped the attention of those higher up the scale, bringing former Army chief Sir Mike Jackson, now upped to Brigadier and Commander Recruiting Group, to observe, 'Not much over £1,000 a month for the private soldier on operations is hardly an impressive figure.'

The basic core of any Army is the infantry and it is into infantry regiments that most young recruits choose to enlist. Throughout the world, the British Army is recognised as the most professional and its infantry training especially is seen as second to none. The Headquarters School of Infantry (HQ SCHINF) oversees the training of all infantrymen joining the British Army and produces, without doubt, the most capable and qualified infantry soldiers in the world. Located in the dales of North Yorkshire, the School of Infantry oversees the three core sites of Catterick, Brecon and Warminster. The Infantry Training centre (ITC) at Catterick conducts both Phase 1 and Phase 2 of the Combat Infantryman's Course

(CIC) with officers receiving Phase 2 training at the Infantry Battle School at Brecon, which also provides Phase 3 training for Infantry Warrant Officers, and Senior and Junior NCOs. Phase 3, which includes support weapons training for officers and soldiers, is conducted at the Support and Weapons School at Warminster.

Basic Phase 1 training is undergone by all new recruits to the infantry divisions of the British Army and no one ever forgets those first myth-dispelling months at Catterick. Here, the new recruit will meet the introductory 1.5 mile circuit, which he is expected to complete in 11 1/2 minutes. Before he leaves, he'll be running that in under 10 1/2 minutes; just as he's gone from 20 sit-ups in one minute to 65 in three. He'll also learn the basic skills of Army life, including how to fit in to the new society of a life under arms. In the words of SAS veteran Lofty Wiseman, 'He'll be taught which feet his left and right boots go on.'

He will then be instructed in basic combat skills. The Combat Infantryman's Course is the framework upon which all regular infantry recruit training is based. Arms and special skills are taught to a level needed to join a rifle platoon ready to deploy on an operational tour after minimal pre-operational training in the field. Successful completion of the CIC marks the end of initial Army training. For line infantry regiments, Phase 1 training lasts for 24 weeks; those opting to join the Foot Guards, Paras and the Gurkhas go on to continuance training to meet the particular needs of those regiments.

The 24-week Combat Infantryman's Course is divided into

three individual phases. Weeks 1–6 are taken up with individual skills, drill, weapons training, fitness and field-craft. Weeks 7–21 see the recruit learning to act as a member of a team. This means endurance training where he learns never to let his side down, long runs and patrolling skills. Weeks 22–24 are taken up with live firing and battle camp at Sennybridge in Wales.

Phase 2, often referred to as 'Special to Arm' training, prepares the new recruits fresh from Phase 1 to take their place in field force units of their regiment or corps (see Appendices). This phase of training has no fixed duration and courses vary considerably in length and are carried out at various training facilities. Infantry Phase 2 training is usually around another 14 weeks in length and is carried out, as Phase 1, at Catterick. However, while training varies, the conditions of service for all British Army soldiers and officers are the same.

As a general rule, all recruits enlist on an Open Engagement, which allows them to serve for 22 years from their 18th birthday or from three months after attestation into the service, whichever is the later, thus qualifying for a pension at end of service. Under this engagement, a soldier has a statutory right to leave after four years reckoned from either his 18th birthday or three months after attestation, provided that he or she gave 12 months' notice of their intention to leave and that no leaving restrictions apply, as in the case of those employments requiring lengthy special training which carry a time bar on leaving as a statutory right.

However, for the recruit who realises they weren't cut out for crawling through mud-filled ditches and possibly having to

challenge an armed enemy – in other words, those with serious second thoughts – the Army provides the process of 'Discharged As Of Right' (DAOR) for the initial period after joining. During this time there is no obligation to stay. The time limit of the DAOR is six months for under-18s and three months for over-18s from the date of turning up at the Army Training Regiment. After that time has expired, the time limit extends to four years. Allowances are also made for medical and exceptional compassionate circumstances, but if you don't want the Army, it really doesn't want you.

5

WOMEN ON THE
FRONT LINE

Current reports suggest that 20 per cent of the 8,000 military personnel serving in Afghanistan are female, even though they make up less than a tenth of total UK military strength. An MoD spokesman approached during research for this book said it was a mistaken concept that women do not take on frontline roles, and qualified the deployment of servicewomen on the battlefield, saying, 'Women can be employed anywhere and are currently involved in every theatre of war involving British troops. What women can't do is any specialisation where the primary duty is to close with or kill the enemy. This effectively means close quarter battle, hand-to-hand combat, or other very close forms of fighting.'

Prior to the1850s, each British Army regiment had its own medical officer. Male orderlies, with no formal training, were seconded from the regiment. During peacetime, the problems

of a localised system were not apparent but the experiences of the Crimean War of 1854–56 highlighted the difficulties caused by lack of equipment and supplies, poor communications, inexperienced staff and badly managed resources.

The Crimean War was a harsh and bloody experience for Britain and was fought in the Crimea, Asia Minor, the Baltic, the White Sea and on Russia's Pacific coast between the armies of Russia, Turkey, Great Britain, France and Piedmont-Sardinia. The Crimean War has been characterised as one of the worst-managed wars in history, with deaths due to illness and malnutrition at four times the rate of those due to enemy action. In September 1854, the *Times* war correspondent William H Russell brought the desperate conditions in the Crimea to the attention of the British public and popularised the call for women nurses to join the forces: 'Are there no devoted women amongst us, able and willing to go forth to minister to the sick and suffering soldiers of the East in the hospitals of Scutari? Are none of the daughters of England, at this extreme hour of need, ready for such a work of mercy?'

In response to the worsening situation in the region, Florence Nightingale was appointed as 'Superintendent of the Female Nurses in the Hospitals in the East' by her friend Sidney Herbert, Secretary of War. Nightingale arrived at the Barrack Hospital in Scutari, a suburb on the Asian side of Constantinople, Turkey, on the eve of the Battle of Inkerman on 4 November 1854, with 38 nurses. The conditions were appalling and Welsh nurse, Elizabeth Davis, reported, 'The first that I touched was a case of frostbite. The toes of both the

man's feet fell off with the bandages. The hand of another fell off at the wrist. It was a fortnight, or from that to six weeks, since the wounds of many of those men had been looked at and dressed... One soldier had been wounded at Alma. His wound had not been dressed for five weeks, and I took at least a quart of maggots from it. From many of the other patients I removed them in handfuls.'

With an incredible amount of hard work the nurses in Nightingale's charge brought the Scutari hospital into better order and 46 more nurses had arrived in the Crimea by December. Despite a rise in the number of nurses, the workload was overwhelming. At one point, less than 100 nurses had 10,000 men under their care. By February 1855, the death rate was running at 42 per cent due to defects in the sanitation system resulting in outbreaks of cholera and typhus fever. The War Office ordered immediate reforms in the sanitary system and by June the rate fell to 2 per cent.

Pay for nurses was notoriously low, even by contemporary standards. A receipt signed by one M A Fabian and now kept in the National Archives reads: 'Mrs Fabian. Received of the Viscountess Canning – this fifth day of April 1855 – the sum of Three pounds Twelve shillings – being four weeks' wages in advance for services as Hospital Nurse at Scutari.'

It wouldn't be until 1917, during the last year of the First World War, that for the first time women were recruited for service with the Army in a non-nursing capacity with the formation of the Women's Army Auxiliary Corps, later to become the Queen Mary's Army Auxiliary Corps when

Queen Mary became its patron. Members of the corps soon proved their worth, serving with the British Expeditionary Force (BEF) in France and winning three Military Medals for gallantry. The corps was disbanded in 1921.

The Auxiliary Territorial Service (ATS) was formed on 9 September 1938, by order of King George VI. More than a quarter of a million members, including the present Queen, then Princess Elizabeth, who was commissioned in 1945, served during the Second World War. The ATS served in most overseas theatres of operation as well as home defence, especially in the Anti-Aircraft Command. In addition, they served as drivers, orderlies, storekeepers and cooks; 72 were killed in action and 313 were wounded. It was acknowledged even before the end of the Second World War that women would be a valuable asset to a peacetime Army and they continued to serve on emergency engagements in the ATS while plans were formulated for a regular Women's Corps.

In 1948, Secretary of State Emmanuel (Manny) Shinwell made a formal submission to the Crown, represented by George VI, for permission to raise a corps of women for both the regular and territorial armies. On 1 February 1949, King George VI gave royal assent and the Women's Royal Army Corps (WRAC) was born. For the first time, women in the Army became subject to all sections of the Army Act. The first Director of the WRAC was Dame Mary Tyrwhitt DBE TD.

The new WRAC was organised into battalions and companies, later to become independent companies and platoons as they became integrated with their parent military

units. However, the concept of women on the frontline was not to be tolerated in the patriarchal society of post-war Britain. Women could certainly fill non-combat roles and free men for the front in time of war, but essentially they were seen as the gentler sex whose ultimate duties in life were to bring up a family and serve Ovaltine at bedtimes. The Corps Charter recognised this when it stated that its purpose was to provide 'replacements for officers and men in such employment as may be specified by the Army Council from time to time'. Such it was that women served in over 40 different trades among 20 separate Arms and Corps. Her Majesty Queen Elizabeth the Queen Mother, who had been Commandant in Chief of the ATS since 1940, became Commandant in Chief WRAC in 1949. Her Royal Highness Princess Mary, the Princess Royal, who had been Controller Commandant ATS, became Controller Commandant WRAC with the honorary rank of Major General. Following the death of the Princess Royal in 1965, HRH the Duchess of Kent became Controller Commandant with the same rank in 1967. Such grandiose titles were dispensed with in March 1950 when Field Marshal Sir William Slim GBE KCB DSO MC announced that, henceforth, female officers would use the same titles of rank as male officers. Previously, women officers had been known as subalterns, junior commanders, senior commanders, controllers and controller commandants.

During the Second World War, women played a major role in the forces and many served in areas of extreme danger but, with the end of hostilities, the perception of the armed services

was still that of a masculine world. The turning point was in 1994, when the Royal Navy first allowed women to serve on seagoing vessels. The early 1990s also saw the scrapping of the WRAC and ATS.

Since 1998, women have been eligible to serve in 73 per cent of Royal Navy posts, 70 per cent in the Army, and 96 per cent of posts in the RAF. Women currently make up nine per cent of the total UK armed forces personnel. However, although many postings are perilously near the front line, they are denied entry to combat regiments such as the Infantry.

The Ministry of Defence describes the contribution of all women in the armed forces as 'essential' and points to recent gallantry awards to women to show they are serving in more demanding and hazardous environments than ever before. There are many arguments raised against the employment of women in armed combat roles, not the least being the old chestnut about male troops being reluctant to leave a wounded female on the battlefield. The fact is in today's Army, no soldier is left on the battlefield by his or her comrades whether he or she is wounded or dead. Witness the efforts of the men of A Company, 2nd Battalion Mercians, to retrieve the body of their dead comrade-in-arms, Johan Botha, at Darvisham when engaged on Operation Pechtaw.

The most telling argument is that of gender differences. Female military personnel are entitled to 52 weeks maternity leave, 39 of which are paid, and they are not considered for deployment within six months of giving birth, unless they volunteer. The argument continues that women on the front

line would be tested against the male enemy in close combat, where they would lack the physical strength, aerobic fitness and sheer aggression to take on a male at close quarters – or as former BBC chief correspondent Kate Adie describes it 'getting stuck in with a bayonet… blokes' fighting, in other words'.

Nonetheless, many posts held by women in today's British Army come with the risk of death on the battlefield. Across the forces, the front line roles taken on by women are many and varied. Some work as interpreters, as medical and media staff, and in intelligence-gathering and policing. They are excluded from joining the Royal Marines Commando Units, and cannot take on combat roles in the Household Cavalry, Royal Armoured Corps, the Infantry or the Royal Air Force Regiment. Nonetheless, women now serve in hazardous posts such as forward observation officers with the Royal Artillery, on communications with the Royal Signals, and with the Intelligence Corps. Many of these involve frontline operations within sight of the enemy. All female soldiers are weapons-trained and there is a chance that some time in their career they will be forced to call upon those skills to get themselves and their comrades-at-arms out of a life or death situation in whichever theatre they happen to be. That may currently be Kosovo, Northern Ireland, Iraq or Afghanistan – and they take casualties in a war where the front line starts at the forward operating base gate.

Twenty-six-year-old Acting Sergeant Sarah Bryant of the Intelligence Corps died along with a signaller and two 21 SAS reservists when their vehicle ran over a land mine near Lashkar

Gah in Helmand Province on 28 June 2008. War in Iraq also claimed the life of a female serving officer when Flight Lieutenant Sarah-Jayne Mulvhill was one of five military personnel to die in a helicopter crash in Basra in May 2006. Staff Sergeant Sharron Elliot of the Intelligence Corps was killed in an attack on a Multi-national Forces boat patrol on the Shatt al Arab waterway in Iraq in November of the same year. Second Lieutenant Joanna Dyer, also of the Intelligence Corps, a graduate of Sandhurst Military Academy where she studied with Prince William, died in a roadside explosion near Basra in 2007 along with 19-year-old Private Eleanor Dlugosz of the Royal Army Medical Corps. All of these women were employed in what the MoD refers to as 'close-combat support'.

Despite the validity of refusing women front line combat roles, there is no apparent shortage of courage when the chips are down. In the Iraq theatre of war, Flight Lieutenant Michelle Goodman landed her helicopter in the middle of a four-hour battle between British troops and rebels to rescue a severely injured rifleman who had minutes to live without surgery. The 26-year-old pilot from 28 Squadron based at RAF Benson in Oxfordshire received the Distinguished Flying Cross for her bravery under fire. And in 2006, Private Michelle Norris, a 19-year-old Army medic, became the first woman to be awarded the Military Cross, Britain's top medal for gallantry, for braving sniper fire to give first aid to her seriously wounded commander during a firefight in al-Amarah, southern Iraq.

The MoD is always careful to stress that there exists no

special treatment for women in the armed services. 'Service life is often rough and ready, and women are expected to muck in and get on with it,' said one spokesman. But as vast as the female contribution to British Armed Forces is, there will always be gender differences. For example, the MoD points out that the only time women might be excluded from the theatre for reasons of cultural sensitivity would be if there were to be a conflict in a country like Saudi Arabia. But no such exclusion exists in Afghanistan and Iraq, where British servicemen and women stand together in bearing the brunt of a cruel war and together carry on a proud tradition of the British Armed Forces, resolute under fire.

6

REVOLT AT
QALA-E-JHANGI

The revolt by more than 500 Taliban foreign fighters against their United Front (UF) captors and its subsequent suppression by the intervention of a makeshift deployment of British Special Forces were widely reported by some factions of the world press as a massacre. Certainly, there is no doubt that many died on both sides before the UK contingent arrived to restore the status quo, but the word 'massacre' is used indiscriminately. The prisoners had armed themselves and entered into a firefight with UF and US forces that lasted three days before the British intervention. The events leading to the revolt at Qala-i-Jhangi began with the fall of the Taliban stronghold of Kunduz.

The Battle for Kunduz in northern Afghanistan was fought in November 2001, when the UF forces of the Northern Alliance under General Mohammed Daoud, fresh from their victory at Taloqan, moved to assault the last enclave of the

Taliban in the province. The Alliance, formed of a loose association of tribal leaders and warlords armed and supported by the USA, needed to seize Kunduz to consolidate its hold on the north of Afghanistan and to open up routes north to Tajikistan and south to Kabul. Kunduz was the only town in northern Afghanistan still under Taliban rule.

As the Northern Alliance troops surrounded and besieged the town, its mayor, fearing a massacre should the town be stormed, asked Daoud to delay his advance while negotiations were opened by the mayor with the Taliban occupiers, who were composed mostly of foreign insurgent volunteers, among them Chechens, Pakistanis, Arabs, Uzbeks and Bangladeshis.

Eventually, the insurgents, aware that the Northern Alliance fighters already stood accused of impromptu executions of prisoners, opted not to surrender and reopened the hostilities with rocket and artillery fire on the besiegers' positions. Their fire was rapidly returned as US attack jets and B-52 bombers attacked Taliban positions in and around the city, demolishing the main Taliban command HQ and killing many of the defenders.

According to US sources, the city was defended by no more than 3,000 insurgents, although later figures confirmed a force ten times that amount. It was clear that however many Taliban sympathisers crowded into Kunduz at that time, they were prepared to sell their lives as dearly as possible, expecting no quarter from the troops of the Northern Alliance who had left behind a trail of blood and accusations of the massacres of foreign fighters in their rampage across the northern provinces. In particular, there had been accusations by the UN and the

International Red Cross of hundreds of deaths from mass executions in the city of Mazar-e-Sharif, which had fallen to the Northern Alliance earlier in the month.

The collapse of the ethnic Pashtun Taliban in the minority-dominated north had began on 9 November with the UF seizure of Mazar-e-Sharif, the lynchpin of the Taliban hold on the north. After opposition breakthroughs at Dehdadi to the west of the city and the Marmoul Gorge close to the airport 10km east of Mazar, the Taliban command ordered a general retreat from the city between 18.00 and 19.00 local time. The retreat order also involved abandoning the nearby river port of Heiratan on the Uzbekistan border, 65km to the north-east. To the relief of UF commanders, no attempt was made by the Taliban to blow the vital bridge at Heiratan across the Amu Darya River linking Afghanistan to Uzbekistan.

UF advance elements entered Mazar city between 19.30 and 20.30, encountering light resistance. The fiercest resistance in the city came a day later when UF forces surrounded a large force of mainly Pakistani, Arab and other foreign fighters in the Sultan Razzia Girls High School in the Darwaza-e-Balkh quarter of western Mazar-e-Sharif. In the assault that followed, after calls to surrender had been ignored, at least several hundred – some gave the figure as high as 1,200 – foreign fighters were killed.

It was also estimated that around 5,000 Taliban and their insurgent allies abandoned Mazar and Heiratan, leaving behind them their armour and heavy weapons. Some fled across open desert to the east towards Kunduz Province, a Taliban stronghold

in the north with a significant Pashtun population. Most Taliban, reportedly harried by night-time US air strikes, moved south-east along the highway to Samangan towards Pul-e-Khumri in Baaghlan Province. From there, some units continued south towards Bamian and Kabul while others turned north towards Kunduz. The fall of Mazar-e-Sharif had triggered a complete collapse of Taliban positions across the north.

So it was that the defenders of Kunduz, who gathered around their fanatical leader, Juma Namangani of the Islamic Movement of Uzbekistan, were in a bitter mood as their UF conquerors gathered at the gates and walls of the city, which fell on 25 November after a fortnight of fierce no-quarter fighting following a mass surrender of hundreds of foreign fighters overnight. Juma Namangani and his inner circle evaded capture during a truce when the besieging UF allowed the rapid landing and equally hasty take-off of two Pakistani aircraft the day before the surrender, sparking rumours of a secret deal by Northern Alliance General Abdul Rashid Dostum to allow Namangani and his circle to go free in exchange for a negotiated surrender.

The captured insurgents, who numbered more than 500, were rapidly shipped to a detention centre in the old fort of Qala-e-Jhangi, a few kilometres from Mazar-e-Sharif, now occupied by the UF. The detainees, smarting at defeat and undoubtedly feeling bitter at the fortunes of war that had seen their leader Namangani and his Uzbeks airlifted to Pakistan and safety while their abandoned comrades-at-arms were marched into captivity, were in no mood for compromise.

They also expected little mercy from their captors. Some had secreted hand grenades in their clothing when they were called on to surrender arms. Qala-e-Jhangi was about to erupt.

The first explosion rocked the compound, instantly killing the prisoner who had pulled the pin and several UF guards he had placed himself among before the detonation. The compound erupted. As if the exploding grenade had been the signal, the insurgents turned on their guards, stabbing them to death with knives that suddenly appeared from beneath torn cloaks and ripping the weapons from their dying hands. A CIA operative, John Michael (Mike) Spann, who was in the compound interrogating prisoners, was killed in the first moments of the revolt along with his UF bodyguards. Colleagues also working for the CIA's Special Operational Group (SOG) and Red Cross workers trapped in the compound together with a Reuters television crew barely escaped with their lives by hiding themselves amidst the confusion and scaling a wall of the compound at night to be dragged to safety by Alliance soldiers.

The insurgent prisoners, now armed with weapons taken from their murdered captors, put down a murderous rate of fire against their erstwhile captors now cowering behind the compound walls, and a prisoners' forage party broke away to examine rooms under the compound, one of which contained a UF armoury from which weapons, including Kalashnikovs, heavy machine guns and rocket-propelled grenades were rapidly dispensed above ground.

Smarting at the murder of their CIA kinsman, US Special

Forces assisting UF troops at the fort rapidly called in air support but the air strikes had little effect as the insurgents took cover in the rooms and tunnels below the compound, which was now littered with the dead and dying of both sides caught in the first moments of the firefight. For two nights, the air strikes continued and disaster struck when a rogue 200kg 'smart' bomb missed its target by 180m and exploded among the Alliance forces, killing several UF Afghanis and wounding five US soldiers.

Fighting continued throughout the night with several forays into the compound being beaten back by the Taliban insurgents, all of whom had convinced themselves that they would rather die amid the wreckage of the underground tunnels than surrender to the indignity of imprisonment or, more likely, execution. Bullets cracked, grenades fired by launchers smacked against the compound's inner walls, and RPGs left smoking trails of acrid-smelling propellant before detonating with a fearsome rush of sound that threatened to implode the eardrums of launcher and target alike. Amid the chaos, urgent calls were being made to the American embassy in the Uzbeck capital of Tashkent for help. Some hours later, that help arrived in a convoy of battered Land Rovers carrying members of the SAS and the British Special Boat Service.

Without further delay, the British Special Forces liaised with their US counterparts and assessed the situation. Hundreds of prisoners had already been killed but the survivors still kept up a fierce rate of small arms and RPG fire from barricaded positions leading to the tunnels, which became effective shelters against air and artillery attack. With characteristic

aplomb, the SAS and SBS suggested flooding the tunnels with gasoline and igniting it. As one member later remarked, 'Not even a raghead (the derogatory term employed by the Western armies for anyone of Arab descent) will sit still with his arse alight.' The plan was discussed and discarded in favour of a full-frontal assault on the insurgent positions.

It was thought at the time that no more than a few insurgents had survived the battle but the first sight of the assaulters brought a fierce response of fire. Notwithstanding the spirited defence, the British Special Forces waited until tank and missile fire had been directed on to the positions and then advanced in a skirmish line, firing from the hip with the 5.56mm Minimi light machine gun and the heavier 7.62mm GPMG. Opposition evaporated under such a withering assault and US Special Forces and UF troops moved in quickly to take control.

By Tuesday morning it was assumed that all the insurgents had either been killed or were in captivity but, three days later, on Friday, 30 November, 13 bedraggled survivors emerged from the tunnels and were taken into captivity. After questioning by their captors, the tunnels were flooded, resulting in the surrender of the remnant force the next morning, among them US citizen 21-year-old John Walker Lindh, who 10 months later would be sentenced to 20 years' imprisonment by an American court for supplying services to the Taliban. Several of the British special forces taking part in quelling the prison revolt were recognised for their extreme bravery by Washington DC and awarded the American Congressional Medal of Honor.

7

WARRIORS
OF ISLAM

While it would never be a wise intention to identify all Muslims as enemies of the Western world, the fact remains that there are mosques in British cities that are recruiting grounds for insurgent forces fighting British troops in Afghanistan. It is an anomaly that Muslim youths born in Britain and educated in British schools and, in some cases, employed by British companies should feel the urge to arm themselves and fight against their compatriots in a foreign theatre of war. Although it is the ultimate aim of Islam to convert the world to the teachings of Mohammed the Prophet, the Koran preaches against the needless taking of innocent lives, yet there is no doubt that there are British-born young Muslims who are willing to sacrifice themselves and those around them in a bloody slaughter that achieves no more than the indiscriminate death of innocents and brings terror to the streets of our major cities.

THE BLOODIEST BATTLES

In a BBC *File on 4* programme as far back as February 2004, my journalist colleague Paul Kenyon reported on the recruitment of young Muslims, born in Britain, into the wars of the Middle East and their conversion to suicide bombers, willing, in the name of Islam, to kill themselves by detonating bombs strapped to their bodies among crowds of Londoners and major city commuters. Kenyon's report was both terrifying and depressing. Is the British Government doing all it can to prevent this recruitment taking place on British soil? The answer, regretfully, is no.

Muslim antagonism to the West goes back to the first Crusades of the early 11th century, when the Eastern Orthodox Byzantine Empire made a plea for help against the expansion of the Muslim Seljik Turks into Anatolia. The ensuing response from the Catholic knights in the West was to take the conflict further and recapture Jerusalem and the Holy Land from Muslim rule. As ever, a little plunder wouldn't go amiss and Jerusalem and the Holy Land offered plunder aplenty. For a share of the booty and the convenient removal of political rivals – the Fourth Crusade actually sacked Christian Constantinople and divided the Byzantine Empire between the victorious Crusaders and the kingdom of Venice – Rome was happy to offer its blessings and grant an individual indulgence to each of the Crusaders for their excesses on the field of battle.

In any event, Islam wasn't seen as much more than the fanatical creed of the occupiers of the Holy Lands. It was and still is a religion that originated from the teachings of the

Islamic prophet Mohammed, a religious and political figure of the 7th century. Muslims believe that God revealed the Koran to Mohammed, God's final prophet, and regard the Koran and the Sunnah – words and deeds of Mohammed – as the fundamental sources of Islam. They do not regard Mohammed as the founder of a new religion, but as the restorer of the original monotheistic faith of Abraham, Moses, Jesus and other prophets. Islamic tradition holds that Jews and Christians distorted the revelations God gave to these prophets by either altering the text, introducing a false interpretation, or both. Almost all Muslims belong to one of two major denominations – the Sunni make up approximately 85 per cent and the Shi'a form a 15 per cent minority. The schism between these two distinct groupings developed in the late 7th century following disagreements over the religious and political leadership of the Muslim community. Islam is the predominant religion in Africa and the Middle East, as well as in major parts of Asia. Large communities are also found in China, the Balkan Peninsula, in Eastern Europe and Russia. There are also large Muslim immigrant communities in other parts of the world, such as Western Europe. Surprisingly, only about 20 per cent of Muslims live in Arab countries, 30 per cent in the Indian subcontinent and 15.6 per cent in Indonesia, the largest Muslim country by population. The word 'Islam' means 'surrender' or 'acceptance' and is seen as the concept of returning to God.

This book is not the place to argue the virtues and deficiencies of the European Bill of Human Rights but the fact

remains that there is a certain reticence among British politicians to limit the movements and preaching of certain Muslim clerics in the UK. The result is that gullible, British-born Muslim youths are being drawn into a conflict whose roots are far lost in history. Equally, the small flame ignited by the teachings of these clerics had been fanned into a fire fuelled by the acts of Western governments of the past and present. There are few in Britain nowadays, apart from the politicians, who do not believe that the invasion of Iraq and the subsequent execution of the country's president Saddam Hussein was a grave mistake foisted upon the credible UK and US populations by tales of weapons of mass destruction that the Iraqi dictator allegedly planned to drop on Western cities. Equally, the US-led invasion of Afghanistan was accompanied by Western propaganda that the Taliban administration – apart from the probable truth that it was hiding the West's arch enemy, Osama bin Laden – was destroying Western culture by the introduction into Western society of massive quantities of heroin, the highly addictive drug based on opium produced in the poppy fields of Afghanistan.

In reality, before the Western invasion, the religiously strict Taliban had forbidden the production of heroin and reduced the country's production to a point where, in 2001, chief UN drug control officer Bernard Frahi admitted that the Taliban religious militia had virtually halted opium production to the extent that Frahi 'did not expect' any opium to come out of Afghanistan that year.

While little doubt can exist that bin Laden was a guest of the Taliban regime following the 9/11 attack on the World Trade

Center in 2001, the USA's track record in the Middle East saw little support for an invasion emanating from the Middle East. Even Saudi Arabia, which had gone so far as to deny bin Laden his Saudi nationality following its own falling out with the fanatical firebrand, was reluctant to allow the use of Saudi soil as a base for air attacks into Afghanistan. Recruits to the Muslim cause were easy to find in regions that still smarted with the memory of the Crusades. In India, resentment still smouldered in the recall of the Union Carbide disaster in December of 1984 when the US combine's pesticide factory in Bhopal leaked 27 tons of deadly methyl isocyanate gas into the city's atmosphere, infecting half a million people, killing 20,000 and leaving 200,000 inflicted with blindness, problems with breathing and gynaecological problems. Since the disaster, survivors have been plagued with an epidemic of cancers, menstrual disorders and what one doctor described as 'monstrous births'. But the real tragedy is that the gas-affected people of Bhopal continue to succumb to injuries sustained during the disaster, dying at the rate of one each day.

As was seen in Northern Ireland, military action against a scarcely espoused cause will awake a surge of patriotic fervour and bring recruits to arms flooding in from all points of the country. Thus, with the earlier questionable action in Iraq still in public focus, the invasion of Afghanistan has brought recruits from Islamic countries as well as from the mosques of London's East End. Afghanistan is Britain's Vietnam and, in the words of many veteran soldiers, will be with us for many years to come.

8

THE SIEGE
OF SANGIN

42 Commando provided the first combat troops deployed
to southern Afghanistan following the decision in January
2006 to commit another 3,300 British troops as part of
NATO's planned expansion into the volatile region. As part of
an 850-strong advance party, 150 Marines arrived in
Afghanistan in April 2006. The aim of the advance party, which
also included elements from 39 Regiment Royal Engineers
and three CH-47 Chinook helicopters, was to carry out the
vital function of protecting Army and RAF personnel
employed in building infrastructure critical for the follow-on
deployment of 16 Air Assault Brigade in the summer. Lt Col
Ged Salzano commanded 42 Commando Royal Marines at
the time of the deployment. The current commander (June
2008) is Lt Col Charlie Stickland.

The Royal Marines have a proud history and unique
traditions and are recognised as some of the toughest fighting

troops in the world of armed combat. Although four of the old Army Marine regiments – the Queen's Own Marines, 1st Marines, 2nd Marines and 3rd Marines – took part in the siege of Gibraltar in 1704, the modern Marine Commando came into its own in the war years of 1940 when Winston Churchill devised the plan of specially trained parties of troops to infiltrate the coastal towns of occupied Europe and wreak havoc on German installations.

42 Commando is part of 3 Commando Brigade, which is currently under the command of Brigadier DA Capewell RM. It consists of four regiments, four battalions and one squadron. The brigade Regimental Sergeant Major is Warrant Officer 1st Class AC Jacka. 3 Commando Brigade can trace its origins back to the Second World War, when it was formed as the 3rd Special Service Brigade. The Commandos were created as forces to perform sharp and incisive raids on occupied Europe. Many of these raids were relatively small affairs, but some were very large and of extreme importance in planning the eventual D Day landings of Operation Overlord, such as the 1942 Dieppe raid of 19 August: the disastrous Operation Jubilee that lasted just nine hours and cost nearly 1,000 lives, and the more successful attack (Operation Chariot) on St Nazaire in 1942 to cripple the port's dry dock and limit repairs to enemy vessels. At the end of hostilities, the British Army ceased using troops in the commando role and the Royal Marines took over the task from the Army Commandos.

Over the next 25 years, 3 Commando was at the forefront of many actions, acting as a strategic reserve for the Far East

and Mediterranean region. During the Suez Crisis of 1956, codenamed Operation Musketeer, the Royal Marines were some of the first in action, conducting amphibious landings against Egyptian defences and performing the first British helicopter-borne assault in history.

The 1982 Argentinian invasion of the Falkland Islands again saw the brigade in action, landing at San Carlos Inlet and marching across East Falkland to take Stanley and witness the Argentinian surrender on 14 June. Less than ten years later, the brigade was deployed in a non-combat role in the aftermath of the first Gulf War, to distribute medical and famine aid to the Kurds in the northern part of the country. More recently, the brigade has been involved in two major campaigns, including Operation Veritas in Afghanistan and a return to Iraq for Operation Telic during the 2003 invasion by coalition forces. In 2006, it returned to Afghanistan on Operation Herrick, replacing 16 Air Assault Brigade. A return to the war-torn Helmand Province took place in 2007, when elements of 42 Commando were to become involved in a vicious siege of an Army compound in the town of Sangin by Taliban forces that would mirror the Alamo in the courage and determination of its defenders.

The area had enjoyed a two-month unofficial ceasefire when the Marines arrived in the Sangin compound from a period of rest and recuperation at Camp Bastion. Sangin, a town of 14,000 inhabitants in Helmand Province, is situated in a fertile agricultural area infamous as a centre of opium cultivation. The green zone centred on Sangin is believed to be

responsible for 83 per cent of the country's entire output of opium culled from the indigenous poppy crop of *papaver somniferum papaveraceae*. The area is a centre of Taliban activity, fostered by local opposition to the Afghan Government and to the presence of foreign troops by local tribesmen and drug traffickers who fear that the ISAF troops might destroy the poppy crops from which they reap such huge profits.

Before the British deployment, the area was under complete Taliban control. However, in June 2006, frustrated at the absence of his new Government's mandate in the region, President Hamid Kharzai pleaded for ISAF intervention. The result was that Sangin became the base for 120 British troops, who set up their operational base in a run-down compound occupied by some government offices and a detachment of the Afghan police force. The compound – the designated district centre (DC) – would become the hub of such intense fighting over the next nine months that General David Richards, the NATO commander in Afghanistan, would be heard to observe that Helmand Province was experiencing the fiercest fighting involving British troops since the Korean War. The British troops had a less eloquent way of arriving at the same conclusion. They nicknamed the town 'Sangingrad' in reference to the defence of Stalingrad by Russian troops against the invading German 6th Army in 1942.

The position at the run-down district centre was strengthened. Foxholes were dug round the perimeter and sandbags reinforced the compound walls. At first, there was no contact with the Taliban, and the attitude of the inhabitants

was passive, if not sympathetic to the presence of British troops who were able to patrol the city safely. The situation changed abruptly on 27 June 2006, after a failed raid by the Special Reconnaissance Regiment, during which two soldiers were killed not far from Sangin.

Following the contact, the attitude of the locals changed suddenly and the base was attacked with small arms that escalated into incoming fire from RPG-7 rocket launchers. The RGP-7 is a lethal weapon even in the hands of untrained recruits but the Taliban had cut their teeth on the Russian grenade launcher during 10 years of Russian occupation. Since the 1980s, the weapon had also undergone a modification when Bulgaria developed the GTB-7G grenade with a thermobaric warhead, introducing the potential to expand the basic RPG-7 Knut portable rocket launcher into a true multi-purpose weapon. The thermobaric warhead utilises an advanced form of the fuel-air explosive concept in which the contents of the 93mm diameter warhead are scattered in an aerosol form on impact and then ignited to create a rapidly formed, high-pressure blast wave, equivalent to that produced by the detonation of 2kg of TNT. The blast effect is such that significant damage can be inflicted on structures, including field fortifications, and lightly armoured vehicles.

When launched, the thermobaric grenade has a maximum direct-fire range of 200m, with an initial velocity of 66m/sec with a maximum possible range of 1km. The grenade weighs 4.7kg and is 1.12m long. It can be employed with any RPG-7 launcher once the necessary sight adjustments have been made.

Another recently developed alternative warhead grenade for the fin-stabilised rocket includes variations of anti-personnel high-explosive fragmentation. The rocket launcher itself is manufactured by the Vazov Engineering Plant (Vazovski Mashinostroitelni Zavodi) at Sopot, an otherwise tranquil resort on Poland's Baltic coast, from where it is offered for worldwide use. The thermobaric GTB-7G grenade is now on offer for export.

The proliferation of RPGs surrounding the base also made resupply difficult, now dependent on helicopter flights from Camp Bastion. All roads were cut off and the District Centre compound was effectively under siege for periods as long as five days at a time when Taliban fire made helicopter flights too dangerous for even the bravest pilot to attempt. Nevertheless, despite withering Taliban fire, a unit of Royal Engineers surrounded the whole compound and the helicopter landing pad with a double rampart of Hesco barriers, a blast wall system designed by the Dubai-based Hercules Engineering consortium for use in high-risk zones, but casualties were inevitable.

On 1 July, two signallers, Corporal Peter Thorpe and Lance Corporal Jabron Hashmi, together with an Afghan interpreter, were listening in to Taliban communications when they were killed by a Chinese-made 107mm rocket landing within the District Centre. Jabron Hashmi was the first British Muslim soldier to die during the War on Terror.

Desperately short of supplies and ammunition, the troops fought like demons to repulse attack after attack, assisted by spotters precariously positioned on the DC rooftop to direct

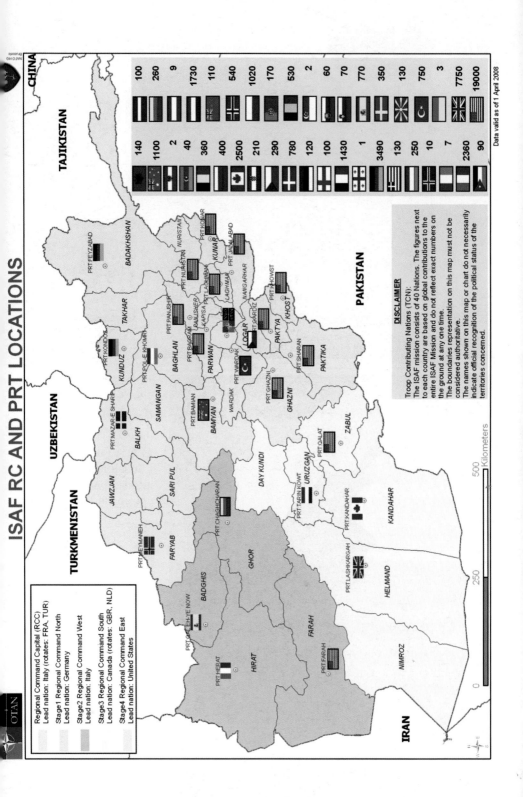

Map of Afghanistan showing troop deployments by nationality.

Above: A SNATCH 2 patrol vehicle armed with L1A1 12.7mm/.50 cal.

©*Crown Copyright/MC*

Left: A Guided Missile Launch Rocket System goes into action against Taliban entrenched in Arghandab.

©*Crown Copyright/MC*

bove: A Challenger II Main Battle Tank.　　　　　　　　*©Crown Copyright/MOD*

elow: Its forerunner, a British Mark IV tank, in action at Cambrai in 1917.

Above: Heavy Metal – the mighty Trojan of the Royal Engineers can clear obstacles an
mines in the path of an advancing army. ©*Crown Copyright/MO*

Below: A Predator unmanned aircraft returns to its base in Uzbekistan, piloted from
thousands of miles away in Langley, Virginia. The aircraft pictured carries only one of it
two Hellfire pod-located missiles (on right pod) and may have been ordered to fire the
other by remote command. ©*USA*

above: A Kabul policeman pays homage to colleagues killed by a roadside bomb.

below: The aftermath of a rocket strike on a Taliban position in Arghandab.

Hearts and minds: a British soldier talks with an Afghan boy during a patrol on the
outskirts of Kabul on July 27, 2008.

©*Shah Marai/AFP/Getty Imag*

bove: A British Army soldier from the 3rd Battalion the Parachute Regiment secures
e helicopter landing strip (HLS) during operation Southern Beast on August 6, 2008 in
aywand District in Kandahar Province.   ©*Marco Di Lauro/Getty Images*

elow: British paratroopers from 3rd Battalion the Parachute Regiment arrive at Camp
agle in the Zabul Province, June 2008.   ©*Marco Di Lauro/Getty Images*

Top: A Desert hawk drone, looking slightly the worse for wear, is recovered after a reconnaissance mission overflying Taliban positions. *©Crown Copyright/MO*.

Bottom: The new Watchkeeper high-altitude drone is expected to be in service in Afghanistan by 2010.

fire from artillery and mortars and call in air strikes from attack helicopters and jets against the Taliban, inflicting heavy losses. The situation had by now become too much for the Afghan police contingent, who began defecting to the Taliban, giving them crucial information on the internal layout of the base.

But temporary relief was to arrive on 16 July when Operation Mountain Thrust, which included support from 700 coalition troops including US, Canadian, Afghan and Estonian forces, saw 200 British paratroops, supported by Apache helicopters, inserted by Chinook into Sangin. In a concerted attack with the aid of the embattled garrison, the siege of the District Centre was finally broken. In a cordon and search operation, the town was sealed off and Taliban compounds were searched and cleared. Ten Taliban were confirmed killed during this operation, and the others were driven out. The operation weakened the Taliban hold on the city, but did not break it. The Siege of Sangin was to last until the late spring of 2007 and would see the Royal Marines in action before the Taliban of Sangin learned the futility of attempting to test the mettle of the British soldier in battle.

Under Brigadier Jerry Thomas DSO MBE, 3 Commando Brigade Royal Marines arrived in Helmand Province in September 2006, at the height of the Sangin siege, to begin a six-month tour as the core of a 4,500-strong UK task force. The area of Sangin at that time was highly complex and volatile, an atmosphere in which the Taliban warrior, the drug trafficker, the tribal warlord and the Afghan farmer were often indistinguishable and, at least, very closely linked. The main

Helmand Battlegroup, 42 Commando Royal Marines, set about easing the pressure on the commercial capital, Gereshk, by dominating the lower Sangin Valley. Attention was then turned to setting the security conditions for a major international development project centred on the nearby Kajaki Dam. This required the seizure of key high ground as well as both company and commando-level operations to clear the enemy from surrounding villages.

The Kajaki Dam, the main watershed for the Sistan Basin, is one of the two major hydroelectric power dams of Helmand Province. Built in 1953, it is located on the Helmand River 90 kilometres north-west of Kandahar City. It has a dual function, to provide electricity while serving to irrigate some 1800 square km of formerly ~~arid~~ land. Water discharging from the dam flows through 500 kilometres of downstream irrigation canals feeding farmland. The structure is 100 metres high and 270 metres long with a storage capacity of 1.2 cubic kilometres of water.

The tour eventually culminated in a successful brigade-level attack to secure Sangin itself. Throughout the tour, the Task Force was in contact with the Taliban for an average of ten hours a day with threats from mines, suicide bombers, ambushes and all-out assaults from a battle-hardened and often well-led enemy. Inevitably, there were casualties on both sides with the far greater portion inflicted on the enemy.

The Royal Marines took up their positions in the relieved District Centre of Sangin after an uneasy ceasefire that had lasted two months. In the words of one combatant, Sergeant

Jason Layton, who was to be awarded the Military Cross for bravery under fire in Sangin, 'After we arrived, the ceasefire came to a crashing halt. Approximately 400 fighters were in the town and they basically tried to take us out. After two days, we came under a huge co-ordinated attack. They were using mortars and small arms fire. It was day and night and went on for 15 days.'

The citation recommending Sergeant Clayton's award of the Military Cross describes how the Welsh-born NCO 'inspired and led his men... knowingly exposing himself to the automatic grenade launcher threat'. Clayton later explained that enemy fire was focused on the observation tower of the District Centre – a strategic target from where an observer could pinpoint the Taliban positions – and not the favourite OP of the members of his troop. Reluctant to place his men in such obvious danger, the tough Marine chose the ingrained philosophy of never ordering a man to do something he wouldn't take on himself and took over the tower watch, subjecting himself to a constant barrage of fire from the grenade launchers and RPGs of the enemy.

Throughout the 15 days of siege, sleep was a precious and scarce commodity. The main attacks continued to be focused on the District Centre and its observation tower. The Afghan police who had occupied a building in the compound were long gone, having fled to their families or to join the Taliban insurgents as they realised the odds were against the besieged defenders, now down to just 100 British personnel, mainly Royal Marines and Royal Engineers.

During their defence of the compound, which each day brought vicious firefights as both sides engaged in a fierce battle of attrition, three men of 29 Commando Royal Artillery Regiment lost their lives. On Saturday, 3 March 2007, Lance Bombardiers Ross Clark and Liam (Paddy) McLaughlin were killed when a rocket burst within the District Centre compound. Five days later, a 39-year-old veteran, Warrant Officer Second Class Michael Smith, was killed by an RPG grenade that exploded just inside the perimeter wall.

Nonetheless, although British blood was inevitably shed to hold Sangin and allow patrols into the surrounding areas, the Taliban hold on the region was broken. The success of 3 Commando Brigade's tour and its impact across the whole spectrum of operations was universally acknowledged – no Taliban spring offensive emerged in 2007, with enemy operations significantly disrupted.

The six-month siege of Sangin was finally broken and an unconfirmed assessment of the firepower employed in what was possibly the fiercest battle to date of the Afghanistan campaign reported that over 1 million rounds of small arms had been used during the engagements.

9

THE GIANT
KILLERS

Although much of the infantryman's engagements with his enemy are tense, close-quarter affairs often carried out in urban environments, deployment in the field has called for the rapid development of weaponry capable of taking out the most dreaded of the infantry's opposition – heavy armour. Over the years, a number of devices have been developed. The earliest tanks had poor protection against anything larger than the standard rifle bullet of the day until the introduction by Germany of the Mauser anti-tank rifle of 1918.

The Mauser Tank Gewehr Modell 1918 was developed in the lull between the introduction of the tank by the British on the Somme in 1916 when 35 Mark 1 tanks, lumbering along at 3mph, attempted unsuccessfully to break through the German lines due to untried tactics and mechanical breakdowns, and the spring of 1917 when the remodelled tanks returned to action. These 30-ton machines of war were to vindicate themselves in

the autumn of that same year when, on 20 November, 300 British Mark IV tanks of the Tank Corps, led by Brigadier Hugh Elles, created a major break in the German Hindenburg Line and nearly reached the town of Cambrai.

However, by this time the 13mm armour-piercing round had been fully developed and the fearsome recoil of the weapon somewhat overcome, the war was over.

Next on the scene was the British Boys Anti-Tank rifle, developed in the 1930s as alarm spread at news of German rearmament. The rifle, developed in secret conditions under the codename 'Stanchion', saw the light of day in 1934 when, at tests, its .55 calibre round successfully pierced 25mm armour. However, the Boys saw little action in the coming Second World War, due once again to the fierce recoil of such a heavy calibre round despite the application of a spring absorber, a muzzle brake and a front support.

It was finally clear that the rifle bullet, however fast, was not the answer, and thereafter all light anti-tank weapons used HE projectiles – the first of these being the infamous Piat, known in sergeant-major speak as the Projector Infantry Anti-Tank.

The Piat consisted of a cylindrical sheet metal body, 610mm long and 76mm in diameter, with a basic T-shaped canvas-covered butt at the rear and a 254mm semi-circular trough at the front. The trough was to accommodate the 1.13kg high-explosive projectile that would be launched up to 320m by the massive internal firing pin attached to the internal spring of the Piat, but woe betide the unfortunate gunner whose hand was on the massive firing lever just to the rear of the tripod,

which was often detached to allow for comparatively easier balance when firing.

Basically, the Piat was fired from the shoulder, fixing the target in the folding sights mounted on the left-hand side of the body. This was a difficult exercise since the weight of the projectile at the front made a steady aim almost impossible. The pull on the massive trigger released the internal bolt that drove the spigot forward with great force so that it entered the tail tube and fired the launch cartridge, upon which the bomb departed with sufficient recoil to hopefully drive the spigot back and re-cock the weapon for the next bomb to be loaded without flattening the firer. The alternative was manual cocking of the Piat, which involved holding the weapon vertically between the knees while standing, placing both feet on the butt then grasping the trigger guard, twisting it anti-clockwise and pulling upwards until the spring was fully compressed and held by the sear. The pull required was 90.7kg or 200lb and ruptures and strained backs were common among operators. Better things were to come.

The entry of the USA into the Second World War in 1941 brought with it the 2.36 inch rocket launcher that would become known as the bazooka after a comic wind instrument played by US radio comedian Bob Burns in the 1930s. The Germans swiftly followed with their checkmate version of the Panzershrek, heavier than the bazooka and outranged by 65m but firing a heavier projectile at 3.18kg to the bazooka's 1.54kg. Both were capable of penetrating 100mm of armour plate and were deadly against the tanks of the day, but

improvements in armour plate would soon call for a heavier weapon capable of pulverising the new metals emerging from the laboratories of the larger nations.

It was from Russia that the new tank killer would emerge, with the production of the rocket-propelled grenade-launcher RGP2 in the years following the Second World War. Based closely on the German Panzerfaust, the RPG2 was a reasonably effective weapon with the disadvantage of a high trajectory that limited its effective range to 100m. Its shortcomings became obvious when used by the Viet Cong against modern US tanks in Vietnam and it was eventually replaced by the RPG7, which today is widely distributed to a variety of guerrilla and subversive organisations and is currently in use by the Taliban in Afghanistan against aircraft, ground armour and personnel. The RPG7 has a range of 900m and fires either the thermobaric grenade or a self-destructing 2.25kg bomb capable of penetrating 320mm of armour plate.

The British Army post-war contemporary of the RPG7 was the 84mm Infantry Anti-Tank Gun, developed from Sweden's 84mm RCL Carl-Gustav. A fearsome weapon, with an anti-tank round weighing 2.6kg and capable of ripping through 400mm of armour, the 84mm IATG has a back-blast of up to 28m and has been steadily replaced by the new high-tech tank killers of the late 20th and emerging 21st centuries.

Today, the infantryman can rely on the onboard computer technology of launch systems like the man-portable Milan anti-tank guided missile system, now outclassed by the American Javelin anti-armour missile which replaced it in 2005.

Until then, the wire-fed Milan had held top ranking in the anti-tank systems list since its introduction in the 1970s. Although capable of piercing all Soviet armour, it was cumbersome in that it required a five-man team to operate it in combat conditions. Nonetheless, it was quick to deploy, although its long flight time meant the operator had to be able to see the target for a full 12.5 seconds at maximum range, which meant, of course, that the enemy could see him. This was because the target system was operated by an infra-red flare in the tail of the £11,000 missile. The flare was detected by a sensor in the sight and its position automatically measured. The position was then compared to the axis of the sight and adjustments sent along the command wire. The Milan flew at a comparatively slow 200m/sec to a range of 2km. At such a slow speed, its force of impact was negligible and damage relied on a specially designed warhead to blast a hole in the tank's armour. The cone-shaped explosive charge could blow a hole in 1m of metal at any range. More recently, the stage has been taken by the Javelin, derivative of the US M47 Dragon anti-tank missile.

The Javelin, which entered into service with the British Army in 2005 with an order for 18 launchers and 144 missiles, is a portable anti-tank weapon, designed in a joint venture by Raytheon Missile Systems (originally Texas Instruments) and Lockheed Martin Missiles and Fire Control. The system is shoulder-fired and can also be mounted on tracked, wheeled or amphibious vehicles. Raytheon is responsible for the Command Launch Unit (CLU), missile guidance electronic

unit, system software and system engineering control. Lockheed Martin produces the missile seeker, missile engineering and assembly.

Javelin entered full production in 1994 and the system was first demonstrated to US Army brass at Fort Benning, Georgia, in 1996. Impressed by the weapon's power, the US Army and Marine Corps and Australian Special Forces deployed the Javelin to devastating effect against Saddam Hussein's armour during Operation Iraqi Freedom in March and April of 2003. To date (summer 2008) more than 1,200 rounds have been fired in combat and the system is in regular use with British troops in southern Afghanistan where it plays a role against defensive positions and in surveillance in the absence of enemy armour. So versatile is the Javelin system and so short on back-blast that it can be fired from within a building, although accompanying troops should avoid the minimised but still appreciable back-blast. Particularly impressive to operators is that it can be fired from the shoulder by one man from a squatting position and does not need to be tracked to the target as did the Milan. The Javelin is a complete fire and forget system, autonomously directed to the target and leaving the gunner free to reposition or reload immediately after firing.

The gunner's controls are on the command launch unit, with a day-sight capacity of 4x magnification and a night-sight capacity of 9x magnification optics. The optimum range of the missile is 2.5km. The missile has recently been upgraded to a block 1 type missile, which includes an improved rocket motor for a shorter flight time to target and an enhanced warhead

effective against a greater range of targets, and improvements to the command launch unit and software. The tandem warhead is fitted with two shaped charges – a precursor warhead to destroy top-plate reactive armour and a main warhead to penetrate base armour.

The gunner's vision of the target is a cursor box that he centres over the target before sending a lock on before launch command to the infra-red guidance system. Lock on is indicated by a high-pitched whine and a cursor crosswire centring on the target. The missile is then launched by the gunner without any post-launch tracking or guidance required. A soft launch system gives the low recoil that allows firing from inside buildings and covered positions. Once the missile is clear of the launcher, the second stage propellant is ignited and the missile assumes one of the two attack modes available to the gunner. The direct attack mode is used against covered targets, bunkers, buildings and helicopters. Top attack is selected against tanks, in which case the missile climbs to a peak altitude of 150m and strikes down to penetrate the roof of the tank where there is less armour.

Javelin now equips the British Army's rapid reaction forces, including 16 Air Assault Brigade, 3 Commando Brigade and mechanised infantry. BAe Systems and a number of other UK companies now provide subsystems for the missiles. In 2007, the Javelin replaced the Swingfire anti-tank guided weapon with the armoured infantry and formation reconnaissance forces in the field.

As with all technological self-destructive systems, the Javelin

is expensive to use, with each missile costing in the region of £60,000, which provoked a sergeant to admonish a soldier who had already fired two missiles at a suppressed enemy position and was preparing to launch a third. 'Oy, you're wasting Gordon Brown's money there, lad,' said the NCO. Back came the reply, 'Yeah? Well he ain't fookin' sitting 'ere... *I* am.'

Other hand-held infantry anti-tank weapons still include the 66mm Light Anti-tank Weapon (LAW), and the 84mm LAW.

10

THE LAST
PATROL

They had lost three here before. On that fateful Thursday, 23 August 2007, Privates Aaron McClure, Robert Foster and John Thrumble had died as the earth of the compound erupted and the American bomb thudded home. It was a disastrous, monstrous error, for these men had not been the enemy – they were men of B Company 1 Royal Anglian and they were heading a drive to clear the Taliban from the village of Mazdurak in war-torn Helmand Province. The 500lb bomb dropped by a US aircraft of fast air support should have landed 500m to the north. Instead, it had touched ground in the compound where men of 7 Platoon were taking cover behind the thick mud walls to lay down fire on the enemy. Three had died and four had been grievously wounded. They had had to return to dig for one brave soul whose lifeless body was lying buried under the rubble at the epicentre of where the US bomb had landed.

There had been no acrimony. This was war and, in its heat, errors were made. The survivors knew that there were Dutch and French pilots up there too and the bomb could have come from any one of their aircraft. Besides, the US pilots had got them out of many tough scrapes before.

Diving at 600mph into the haze of shimmering desert air to release a bomb did not always allow for precision targeting. It was an error, a blue-on-blue. Despite the description, friendly fire is never friendly. That was the risk they all took – and now they were going back. They had not patrolled the area for 10 days and the Taliban were getting cocky.

The enemy radio chatter spoke of them as a disillusioned troop low on morale at the loss of their comrades. Now the Anglians of B Company must show them that they held the day and the night around the Kajaki Dam.

They embarked in the armoured Snatch 2 Land Rovers that would take them to their dropping-off point and left the FOB at 03.30, driving on night vision. The aim of the mission was to reclaim or deny to the enemy any equipment left at Mazdurak in the chaos and confusion following the blue-on-blue incident. The route would take them over the Helmand River, then north for two-and-a-half miles, where fire support teams would deploy to high ground on the east and west to cover the assault. 6 Platoon would lead the assault with 5 and the depleted 7 in fire support.

Once on their start line, the men of 6 Platoon prepared to move cautiously forward under the direction of B Company OC Major Tony Borgnis. They didn't intend to linger long in

the open ground between compounds. Intelligence had warned them of a highly skilled sniper operating in the area. Although the enemy sniper was reported to be using a .50 calibre weapon, almost certainly the weapon employed would be either the 7.62mm Soviet Mosin-Nagant or the Dragunov SVD. The Soviet skill in the production of accurate bolt action and semi-automatic long-range firearms has developed over many years, buoyed by the success of Soviet snipers in the defence of Stalingrad in the Second World War. The semi-automatic Dragunov in particular can deliver a 7.62mm round over 1.2km with devastating results and pin-point accuracy. In the hands of a trained marksman, it is instant death. Crossing the dead zone towards the forward line of enemy troops (FLET) every patrol member had reason to fear the dawn.

Before the advance, they would await the dropping by the RAF of a 1,000lb bomb on the compound where their comrades had died just 10 days before. But enemy radio chatter had identified a group of possibly 12 Taliban, designated as 'Paks' by the British troops, lying in wait for the advancing patrol before the target compound. The enemy spoke of a 'special surprise' awaiting the British troops. Major Borgnis leading the assault smiled grimly at the news. The Taliban had given away both their position and their intent. The 'special surprise' might well be in their camp before the battle was over. Calmly, he ordered an air strike on the enemy ambush position. The RAF pilot paused to identify 7 and 5 Platoons' fire support positions marked by Firefly strobes.

The last time the Anglians had called in for help from the

high-flying F15s and F16s riding the diamond-clear air above them, three of their number had died. Now they watched with trepidation as an RAF military jet prepared for its delivery of death from on high. Firefly strobes had identified the fire support groups and company sections on the ground and their positions were acknowledged by the pilot as he brought his aircraft into a high-altitude bomb delivery drive. The 1,000lb load zeroed in on its helpless target and scored a direct hit on the Taliban position. Cheers erupted from the British positions as poetic justice curled and flamed around the enemy position and figures were flung high into the air in a macabre ballet of death.

With the ambush site cleared, it was now time for the scheduled air strike on the targeted compound. Again, they heard the pilot's 90-second warning as the bomb was released and the F15 bucked skyward with the release of weight. The compound disintegrated as the bomb struck and 6 Platoon moved forward to engage the enemy left alive in Mazdurak and to push through to nearby Khvolehabad in the north-west.

As they advanced through the scattered compounds of Mazdurak, their progress was followed by two stray dogs that had adopted the Anglians when their late owners, the Marines, returned to the UK and now followed them everywhere, including on the noisiest and most dangerous of operations. A soldier ducking out of fire while being spattered by mud chips flying from the thick wall that provided him with nevertheless scant protection from a high-velocity round was likely to find himself at the receiving end of a couple of licks of bad-breath encouragement from either one of the troops' canine supporters.

THE LAST PATROL

An Afghanistan settlement has little resemblance to the organised urbanisations of the West. Here, a man built where he grew his crops and the deserted family compounds were separated by exposed tracts of land where narrow tracks wound through the fields of desiccated poppies, once the cash crop of the region. The patrol moved from compound to compound, lobbing grenades into the low, dark doorways and following the ear-splitting detonation up with a burst of fire from a light machine gun or personal weapon on automatic until eventually they found themselves facing the enemy across a 400m wadi.

The Taliban troops were hidden behind a low wall from where they directed a sustained burst of accurate fire on the advancing patrol. Sergeant Ben Browning leading the assault ordered his machine-gunners up on to the roofs of the mud buildings to deploy rapid fire against the enemy position. The gunners set up their GPMGs along the long, low wall of a roof as the Taliban rounds thudded into the crumbling structures, punching holes through the baked mud. The smoke of battle was tinged with the acrid bite of cordite as guns overheated in the rising temperatures and were cooled by a drenching with precious water from the men's canteens. Rapid fire thudded into the Taliban positions and shoulders ached with the drumming recoil as the machine guns spat their rounds at the enemy. Ricochets were absorbed by the soft-baked mud of the buildings but each heavy round ripping through the walls released a cloud of choking dust that clogged the back of the throats of the men engaged in the desperate battle for

supremacy of the area. The Taliban fire began to lessen but the thought that the enemy were weakening was tempered by the reality that the Anglians' ammunition was running short. It is always a difficult choice whether to conserve ammunition and alert the enemy to an impending loss of firepower or to lay down a defiant cover of rounds and organise a tactical fast extraction before the enemy realises that ammunition is short and they could be about to win a tactical advantage.

Ben Browning decided to withdraw his men of 6 Platoon and ordered a last barrage of fire before the withdrawal began. But the day had been won. Eight wounded Taliban had been seen limping from the scene of the first bomb strike and B Company snipers had taken their toll on the Taliban forces, one sniper dropping a Taliban fighter as the insurgent was on the point of launching an RPG 7's lethal thermobaric grenade at the platoon position. Now 6 Platoon made a hurried extraction to the safety of the dried river bed beyond Mazdurak.

The Anglians had not lost a man to death or injury and morale was high. It had been their last patrol before they turned the defence of the Kajaki Dam over to the men of the Royal Marines and returned to the UK. They had struck a blow that the Taliban would not forget for many months to come and their dead on the tour – they had lost nine men during their six-month in Afghanistan – had been revenged in enemy blood.

11
DRESSED
TO KILL

The duty of any parent is to provide their offspring with the equipment to help them through life and the British Army sees its duty towards its recruits as no less. As part of the most recent settlement of the annual spending review, the Defence Budget is set to increase from a baseline of £32.6 billion in 2007/08 to £36.9 billion in 2010/11 in Total Departmental Expenditure Limit (Total DEL). In real terms – i.e. after inflation – it represents an average annual growth of 1.5 per cent. By 2010/11, the budget will be 11 per cent higher in real terms than in 1997, and represents the longest period of sustained growth since the 1980s. Spending an average of £22,000 on the training of a new soldier would mean little without providing suitable kit to get the job done and to provide suitable protection during its execution. Once kitted out suitably with uniform and special clothing for his or her service role, and having been well fed and housed

(although the latter is often the target of much criticism), the new recruits must devote themselves to weapons handling and become familiar with the huge range of ordinance, large and small, with which they will be expected to go to war.

The first and most familiar is the infantryman's best friend, which any sergeant major on arms drill will insist is the rifle. This most familiar of weapons has undergone a long and changing development since the late 19th century, when British experience in the South African War of 1899–1902 showed the need for a short rifle for universal use. The model that emerged in 1907 was the Short Magazine Lee-Enfield Mark II.

The bolt-operated Lee-Enfield would go on through many stages of development to become the familiar weapon of the British Infantry in the conflicts of the 20th century until replaced by the NATO-inspired FN-FAL, the Self-Loading Rifle (SLR) whose modified national designs – the British version is the SLR L1A1 – saw service with both Argentinian and British troops in the Falklands. Nonetheless, its 20-round 7.62mm magazine was barely matched by the 10-round charger of the Lee-Enfield and its slightly heavier .303 round, which wrought such devastation on German infantry when operated at the standard British infantry rate of fire of 15 aimed shots per minute. But those who mourned the passing of the Lee-Enfield, whose Model 4 is still incidentally in use by the British Army as the 7.62mm L4A1 sniper rifle, would equally mourn the replacement of the SLR by the SA80. The latter weapon, which fired a 5.56mm cartridge from a 30-

round magazine, received much criticism, especially from Special Forces who rejected the weapon outright in favour of the American-built M16 and the Colt AR15.

The L4A1 sniper rifle mentioned above, although a firm favourite, is also now being replaced. The L115A3 long-range rifle (LRR) is a high-accuracy, bolt-action sniper system, based on the Accuracy International AWM rifle, which supersedes the L4A1and the standard L96A1 sniper rifle in power, accuracy and range.

In the current climate, the need for snipers on operations has increased. They are vital in helping to engage targets at a range sufficient to keep the threat at a safe distance. The L115A3 fires a heavier cartridge designed to maintain velocity over long ranges, delivering accurate point fire out to 1,100m. Muzzle brakes are fitted to reduce recoil, jump and flash and act as a base for optional iron sights and suppressors. The rifle has a state-of-the-art telescopic sight with twice the magnifying power of the old version. It is also equipped with brand-new all-weather day and night sights, which gives snipers round-the-clock capability, something that they have not had before.

One of the problems with the SA80 was that for use in the army of a nation where 10 per cent of the population is left-handed, the empty cases are ejected on the right of the weapon from a port opposite the firer's face, thus making it impossible to fire left-handed. The angle of the ejected cases also varies considerably as the weapon heats up and the rate of fire changes, calling for a larger opening of the ejection port and the resulting problem of fouling by sand in desert conditions.

The situation was made worse by the insistence of the manufacturers in producing 5.56mm ammunition using chopped tube rather than ball powder. The chopped tube – made by propellant being compressed into a cylinder then 'chopped' into appropriate lengths for insertion into a cartridge body during the manufacturing process – gives a lower port pressure and corresponding lower rate of fire. The 'girder' under the light support weapon (LSW) barrel came about as the Army wished to fire two-round bursts from it. With the original bipod which was attached to the gas block, one round went high right and the second low left. Firing a succession of double taps gave two distinct groups and the additional ironware and the muzzle-mounted bipod was the final solution.

Another disadvantage which led to its rejection by the SAS and SBS was the safety catch, which entailed the use of the left hand instead of the firer using the thumb or index finger of the right, or 'trigger' hand. A further complaint originated from the placing of the fire selector, again on the left-hand side, which meant the weapon had to be brought off target to effect a change for automatic to single-shot repetition. But an advantage of the SA80 was that it was the first combat weapon to be issued to front line troops with a telescopic sight as standard fitting. The sight, denominated in Army parlance as Sight Unit Small Arms Trilux (SUSAT) gave a 4x magnification and came fitted with a rubber eyepiece. Through this the shooter saw a pointer that was dark in daylight and illuminated by the radioactive Trilux lamp in poor light.

Eventually, German arms manufacturer Heckler & Koch was approached to redesign the SA80 in a £92 million modification plan after it was suspended from the NATO recommended weapons list in 1997. The result was the improved SA80-A2 , designated the L85A1 in its role as a personal weapon, which is still suffering from stoppage problems and has featured in formal equipment failure reports filed by troops in Afghanistan. The SA80 was originally designed and produced by the Royal Small Arms Factory at Enfield Lock. In 1988, production was transferred to the Royal Ordnance's Nottingham Small Arms Facility, now BAe Systems, Land Systems Munitions and Ordnance.

Other small arms in common use by British forces are the adopted P226 Sig-Sauer Pistol, the Browning Hi-Power Pistol, the Heckler & Koch MP5 submachine gun (the much-loved 'Hockler' of Special Forces), the Heckler & Koch 53 Assault Rifle, the SA80-A2 derivative Light Support Weapon, the MINIMI light machine gun, the GPMG general-purpose machine gun, and the .50 calibre Browning heavy machine gun, as well as specialist sniper rifles like the recently introduced L-96 and the long-range 8.59mm L115A1. The Sterling submachine gun, although still in use by some elements of the Army, has mainly been superseded by the SA80-A2, the improved variant of the SA80. All of these weapons, as long proven in service as most of them were, would inevitably come up against an excellent import from behind the defunct Iron Curtain that first came into use with the Russian Army in 1951. It was the invention of a Russian

Army sergeant, Mikhail Kalashnikov, and soon would be in the arsenal of 50 armies worldwide as well as numerous terrorist groups. The weapon was the Avtomat-Kalashnikova, denominated the AK47.

The earliest versions of the AK47 had wooden butts. These, like those of so many early Soviet arms, were made of poor-quality timber which detracted greatly from the otherwise excellent quality of the weapon. Soon after, as a variant, the butt was replaced by a folding metal butt that could be turned forward under the weapon without affecting its use. Although probably destined originally for use by airborne troops, the compactness and resulting easy concealment of the AK47 variant made it the ideal choice of guerrillas, terrorists and irregular forces the world over, when combined with the weapon's robustness and simple construction.

The gun, internationally dubbed the 'Widow Maker', can shoot its 7.62mm rounds accurately to 400m and has the additional advantage of automatic fire at a rate of 600 rounds per minute. Although outranged by most conventional armies' weapons of the same class, the fact that firefights seldom take place at ranges of more than 300m and often at much less makes the Kalashnikov the ideal weapon to hand when the rounds start flying.

But accurate weaponry, even in the hands of crack shots, is not how war is fought. The infantry recruit has first to learn how to advance over disputed ground with his section or platoon. In this he is aided by the Personal Role Radio (PRR), a small transmitter-receiver that allows infantry

soldiers to communicate over short distances – even through thick cover or the walls of buildings – without shouting, hand signals or relaying messages. The PRR enables section commanders to react quickly, aggressively and efficiently to rapidly changing situations including contact with the enemy – greatly increasing the effectiveness of infantry fire teams. A PRR is issued to every member of an eight-strong infantry section, and will be available to other troops in due course. At 1.5kg it is far lighter than more conventional transceivers, has a battery life of 20 hours and can operate on any one of 256 channels up to a range of 500m.

In the British Army, a section consists of eight men, one of whom, usually a full corporal, is the section commander. Allowing for many variations, depending on the disposition of the enemy, the section is usually divided into a six-man Rifle Group and a two-man Machine Gun Group, the latter comprised of the section's second-in-command, usually a lance corporal, and the gunner. The machine gun will almost invariably be the General Purpose Machine Gun – aka the GPMG or Gimpy – which can provide more firepower than the rest of the section put together. Each man in the section is trained on the GPMG to take over if the gunner is killed or wounded.

In normal patrol or battlefield scenarios, the section will form and follow various formations to advance over ground. The arrowhead formation sees the Machine Gun Group deployed on the flank of the inverted V from which attack is most likely, with the more open spearhead stationing the MGG at the rear for immediate weapon deployment when the

point of the spearhead breaks. Other formations include the extended line of battle used when assaulting enemy positions, the diamond for crossing open ground at night, and the file and single file for moving along hedgerows and tree cover. All these and other infantry skills must be incorporated in the infantryman's Phase 2 training, as well as practice in escape and evasion and survival techniques.

The days of ration packs carried on operations are seen more as a rarity in today's Army. Now efforts are made to provide a cookhouse and mess facilities in areas central to areas of operation, with patrols taking food provisions only if their remit requires days away from base. Sensibly, this allows for the carrying of more ammunition to replace the dead weight of tins and freeze-dried packs and also means prepared hot meals at the end of the day or night patrol. Even so, to be 'dressed to kill', the infantryman must often carry heavy loads of other essential equipment. For this, his mentors have thought long and hard and come up with the Personal Load Carrying Equipment (PLCE).

The standard issue kit is two double ammunition pouches, a water bottle pouch, utility pouch, and a bayonet frog. On receiving their kit, most recruits take the advice of older hands and head for the army surplus stores in town or specialist suppliers to buy an extra water bottle or utility pouches and hip pads to cope with the burdens to come.

A major failing of PLCE recounted by sweat-soaked squaddies returning from a 10-mile plus-run with jangling kit is that the belt is prone to slipping. Eventually, the much

maligned plastic buckle – a result of 21st century bean-counting – is replaced by a privately bought or liberated Roll-Pin fastener, which allows the belt to be threaded and tensioned each time the webbing is worn. Another example of the customising genius of today's fighting soldier is the way in which the dividing strip between the compartments of the older issue two-magazine pouch is removed to make for easier insertion and removal and to allow three magazines to be squeezed in at a pinch, giving a total capacity of 12 magazines per man in standard four-pouch combat configuration. The newest magazine pouches contain no dividers, an example of following the lead of the men in the field, and carry three magazines per pouch. This allows an extra four magazines to be carried into battle, a vital extra 120 rounds to be employed in sustained firefights with the enemy.

In conducting trials with PLCE, the Infantry Trials and Development Unit (ITDU) divided the carrying equipment into three orders – Assault, Combat and Marching Orders.

The Assault Order, for operations and patrols of short duration, consists of essential ammunition, water bottle, entrenching tool, helmet and NBC clothing, the latter being carried in a detachable side pocket of the rucksack. Combat Order is Assault Order with the additional means of stowage for rations and personal equipment to enable the infantryman to live and fight for 24 hours with a second detachable side pocket from the rucksack providing the extra space required. Marching Order, heavier yet, is Combat Order plus rucksack and is carried on operations of up to two weeks' duration

without resupply, except of ammunition, rations and water. Combat Order calls for use of the complete Bergen.

The basis of PLCE is the belt, which has two D-rings at the back to attach to the six-point yoke and many rows of vertical slots for the pouches. Constant development has seen the modern PLCE replacing the old 58 webbing pattern used by British infantry in the Falkands. The 58 webbing was heavy, uncomfortable and shrank when wet, problems that were well noted by those forced to lie to seek cover amid the soaked marshlands and peat bogs of the Falklands in 1982.

The first PLCE 90 Pattern appeared around 1988. The 95 Pattern has been on issue since 1992. It should be noted that the British Army continues to use belt-based webbing as standard when most other countries are switching to modular systems. While vests and chest rigs may be more suitable for mechanised infantry and urban operations, the load-carrying ability and capacity of PLCE makes it well suited to conventional dismounted warfare. A special infrared reflective (IRR) coating is applied to all fabric and webbing to reduce the signature to that of foliage when viewed through IR night vision systems.

But whatever patterns have been developed and discarded over the years, the fact remains that today's British soldier carries his home on his back. What he carries and how he carries it is therefore of prime and vital importance to the individual's operational effectiveness. Loads vary according to the type of operation to be undertaken, the environment, duration and the individual combat role of the carrier. The Complete Equipment

Marching Order (CEMO) known to every soldier is carried in the large pack or Bergen, plus webbing.

Although basic rations are carried in the webbing, the majority of operational rations go into the Bergen. Tinned meals are favoured for packing on operations lasting more than three days along with a few packets of biscuits. Dehydrated packs, though nourishing, are not popular due to the constant demand for water in cooking, as well as heating to make the meal more palatable, whereas tinned food can almost be eaten on the run and, ounce for ounce, provides an equal amount of nutrition as dehydrated rations.

Taking up the largest amount of space in the Bergen is the 2.5kg GS sleeping bag inside its own waterproof holder. Along with this goes the poncho or bivvy bag, since it's considered sensible not to separate shelter from sleeping bag since one will not normally be used without the other. Spare clothing follows but is best kept to a minimum such as spare socks and underwear and a warm pile jacket, as well as something dry to sleep in. A certain legendary UK Special Forces operative used to produce waves of envy whenever he produced a well-washed pair of overalls reeking of fabric softener – he had joined the regiment from the Royal Engineers – to sleep in.

Personal Admin in the strange acronymic tongue of the British Army barely escapes being called PA and relates to articles of personal hygiene such as washing and shaving kit, boot brush and polish, toothbrush and soap, etc. During training, Personal Admin items are carried in the webbing but this is not always practical in combat. Despite its obvious

importance, the weight is kept to a minimum – half a bar of soap, half a toothbrush (no handle) half a towel, and so on.

Ammunition is the most important item along with water, rations and medical kit. These need to be easily accessible and are therefore carried on the belt, the familiar Belt Order of jungle warfare, while a large amount of ammunition is carried in the Bergen, giving truth to the horror stories of 55kg loads. A specific problem with heavily packed Bergens is to do with the back height of the carrier. Those blessed with long backs have no problem other than to bear the weight, but a soldier who is short between the belt and the neck may find adopting the prone position to fire his weapon difficult as the Bergen creeps up the back and tends to push the head into the ground – usually mud.

Two pints of water are also carried in the Bergen, along with two pints on the belt, making up half a gallon that can easily go within hours of intense movement in hot conditions. Constant resupplies are necessary.

Specialist equipment depends on the individual's role and may be radios, explosive devices or surveillance equipment. The thing all have in common is that they are bulky and heavy and usually require batteries, which are distributed to be carried among the section.

The standard anti-personnel hand grenade of the British Army is the L109A1, which replaced the L2A2 in 2001. It weighs 465g and has a fuse delay of 3–4 seconds. The grenade is filled with RDX explosive and, on detonation, the steel shell bursts and fragments outwards at high velocity. Signal smoke

grenades, designated L64, L65, L66 and L67, are designed for signalling purposes. Troops typically use the coloured smoke released by these grenades to mark their own positions and to mark out aircraft landing zones. Screening smoke grenades such as the L50A1, L72 and L83 are designed to release a large volume of smoke in a short period of time. These grenades are used to screen movement from enemy fire.

It is standard operating procedure of most British patrols when in a sudden contact with the enemy to lay down a smoke screen while withdrawing to a rallying point. A much feared member of the grenade family is the white phosphorus grenade which has both an offensive and defensive application. The grades contain phosphorous, which, as any schoolboy who pays attention in his chemistry classes knows, ignites on contact with the air, burning at high temperatures and producing voluminous clouds of white smoke. Besides being used to create smoke screens, white phosphorous grenades can be used as anti-personnel grenades and are used to clear trenches, foxholes and buildings where the risk of fire is not considered to be a problem.

The final grenade in the armoury is the flashbang or stun grenade, employed by UK Special Forces to stun and disorientate the target during anti-terrorist operations. The G60 stun grenade emits loud explosions accompanied by bright lights that leave the enemy temporarily deaf, blind and incapable of coherent thought or co-ordinated movement for the brief seconds necessary for the attacking force to enter the area and neutralise the opposition.

The personal medical kit, carried along with the standard issue previously mentioned, is where the ingenuity of the British Tommy comes into its own and shows a skill obtained and passed on over many years from the days of the First World War and before. Even ordinary tampons to be pressed into a gunshot wound have found their way into the makeshift medical kit along with pills for headaches, colds and diarrhoea, along with scissors, scalpels, spare blades and tweezers. Many of these items will be carried by the section or platoon medic but, under fire on an uncertain battlefield, it's good to be self-sufficient.

Probably the sum of all this information is that the standard British Army Bergen is a failure when it comes to coping with infantry loads. Many soldiers prefer to buy their own civilian packs or opt for the larger Para Bergen designed for airborne forces. The standard large pack that connects to the 58 webbing is practically useless and is often discarded after training, leaving the Para Bergen as the most popular choice of kit in infantry battalions.

12

OPERATION
PALK WAHEL

Next to Helmand Province lies the province of Kandahar from where, in August 2007, ISAF launched Operation Palk Wahel. The name alone should have warned the enemy what they were in for. Palk Wahel in Pashtun means 'Hammer Blow'.

The aim of the operation was to clear a section of the notorious Green Zone in Helmand's Upper Gereshk Valley. The troops chosen for the job had recently arrived in Afghanistan as part of the Army's autumn troop rotation and were well suited to the task. The Royal Gurkha Rifles had left their base in Serai in Brunei and were preparing to go into action in Afghanistan.

The fierce Nepalese mountain dwellers known as the Gurkhas have been part of the British Army for almost 200 years. The potential of these warriors was first realised by the British at the height of their empire-building, the Victorians

identifying them as a martial race and perceiving in them particularly masculine qualities of toughness.

Gurkhas have been recruited into the British and Indian armies since 1815, following the success of the East India Company in obtaining possession of the southern slopes of the Himalayas the previous year. As part of the treaty to end hostilities, the acquisitive East India consortium was forced to recognise Nepal's independence but was allowed to recruit from the country's former Army.

Gurkhas served as troops of the East India Company in the Pindaree War of 1817, in Bharatpur in 1826, and the First and Second Sikh Wars in 1846 and 1848. During the Sepoy Mutiny in 1857, the Gurkha regiments remained loyal to the British and became part of the British Indian Army on its formation. At the height of the unrest, the 2nd Gurkha Rifles (the Sirmoor Rifles) were deployed for over three months to defend the house of a prominent Hindu loyal to the Queen, losing 327 out of 490 men. The 60th King's Royal Rifle Corps, later part of the Royal Green Jackets, fought alongside the Sirmoor Rifles and were so impressed that following the mutiny they insisted the 2nd Gurkhas be awarded the honours of adopting their distinctive riflemen's green uniforms with scarlet edgings along with rifle regiment traditions and that they should hold the title of riflemen rather than sepoys. Twelve Gurkha regiments also took part in the relief of Lucknow.

Since then, the Gurkhas have fought loyally for the British all over the world, receiving 13 Victoria Crosses between them. More than 200,000 fought in the two world wars and, in the

past 50 years, they have served in Hong Kong, Malaysia, Borneo, Cyprus, the Falklands, Kosovo and now in Iraq and Afghanistan, where they serve in a variety of roles, mainly in the infantry but with significant numbers of engineers, logisticians and signals specialists. The name 'Gurkha' comes from the hill town of Gorkha from which the Nepalese kingdom expanded.

Time and again, Britain was to appreciate the diplomacy of the long-defunct East India Company when all Gurkha regiments served in the First World War on the Western Front, in the Middle East, and on the north-west frontier of India. In the war of 1939–45, they were to see service in North Africa, Italy, Burma and Malaya. When India and Pakistan gained independence in 1947, following an agreement between Nepal, India and Britain, four of the Gurkha regiments were assigned to the British Army, mainly for service in the Far East; the remaining six regiments were absorbed into the Indian Army. The 3 Gurkhas are now based at Shorncliffe near Folkestone – but they do not become British citizens after service.

The soldiers are still selected from young men living in the hills of Nepal – with about 28,000 youths tackling the selection for only 270 places a year. The selection process has been described as one of the toughest in the world and is fiercely contested. Young hopefuls have to run uphill for 40 minutes carrying a wicker basket on their back filled with rocks weighing 34kg (75lb).

The ranks have always been dominated by four ethnic groups – the Gurungs and Magars from central Nepal, and the

Rais and Limbus from the east, who live in hill villages of impoverished hill farmers. They keep to their Nepalese customs and beliefs, and the brigade follows religious festivals such as Dashain, in which, in Nepal, goats and buffaloes are sacrificed; the practice is outlawed in the UK.

All ranks carry into war the fearsome *kukri*. The *kukri* is designed for chopping and in use resembles a cross between a knife and an axe. The blade of the fighting *kukri* tapers from 3–10cm in width and is 30cm long, excluding the tang. Blades are deflected inwards at an angle of 20° or more, with a thick spine and a single sharp cutting edge; this causes the end section of the blade to strike square on, greatly increasing chopping effectiveness. They also have a hard, tempered edge and a softer spine. This enables the weapon to maintain a sharp edge, yet tolerate impacts. It is balanced so that it will rest in a vertical position if supported on a fulcrum, e.g. a finger.

In times past, it was said that once a *kukri* was drawn in battle, it had to 'taste blood' – if not, its owner had to cut himself before returning it to its sheath. Now, the Gurkhas say, it is used mainly for cooking but that must be little consolation to the Taliban insurgents on the receiving end of Operation Palk Wahel who felt the cut of the *kukri* in the fierce hand-to-hand fighting that accompanied the campaign.

Another distinctive feature of the Gurkha is the officers' hat, identified in army-speak as the 'Hat Terai Gurkha'. This headgear is worn by officers of the Gurkha contingent in Singapore attached to the Singapore police force and is named after the Rai region in Nepal from where many recruits to the

Brigade are drawn. Worn only during guard duty and on parades, the hat is made of khaki-coloured felt with a dark blue-coloured *puggaree* wound around the hat with six folds. It is always worn with the chin strap and is deliberately tilted to the right so that the brim touches the right ear.

Gurkha numbers have been sharply reduced from a Second World War peak of 112,000 men, and now stand at about 3,500. During the two world wars, 43,000 young men lost their lives fighting for the British Empire, which sadly has not rewarded the survivors. Newspaper stories often recount the tales of frail veterans walking for days to the nearest town to pick up their meagre pensions from the British Army. There is also the problem planted by immigration, where the UK, although compliant with EU requests to open its doors to economic immigrants or the descendants of citizens of a past colony, regularly refuses entry to retired Gurkhas on the grounds that, although not to be judged as mercenaries under Protocol 1 of the Geneva Convention of 1949, they are subjects of an independent monarchy and therefore have no automatic right of residence in the UK. In London on 19 March 2008, this led to a protest by hundreds of Nepalese Gurkha soldiers outside the Houses of Parliament, demanding better pensions and the right to stay in the country they served. This sparked a national petition to entitle them to British citizenship when their service ends. Sadly, the petition was only partly successful. In 2004, then Prime Minister Tony Blair said that retired fighters of the Gurkha Brigade would be allowed to settle in Britain. But the law applied only to those

demobilised after 1 July 1997, the day Britain disbanded its Hong Kong regiment and returned the city to Chinese control, and excluded the disbanded Hong Kong garrison and anybody who had previously served in Britain's four Gurkha regiments before that date.

Due to the Hong Kong handover from the UK to China, the Training Depot Brigade of Gurkhas (TDBG) was closed down in December 1994. However, it was reconstituted immediately as the Gurkha Training Wing (GTW) at Queen Elizabeth Barracks at Church Crookham, Hampshire, in the UK. In December 1999, the GTW moved to Helles Barracks at Catterick Garrison in North Yorkshire and became Gurkha Company, 3rd Battalion, Infantry Training Centre (ITC). Organised in two wings, A (Imphal) Wing and B (Meiktila) Wing, the company currently maintains 72 permanent staff of all ranks and 230 recruits.

The salaries and hard-won pensions of the Brigade of Gurkhas is an important source of income for Nepal. Recruitment is fierce and competitive, overtaking the SAS selection course in comparison to the ratio of applicants to passes.

Hill selections are held at various locations in Nepal. There are usually 30 applicants for every place available at this stage. Potential recruits must satisfy the following requirements before proceeding to the second stage:

Age between 17 and 22
Height at least 1.57m (5ft 2in)
Weight at least 50kg (110lb)

Good health

Educational requirement

The second stage is held at the Pokhara Selection Centre. This stage of the selection process lasts for three weeks. All candidates must pass the following tests in order to proceed further:

English grammar

Mathematics

Fitness test, which includes exercises and a 'doko race', which consists of carrying 34kg of stones while running up a 4.2km steep mountain course

Initiative test

Final interview

(Candidates for the Gurkha Contingent, Singapore Police Force, are also selected at this stage.)

The third stage consists of basic training at GTW Infantry Training Centre, Catterick. This is a nine-month-long training course that includes:

Language training (three months)

Military skills

Western culture and customs

The graduation of successful recruits is marked by a Passing Out parade at the end of the basic training course. Based on their progress and results, the new entrants are then allotted to

various positions within the Brigade of Gurkhas. In general, those who obtained better results in the mathematics test during the second stage of selection are offered postings to the Queen's Gurkha Signals or the Queen's Gurkha Engineers.

Although hardened by their lives in the hill communities of Nepal and trained to face an enemy of the Crown with all the inherent warrior skills of their ancestors, many of the fierce soldiers of the Gurkha Brigade involved in Operation Palk Wahel had never experienced combat before arriving in Afghanistan. Nonetheless, their motto in Gurkhali: '*Kaphar hunnu bhanda marnu ramro*' which translates as 'Better to die than live as a coward' was uppermost in each of their minds as they prepared for combat.

The Gurkhas in battle are not motivated by hatred of their enemy – many of the Afghanistan deployment spoke Hindi which would allow them to communicate with the Urdu and Pashtun speakers in the area and they had made friends among the Muslim community during postings to Brunei – but rather by their determination to fight fiercely and die bravely if necessary and be honoured by their families. A Ghurka who dies or is wounded in battle is revered by his people; look no further for proof than the 13 Victoria Crosses awarded to the Brigade since its formation.

The Gurkhas began their deployment in September 2007 in the Palk Wahel offensive to drive the Taliban from key areas in the Upper Gereshk Valley. This was the first time the Gurkhas, led by Lieutenant Colonel Jonny Bourne, Commanding Officer of the 1st Battalion Royal Gurkha Rifles, had deployed

from Brunei as a formed battalion, although the unit has been involved in operations elsewhere to varying levels, including Iraq, Sierra Leone and the Balkans. The newly arrived Gurkhas were ideally suited to the operating environment in Afghanistan which, in some ways, they found similar to the mountains and plains of Nepal. In addition, their experience of operating in the Brunei jungle meant that they were able to acclimatise quickly and prepare themselves for the task ahead, which was to exploit previous gains against the Taliban and to clear the ground into the Upper Gereshk Valley from the north-east.

The clearing operation was also aimed at relieving the pressure on Royal Marines tasked with guarding the Kajaki Dam where they were constantly under long-range mortar and rocket attack from Taliban forces operating in the area. The Kajaki Dam, which had seen fierce fighting between NATO forces and Taliban insurgents earlier in the year, had been badly damaged by US bombing raids prior to the invasion and had been hurriedly repaired to provide power to the region. Its strategic importance to the region was enormous as one of the two major hydroelectric power dams of Helmand Province with a potential to provide electricity for 2 million people, and its waters irrigated more than 650,000 acres of formerly arid land. A breach of the structure would bring a loss of power and havoc to the region and such an event was inscribed in blood on the Taliban calendar.

Initially, the Gurkhas met stiff resistance in the Gereshk Valley but this was soon overcome. Regular patrols were

conducted throughout the area and the civilian population, who had previously tired of living in a battle zone and fled the area, began to return. But an incident was to occur that would cause the green valley of Gereshk again to reverberate with the crash of warfare and echo to the screams of dying men. And a new legend was about to be created in the annals of the Gurkha Brigade.

The Nepalese troops took up their positions in a compound, denominated as the district centre in the battered township of Gereshk. The compound was in the centre of the town but the troops immediately noticed the silence. No one sat in the shadows to escape the gruelling heat of the midday sun, no small children clustered around the soldiers begging for *baksheesh*, no shepherd drove his goats to crop the sparse grass and roots that pushed up through the sun-baked earth between the mud-walled buildings. Gereshk was a ghost town.

The civilians had left in the face of a coming conflict and the Gurkhas braced themselves in that knowledge. Eyes watched them from beyond rifle shot, sometimes they heard a furtive fluttering as a figure flitted between the entrances of the 'rat runs', tunnels dug by the Taliban to bring them almost within touching distance of the district centre walls. Ammunition was distributed and those on guard duties kept their eyes moving over the rough terrain outside the compound walls, always looking slightly to the right or left of a suspicious site since direct vision tends to distort the view.

Tension grew with the passing hours and the slightest clink of metal on rock would bring all ears to focus on the sound,

for bolts to be pulled back, racking bullets into their chambers, and for safety catches to be snicked off as personal weapons came to the shoulder, poised to fire. The first night passed with men watching the darkness and with no other sound than the whispered exchanges between sentries and their officers.

The expected attack came at first light as the men of the 1st Rifle Brigade awoke to a dawn promising yet another day of temperatures between 35° and 40°C. The first rocket-propelled grenades struck the walls and buildings around the key strategic post in Gereshk, southern Helmand Province, and sent men diving for their personal weapons, which had never been more than an arm's length away. Troops took cover as a sniper's rifle cracked a mere two seconds after the high-velocity round slammed into a sandbag barricade, giving warning that the sniper was firing from as near as 700m and looking for an unwary target. Men watched cautiously for the puff of smoke or movement of dust whipped up by the passage of the bullet from the muzzle that would give away the sniper's position. Such a high-velocity round was capable of decapitation or amputation of a limb. An eddy of dust was spotted just below an aperture at ground level in the wall of an outhouse around 650m from the compound and a Gurkha sniper fired at a flash of movement from within. The Taliban sniper fell silent.

The RPG positions of the Taliban fighters were gradually identified as men peered from between cover, through the dust of rocket strikes to follow the tell-tale exhaust of the launched rockets back to their launch points. Heavy fire was directed at

the sites until the enemy either fell wounded or dead or lived to crawl away and set up another firing position. The guns of the Gurkhas grew hot under the searing morning sun and sweat ran from the brows of men born in the cool heights of the Nepalese mountains. Heavy and light machine guns met in a duel of fire accompanied by the sharp crack of small arms fire.

After two hours, the Taliban withdrew, leaving ten dead, lying in their blood where they had fallen. The Gurkhas had been blooded and more was to come. Over the next four days, the Gurkha contingent was to face 28 concerted attacks lasting from one to six hours each, including five full-scale efforts by hundreds of Taliban fighters to overrun their compound. Taliban fighters, caught in the devastating fire from the Gurkhas as they attempted to storm the compound, lay dead or dying on the surrounding blood-soaked ground. Smoke and dust stung the eyes and sweat dried to caked mud as it mixed with the dirt thrown up constant rocket strikes and grenade bursts. The Gurkha warriors returned a sustained and deadly onslaught in the face of a barrage of heavy machine gun fire, rocket-propelled grenades, sniping and tunnelling as the Taliban grew more desperate to storm the defensive position. After 160 hours of bloody battle, the Taliban withdrew and abandoned Gereshk. The result of the prolonged firefight was a crushing defeat for the insurgents, who had lost 100 of their number to only 3 injuries to the men of the Gurhka Rifles.

The withdrawal of the defeated Taliban had been urged earlier when the Gurkha philosophy of battle was summed up in a message sent by the Ghurka officer to the Taliban using a

police radio. It warned the attackers: 'You have two paths here – if the attacks continue, you will suffer. We are being restrained. We take no pleasure in this. We are here to help you if you want a better life. It is in your hands.' The message was understood and the Taliban fighters wondered at these fierce fighters who came from a region far to the north of neighbouring India. The legend of the Gurkha would be passed from man to man around the smoking campfires of the Kush. The tribesmen withdrew, mourning their fathers, uncles and brothers lying dead before the walls of the compound. They knew in the height of their battle fever that they had met their match.

13

THE FLOWER
OF WAR

Western civilisation, especially in the UK, recognises the poppy as a symbol of the futility of war. Many thousands of paper and linen copies of the red Flanders poppy are worn with pride on November's Remembrance Sunday in the UK and in the Continental countries that sent their young men to die on the battlefields of France and Belgium in the First World War. On the 11th hour of the 11th day of the 11th month in each year, the Flanders poppy becomes a symbol of recognition and respect for our war dead. Yet ironically another species of *papaver*, this time the beautiful pink and white flower that grows in the southern plains of Afghanistan, now finances the purchase of the weapons of war that leave Britain's fighting men and women and their enemies dead on the fields of a far-flung foreign country. For opium, the fabulous cash crop of the East that finances the Islamic wars, in its purest form is derived from the seed pods of *papaver somniferum*, the opium poppy.

To anyone with the briefest knowledge of the Latin language, the name infers sleep. The source is an extract of the exudates obtained from the body of the flower by inflicting small cuts into the seed pod. The dark, rubbery exudates that bleed from the pod form the basic cash crop of farmers in the Afghanistan Province of Helmand, which last year accounted for 93 per cent of the entire world production of opium.

In 2005, Afghanistan was estimated to be producing 87 per cent of the world's supply of opium (4,519 tons, down 2 per cent from 2004), with nearly half of the country's US$4.5 billion economy coming from opium cultivation and trafficking – a far cry from 2001, when the emerging Taliban Government, then hailed by the West as the new face of Islam in the east, banned poppy farming in Afghanistan. Times have indeed changed, with the money from opium financing much of fundamentalist terrorism.

In the same year of 2005, a leading article in the *Asia Times* criticised the inaction of the allies over the world drug crisis created by the invasion. The article pointed out:

> '*By early 2003, it had become evident that US troops had forged alliances with many reigning Afghan warlords, who ostensibly provided support to American troops in their battle against the various anti-US elements conveniently lumped together as the Taliban. Some of those dubious allies of the US troops and the North Atlantic Treaty Organization-led (NATO) coalition forces are suspected to be among Afghanistan's biggest drug traffickers, controlling networks that include producers, criminal gangs and*

even members of the counter-narcotics police force. US-backed Afghan President Hamid Karzai has also brought some of these warlords into his popularly elected Government, in recognition of their clout.

But the EU, perfectly in sync with the US approach toward Afghanistan following September 11, has put no pressure on the US to take definite steps to reduce opium production in Afghanistan. In fact, hardly a peep on the subject has been heard from the top political leaders of Britain, France or Germany – Europe's most powerful nations.'

But the production of opium is not new. The plant was cultivated in the ancient civilisations of Persia, Egypt and Mesopotamia. Archaeological evidence and fossilised poppy seeds even hint that the Neanderthals may have been into the effects of the potent drug 30,000 years ago, which might account for all those handprints over cave walls as they groped to find the exit.

The first written reference to the poppy is found in a Sumerian text dated around 4000BC. Then the flower was known as *hul gil*, the plant of joy, and the Egyptian Eber papyrus of 1500BC suggests the use of the condensed juice of the unripe seed pod as an aid to the rigours of infant teething or simply 'to prevent the excessive crying of children'.

The opium-producing poppy has evolved through centuries of breeding and cultivation of the Mediterranean wild strain, *papaver setigerum*, which has been identified as a minor morphine-bearing strain by the United Nations Office on

Drugs and Crime (UNODC), the New York-based organisation which has field offices monitoring drug production all over the world.

Two of the many refined derivatives of opium are morphine and heroin but, in the 19th century, pure opium was used as a reliever of pain and accepted as a general cure-all for nearly all medical conditions in the form of laudanum, the classic formula of which is 2oz of opium, 1oz of saffron, and a drachm (equivalent to one-eighth of a fluid ounce) of cinnamon and cloves, all dissolved in a pint of sweet, white Canary wine. Nowadays, opium is the basis of derivatives morphine and heroin and the long line of processed drugs too numerous to name here that are sold on streets all over the world.

But the story was far different in 2001, the year of the US-led intervention in Afghanistan following the attacks on the Twin Towers of New York and the Pentagon. In that year, a UN survey revealed that the Taliban had completed one of the quickest and most successful drug elimination programmes in history. The area of land given over to growing the opium poppy in 2001 fell by 91 per cent when compared to the previous year and production of fresh opium, the raw material for heroin, went down from 3,276 tonnes to 185 tonnes. In fact, almost all Afghan opium in 2001 came out of territories controlled by the West's ally in the assault on Afghanistan, the Northern Alliance. Due to the overall ban of poppy-growing by the Taliban, only 4 per cent of opium poppy farming took place in areas controlled by the Taliban. So what went wrong?

The warlords of the Northern Alliance, freed of the yoke of

the Taliban by Western intervention, were now able to renew planting of the profitable poppy fields under the cover of war. Even the October launch of the invasion by US forces allowed farmers to exploit the last weeks of the sowing season for both poppy and marijuana crops, which fall in October and November. While the bulk of the drug was being produced in alliance strongholds, the farmers in the southern provinces also saw themselves free of anyone to enforce the ban imposed by the besieged Taliban regime as it reeled before the US onslaught.

The autumn of 2001 saw a return to the record levels of opium produced and was a major embarrassment to George W Bush and British Prime Minister Tony Blair, who had both repeatedly and incorrectly cited the Taliban's involvement in the drugs trade as a further justification for military action.

By 2004, the re-emergent opium trade in Afghanistan had become the biggest single threat to the establishment of democracy in the post-Taliban era. The country's soaring drug profits equalled 50 per cent of the gross national product and had become the principal source of funds for reconstruction, outpacing foreign aid. In addition, there was no doubt that in displacing the Taliban's harsh regime, the US-led coalition had opened the door to drug-fuelled corruption at the highest levels of government, involving army generals and other top officials who routinely worked with the coalition's military on anti-terrorism operations. Thus the Taliban effort to discourage drug production, which in its early years it had justified on the basis that the drugs were consumed abroad by unbelievers, was undone. The mind-change of the regime,

which had apparently been made in the hope of winning credit with the UN and strengthening its claim to Afghanistan's seat in the General Assembly over that held by the Northern Alliance, was lost in the dust of war, and Helmand Province returned to being the key producer of a drug that was sapping the strength of the Western world and financing the *jihad*. The brown paste extracted from *papaver somniferum* by the farmer now sells for a minimum of $340 dollars a kilo in the market place, a good profit for the farmer whose return from his crop of onions and emaciated beef cattle under the Taliban would bring him less than $6 a month. It was no wonder that those who were glad to see the Taliban go were reluctant to follow the same rules imposed by their liberators. It is no secret that many of the candidates elected to the new democratic parliament under President Hamid Kharzai are movers and shakers in the drug trade.

Meanwhile, the man who sparked the US invasion of Afghanistan by taking refuge in Kabul after the bombing of the World Trade Center must be well pleased with the results of the past seven years. As long as the profits of the drugs trade shine before the eyes of the country's indigenous population, the presence of the occupying coalition will be unpopular and hearts and minds will never be won. In the words of one soldier, 'Afghanistan has become the new Vietnam and we'll be here year in and year out. The men on a tour here now will be back again and again because there's no way out and no end to it.'

In themselves, those words form a sad epitaph for the young men and women who now fall amid the poppy fields of

Afghanistan, re-enacting the spillage of the blood of their great-grandfathers that drenched the red poppy fields of Flanders.

14

WINGS OF MERCY

No tales of the blood-soaked plains of Afghanistan would be complete without the retelling of an adventure that epitomises the fortitude, courage and compassion of British troops under fire. It occurred in January 2007 as the result of a heavily contested attack by Royal Marines on the Taliban-held Jugroom Fort near Garmsir, in the south of Helmand Province.

They had struck on the dawn of 15 January. Z Company, mounted in Vikings and supported by C Squadron of the Light Dragoons, crossed the Helmand River to the south-west of the fort at a crossing point previously secured and now held by 3 Commando Brigade Reconnaissance Force. Once across the river, the Marines had left the protection of the Vikings to engage the enemy with small arms fire. The attack was supported by elements of 29 Commando Regiment Royal Artillery, 59 Independent Squadron Royal Engineers, and

elements of 32 Regiment Royal Artillery, supported by Apache attack helicopters and aircraft.

Earlier, I Company, along with the Afghan National Police, had attacked further to the north of the fort. Now the UK Task Force was meeting a solid defence from the Taliban on all sides of the mud-walled fortress. The troops of Z Company, meanwhile, withdrew back to the far side of the Helmand River, having successfully completed their objective. The entire engagement lasted five hours with an undefined number of the Taliban targets, high-ranking officers in the Taliban chain of command, killed.

Once across the river, the men of Z Company 45 Commando assembled for a roll call before taking in water and re-arming and cleaning their weapons in the event of being called to another assault. The mission had been long and arduous but morale was high. They had accomplished their mission and drawn blood from the enemy and, apart from a few superficial wounds – many of which were minor scratches from rock splinters thrown up by bullet strikes – they appeared to have taken no casualties. But consternation grew when the roll call revealed to the Marines that their colleague Lance Corporal Matthew Ford was missing in action. Speculation was aroused as to just where the 30-year-old had fallen. An Apache attack helicopter was immediately sent to overfly the battle sector where 1 Assault Group had launched its attack and its pilot reported a crumpled figure huddled against a broken wall, apparently undiscovered by the enemy who appeared to be still cowed from the fury of the recent assault, but literally within scant metres of their position.

Consternation turned to horror. Every British serviceman and woman serving in Afghanistan knew that the Taliban men, and especially their women, had been known to act mercilessly when encountering wounded individuals from enemy forces. There was no doubt in their minds that Matt Ford was not going to meet that fate and volunteers for a rescue mission were many. 'No one gets left behind' was the unspoken motto in the mind of everyone present on that morning to the south of Garmsir. But how could the extraction be accomplished?

They had regrouped four miles from the fort over the river and they would have to return and face a prepared enemy. The Viking vehicles would offer little protection against an expected barrage of heavy machine guns and RPGs. It was then that an Apache attack helicopter pilot, identified later only as 'Tom', pointed out that the quickest insertion and extraction would be achieved by helicopter.

But here there was a snag. The helicopter with enough firepower and fast enough for the task was obviously the WAH-64 Apache, but the Apache can carry only its crew of two with no more room available in the cabin for even, as it was pointed out at the time, a mosquitom, let alone a hefty armed Marine. Insertion of personnel by an Apache had certainly been considered by the MoD, and a design team had previously produced the Avpro Exint Pod for special forces insertion and extraction.

Avpro of UK had cleared the Exint ballistic transport pod for use with AH-64 at the start of 2000, but certification to carry personnel is still required. In its special forces insertion

role, the Apache can carry a maximum of four pods, each able to accommodate a 226kg payload. However, despite questions being raised in Parliament (*Hansard* 26 July 2000) the pod is still not in general service. But who needs a pod when the Apache has D-rings welded on to the chassis for miscellaneous cargo – and what was more miscellaneous than four tough soldiers going in to save a mate? The decision was made, now it only remained to select four men from the many volunteers.

It was decided that two men would ride each of two helicopters with a third aircraft in defence. The WAH-64 Apache carries a Boeing M230 chain gun 30mm automatic cannon located between the main wheel legs in an under-fuselage mounting, which provides 625 rounds of high explosive dual-purpose ammunition a minute as well as up to 16 Hellfire 2 anti-tank missiles or up to 76 2.75 inch FFAR (folding fin aerial rockets) in their launchers or an alternative combination of Hellfires and FFAR.

The men chosen for the death-defying mission were Plymouth-based Royal Marine Sergeant Major Colin Hearn, a 45-year-old veteran of the landing force command support group, and Marine Gary Robinson from Rosyth, Fife. On the second Apache were 19-year-old signaller Chris Fraser-Perry from Southport and Royal Engineers Captain Dave Rigg, a 30-year-old veteran from Newton Ferrers in Devon. All four men were strapped to the helicopters' fuselage using D rings and tested their fastenings before take-off. Seconds later, they were winging their way across the Helmand River and back to Jugroom Fort, buffeted by the fierce headwind created by the

helicopters' onward flight and downward blast from the rotors, despite the pilots holding their speed down to under 100kph to reduce the rush of air.

As the aircraft approached the fort, Taliban snipers, alerted by the strange silhouettes of the men mounted at each side of the helicopter cabins and expecting some bizarre new weapon, opened fire. Rounds cracked past the rescuers' ears as the Apaches began to settle and one pilot radioed the support helicopter to put down rounds on a building containing the snipers. The defence helicopter's chain gun rattled its defiance and the sniper fire ceased as the Taliban threw themselves into cover. Meanwhile, all four soldiers had unstrapped themselves from their metal 'steeds' and Fraser-Perry and Rigg received covering fire from Sergeant Major Hearn and Gary Robinson that allowed them to advance to where Matthew Ford had been seen to be lying. The lance corporal had received a burst of sustained small arms fire to his chest in the initial advance on the fort. He was later assessed to have died instantly from his wounds. Now the mission became one of urgency to retrieve the body and retreat to the helicopters for extraction.

The tempo of the firefight increased as the Taliban defenders in the fort saw an apparently wounded soldier being carried to the waiting helicopters and railed at being robbed of a prize that had been lying unseen under their noses. The chain gun and FFAR rockets of the Apache circling overhead kept them at bay as Fraser-Perry and Rigg strapped their fallen comrade to the helicopter and fastened their own straps to the fuselage. A quick rap on the helicopter side screen and a thumbs-up

from both men sent the Apache's rotors beating skyward, followed by the second Apache carrying the fire team of Hearn and Robinson. The third aircraft covered their escape with a final defiant burst of fire at the Taliban cowering behind the cover of the smashed walls of the fort and then pivoted on an 180 degree axis to join the other Apaches as they turned for their journey back across the Helmand River to Garmsir where the helicopter carrying the fire team of Colin Hearn and Gary Robinson and the support helicopter landed. The helicopter carrying Captain Rigg, Fraser-Perry and Ford's body went on to land at Camp Bastion with the aircraft virtually flying on fumes from an almost empty tank.

Lance Corporal Ford was later pronounced T4, having probably died instantly from his wounds. His rescuers, whose mission would enter army legend as 'Flight of the Phoenix', had shown the grit and determination which is intrinsic in the British fighting man and never more apparent than in the Middle East conflicts of today – and a new legend had been born.

15

CHARIOTS OF WAR –
PART ONE

Ever since the days of the Saxon shield wall, in which the most stalwart warriors linked their shields together, right edge over left, and withstood an enemy charge while their tallest men-at-arms swung those massive battle-axes over the heads of the defenders, to the Roman *testudo*, the tortoise-inspired battle formation when the rectangular shields were held overhead and at the sides to form a mobile unit impregnable to the arrows and spears of the enemy, the organised fighting man has sought protective armour.

For the British infantryman serving in the field of combat, the protective kit of choice would be Combat Body Armour, which can be further reinforced with ceramic armour plates. This is known as the Osprey body armour kit, standard equipment for all British army personnel on operations. The Osprey is complemented by the new Enhanced Body Armour or Combat Body Armour helmets, soon to replace the standard

Mark 6 combat helmet. As with the Mark 6, the new helmets will continue to provide outstanding ballistic protection while allowing the soldier to wear a respirator, ear defenders, goggles and a radio set as necessary. But not even Enhanced Body Armour is a defence when the infantryman hears that clunk and rattle of metallic treads that strike fear into the bravest hearts – the advance of the heavyweight killer tank.

Britain's latest and most deadly in that role is the Challenger 2 (CR2) Main Battle Tank, named in an extraordinary moment of army logic and based on the Challenger 1 that saw rugged operations during the Gulf War and in the Balkans. So many modifications were made in the production of the Challenger 2 that only five per cent of components are interchangeable with its predecessor, Challenger 1. The modifications – 150 in all – included a completely restructured turret, an L30 CHARM 120mm gun, and the excellent missile-deflecting second-generation Chobham armour.

The L30 gun is made from electro-slag refined steel (ESR) and is insulated with a thermal sleeve. It is fitted with a muzzle reference system and fume extraction. The turret is capable of 360° rotation and the weapon elevation range is from -10° to +20°.

There is capacity for 50 120mm projectiles, including Armour-Piercing Fin-Stabilised Discarding Sabot (APFSDS), High-Explosive Squash Head (HESH) or smoke rounds. The L30 gun can also fire the Depleted Uranium (DU) round with a stick charge propellant. With the DU round, the L30 is part of the CHARM 3 gun, charge and projectile system. The gun

control is provided by an all-electric gun control and stabilisation system from BAe Systems. Challenger 2 is also equipped with a Boeing 7.62mm chain gun, which is located to the left of the main tank gun. The loader has a 7.62mm GPMG L37A2 anti-air machine gun mounted on the cupola.

The turret is protected with second-generation Chobham armour, and comprises a nuclear, biological and chemical (NBC) protection system located in the turret bustle. On each side of the turret are five L8 smoke grenade dischargers, from Thales AFV Systems Ltd (formerly the Helio Mirror Company). Challenger 2 can also set a smoke screen by the injection of diesel fuel into the engine exhausts.

Challenger tanks fitted with this system were deployed to Iraq in early 2006. In 2006, the Challenger lethality improvement programme set about upgrading the main gun of Challenger 2 from its then current 120mm L30A1 rifled gun to the 120mm Rheinmetall L55 smoothbore gun currently used by the Canadian Leopard 2 A6. The use of a smooth bore now allows Challenger 2 to use more lethal rounds developed in Germany and the USA.

The commander of a Challenger 2 has a panoramic VS 580-10 gyro-stabilised sight from SAGEM (formerly SFIM Industries). A laser rangefinder is incorporated into an intermediate assembly. Elevation range is +35° to -35°. The commander's station is equipped with eight periscopes which provide 360° vision. Night vision is provided by a Thermal Observation and Gunnery Sight II (TOGS II), from Thales (formerly Pilkington) Optronics. The sensor is based on UK

TICM 2 common modules. The thermal image, with 4x and 11.5x magnification, is displayed in the gunner's and commander's sights and monitors. The gunner has a Thales Optronics stabilised Gunner's Primary Sight, consisting of a visual channel, 4Hz laser rangefinder and display. The laser rangefinder has a range of 200m to 10km. The driver is equipped with an image-intensifying Passive Driving Periscope (PDP) from Thales Optronics for night driving.

The Challenger 2 has a 12-cylinder, 1,200hp Perkins Caterpillar CV12 diesel engine and a David Brown TN54 gearbox, with six forward and two reverse gears. Second-generation Hydrogas suspension and hydraulic track tensioners are fitted. The maximum speed by road is 59kph and 40kph cross-country. The range is given as 450km by road and 250km cross-country.

The latest Challenger 2E has a new integrated weapon control and battlefield management system, which includes a gyro-stabilised panoramic SAGEM MVS 580 day/thermal sight for the commander and SAGEM SAVAN 15 gyro-stabilised day/ thermal sight for the gunner, both with a laser rangefinder. This allows hunter/killer operations with a common engagement sequence. An optional servo-controlled overhead weapons platform can be slaved to the commander's sight to allow operation independent from the turret. The power-pack has been replaced with a new 1,500hp Europack with a transversely mounted MTU 883 diesel engine coupled to Renk HSWL 295TM automatic transmission. The smaller but more powerful engine allows more space for fuel storage, increasing the vehicle's range to 550km.

oyal Marines from Zulu company, 45 Commando prepare to leave their base,
M Condor, for Afghanistan, October 2, 2008.   ©*Getty Images*

Top: A Taliban fighter, accompanied by other prisoners, looks at the light coming from hole in a room of a jail in Bamiyan, 5 February 2002.

©*Jewel Samad/AFP/Getty Imag*

Right: Taliban killed during the Northern Alliance advance following the fall of Kunduz.

above: The Zhawa Kili cave complex in eastern Afghanistan, believed to have been an early hiding place of Osama bin Laden.

below: An Afghan army soldier stands by as British forces unload supplies from a helicopter after arriving at Kajaki on March 12, 2007 in Southern Helmand province.

Above: A British soldier walks near the side of a suicide bomb attack in Kabul, 6 October 2007.

©*Massoud Hossaini/AFP/Getty Imag*

Below: Taliban fighters in the streets of Kandahar.

bove: British 29 Commando Royal Artillery soldiers at Bagram Air Base in fghanistan, 2002.

©*Joe Raedle/Getty Images*

elow: Crowds gather to greet the Royal Marines as they arrive at Exeter International irport on April 8 2008 after a six month tour of duty in Afghanistan.

©*Matt Cardy/Getty Images*

Above: A British Army Theatre Military Working Dog Support Unit during an operation to capture Taliban leaders in Kandahar Province, July 2008.   ©*Marco Di Lauro/Getty Images*

Below: A joint UK and USA patrol in Helmand Province. FOB Sangin is in the background.

Above: A Major presents campaign medals to men of the 246 Ghurka Rifles. ©*Crown Copyright/MOD*

Left: The deadly *kukri* fighting knife of the Ghurkas. Ancient tradition demanded that, once drawn, the blade must taste blood. In the hands of a contemporary Ghurka warrior it is still a fearsome weapon although its modern day uses are manifold. Depending on the purpose, its design and manufacture varies. Blades are usually 3 – 10 cm wide and 30 – 38 cm long, but size varies depending on its purpose. Blades are deflected at an angle of 20° or more, with a thick spine and a single sharp cutting edge; this causes the end section of the blade to strike square on, greatly increasing chopping effectiveness. Night attacks by kukri-wielding Ghurkas on German trenches in WWI earned the small of stature Nepalese warriors the nickname of 'Poison Dwarfs' from the terrified enemy.

©*JOHN D MCHUGH/AFP/Getty Images*

Above: The General Purpose 7.62 calibre Machine Gun, aka the GPMG, a heavy-hitter that has served with the British Army since the '60s.

Below: The SA80-l85a2 Individual Weapon of the Infantry.

The tank is built by BAe Systems Land Systems, formerly Vickers Defence Systems and then Alvis Vickers Ltd. Challenger 2 is now in service with the British Army and the Royal Army of Oman. The UK placed orders for 127 Challenger 2 tanks in 1991 and an additional 259 in 1994, with the new leviathan entering service in June 1998. Since that month and year, Challenger 2 has seen operational service in Bosnia and Kosovo and the new tanks were deployed on active service in Afghanistan's near neighbour in Operation Iraqi Freedom.

Currently, there are seven Challenger 2 armoured squadrons comprising around 100 tanks, with one Challenger 2 regiment forming an armoured reconnaissance regiment. Challenger 2E, the latest development model, has been designed for the export market and is suitable for harsh environmental and climactic conditions. The 2E has been extensively trialled in Greece, Qatar and Saudi Arabia.

Just behind the Challenger 2 Main Battle Tank in firepower and infantry support comes the Warrior Infantry Fighting Vehicle, which can keep up with its big brother over the most difficult terrain. The Warrior (WR) family of seven variants of armoured vehicles entered service in 1988 and has proved a resounding success for armoured infantry battlegroups in the Gulf War, Bosnia and Kosovo and Iraq. They provide excellent mobility, lethality and survivability for the infantry and have enabled key elements from the Royal Artillery and Royal Electrical and Mechanical Engineers to operate effectively within the battle group.

A highly successful armoured fighting vehicle, Warrior can

be fitted with enhanced armour and is continuously being updated; for example, the Battle Group Thermal Imager (BTI) is being fitted to increase its night-fighting capability. Warrior infantry command and section vehicles carry a turret-mounted 30mm Rarden cannon that will defeat light armoured vehicles engaged up to a range of 1.5km. An 8x magnification image-intensifying night sight is fitted, and eight 94 mm light anti-armour weapon (LAW) HEAT rockets can be stowed in the vehicle. Warrior variants include an artillery observation post vehicle and command post vehicle, and a Royal Mechanical and Electrical Engineers' recovery and repair vehicle. All variants are equipped with a 7.62mm chain gun. Both chain gun and Rarden cannon have an anti-helicopter capability.

The most impressive feature of Warrior is its power. The 550bhp diesel engine gives a power-to-weight ratio of 23.5bhp/ton resulting in a road speed of 75kph and a cross-country speed of up to 50kph. This is 30 per cent better than the FV432 and with the improved suspension and a lower ground pressure it allows Warrior to keep pace with Challenger 2 across the toughest terrain, and the Warrior can wade to a depth of 1.3m.

The armour is designed to withstand a 155mm shell at 10m and direct fire from machine guns up to a calibre of 14.5mm. During the first Gulf War and operations in the Balkans as well as more recently in Iraq, additional armoured protection was fitted. Collective chemical, biological, radiological, and nuclear (CBRN) protection is provided when closed down and the

section should be able to remain fully closed down for 48 hours. For those calls of nature produced by the vagaries of life under fire, a toilet is also provided in the vehicle.

16

ENCOUNTER IN URUZGAN

It was 3 June 2008, and the convoy wound its way back to its operating base near Kandahar. The 50 men under the command of Lieutenant Fraser in the 17-vehicle convoy of fusiliers from the 1st Battalion, Royal Welsh, were on their way back to Kandahar after heavy fighting supporting Dutch troops of the ISAF in their battle to disrupt Taliban supply lines and disperse drug smugglers in the province of Uruzgan, 100 miles to the north of Kandahar. Dust thrown up by the convoy clung to skin damp from sweat and laid a thin film across the lens of the heavy desert goggles that the fusiliers wore as part of their kit, making visual scanning of their route difficult.

The Royal Welsh is a young infantry regiment and one of the largest in the British Army. It was formed on St David's Day, 1 March 2006, two years after the announcement of its formation by the Ministry of Defence and the then Army Chief-of-Staff General Sir Michael Jackson as part of the

restructuring of the infantry. The Royal Welsh consists of two regular battalions and a Territorial Army battalion, all of which wear the regiment's cap badge bearing the arms of the Prince of Wales and the motto, 'Ich Dien', formerly the cap badge of the Royal Regiment of Wales. The distinctive hackle of the Royal Welsh Fusiliers is worn by all NCOs and other ranks.

Of the regular battalions, the 1st serves a light infantry role and the 2nd is an armoured battalion. The 3rd (Territorial Army) battalion is a reserve battalion based in Cardiff. Recruited almost exclusively from Wales, it's possible that some of the 50 fusiliers making up the returning convoy may have had ancestors among the 19 Welshmen who fought at Rorke's Drift as members of the 24th Regiment of Foot of the 2nd Warwickshire, later to become the Royal Welsh Borderers. During the 22 and 23 of May 1879, 139 British and colonial troops successfully defended their small garrison against an estimated 5,000 Zulu warriors, the *impis* of King Cetshwayo. Now, in the torrid heat of 21st century Afghanistan, awaiting the Royal Welsh was a battle every bit as fierce and unforgiving. Certainly, at 3 to 1, the odds were more favourable, but in 1879 the men of the 24th of Foot knew what was coming over the brow of the hill.

Here, the warning of the ambush came with the ear-numbing detonation of a landmine as a Snatch 2 Land Rover was thrown into the air and flipped on to its back by the blast, its driver and gunner tossed like rag dolls to lie motionless at the side of the rutted track. Before the wreckage had settled, the air became alive with the crack and hum of small arms fire

and the whoosh and detonation of rocket-propelled grenades as the Taliban fighters opened fire from their prepared ambush positions around the convoy.

From his position on his vehicle, fusilier Damien Hields saw only smoke and confusion as the British troops took cover where they could from the ferocious incoming fire. Apart from being extremely accurate marksmen, their skill with arms honed by decades of modern warfare, the Taliban are well skilled at the psychology of ambush. The detonation of the landmine had acted just as the flash and bang of a special forces' stun grenade. When the 22 Special Air Service set up its Counter-Terrorist Wing back in the 1970s following the massacre of Israeli athletes in Munich, it sent a specification for a stun device to Royal Ordnance Enfield. The result was the G60 stun grenade, or 'flash bang'. The aim of the flash bang is to disorientate and distract hostiles in an enclosed environment, giving the entry team a few precious moments in which to enter and neutralise any threats.

Now the besieged fusiliers, their ears ringing from the detonation of the landmine, coughed and groped their way to their weapons through the billowing dust clouds, as the insurgents' bullets began to take their toll. The convoy was taking hits and the air rang with the cries of wounded men calling for a medic. The convoy's medical team was led by Combat Medical Technician Lance Corporal Carley Williams from Llanelli, an attractive young woman whose courageous efforts to treat wounded men under fire and to organise first aid would earn her a joint commander commendation along with Lieutenant Fraser.

Amid the acrid fumes of cordite and the choking smoke emitted by the exhaust gases of rocket-propelled grenades, L/Cpl Williams crawled from man to man supplying the instant nirvana of morphine, administered by a self-injecting syrette, to ease the pain of gunshot and shrapnel wounds. She recalls, 'The lads were screaming at me to get into cover. They said they actually saw one round pass between my legs.'

One man, Fusilier Damien Hields of Denbigh, North Wales, was still at his position of a vehicle-mounted automatic grenade launcher. Hields was a 24-year-old career soldier who had joined the Army at 16. Now married with a four-year-old son, Hields lived and breathed Army life. Now all that he had trained for was happening around him, and his mates and Carley Williams were under fire.

He saw the curving exhaust of an RPG-launched grenade and marked the firer's position, then swung his automatic grenade launcher on to the target and fired two rounds in quick succession to home in on the position. Once he saw his rounds were hitting the mark, he switched to automatic fire. A grenade machine gun has a box with 32 grenade rounds. 'I emptied a box on to that position and you could see all the dust and smoke flying about where they hit,' he later reported. 'After that, no fire came back from that position and I moved on to the next one. One or two rounds until I got on to the target, and switch to automatic and empty the box.'

Fusilier Hields was helped by his vehicle driver who, noting the Taliban targets, drove out of the convoy to reposition the vehicle without a thought that he was placing the grenade

gunner and himself in dreadful danger from the Taliban gunmen who were now realising that the persistent grenade gunner was their major threat and were homing in with their RPGs, Dushka machine guns, and Kalashnikov automatic rifles.

Fusilier Hields by this time had emptied six magazines, nearly 200 grenades, at the enemy and had taken out seven positions. 'We were winning the fight,' he insists. 'They started it and we were going to finish it.' But it was then that one of the thousands of bullets directed towards him and his driver – their vehicle was later reported to 'resemble a teabag' from the rounds pumped into it by the desperate enemy – found its mark. Says Hields, 'I was bending down to reload when I felt a sharp punch in the kidneys on my right side. I looked down and saw a hole in my body armour and a bit of blood.' The bullet had smashed a rib and exited without damaging major organs and Hields was still at his gun and bleeding profusely when L/Cpl Carley Williams reached him. Both the medic and the grenade vehicle's driver had to drag the wounded soldier to safety as he fought to return to his gun. They pulled him 20m to cover as the convoy, relieved of pressure by the savage effect of Hield's fire on the enemy, prepared to continue its journey to its base at Kandahar airfield. The wounded, meanwhile, were evacuated ahead by helicopter.

There can be no doubt that the bloody engagement on the road in Uruzgan Province was aimed at striking a crushing blow on British Army operations in the area. The loss of 17 armed and armoured vehicles to the enemy and the deaths of 50 soldiers would have had a disastrous effect on logistics and

morale, but the courageous stand of a Welsh fusilier, firing his grenade launcher at the enemy with lethal effect while he stood bloodied and wounded, saved the convoy. His commanding officer, Lieutenant Colonel Huw James, had no doubt that his fusilier had won the day. 'The Taliban did everything in their power to neutralise him and Fusilier Hields was having none of it. His actions allowed his patrol to come out of the ambush in which they were outnumbered by three or four to one and probably saved a lot of lives.'

Fusilier Hields recovered from his wounds and immediately asked to be returned to operational duties. For his actions that day, he was awarded not only the Military Cross, the third highest award for gallantry, but also the NATO Meritorious Service Medal for his actions, which were part of a NATO operation. However, he will not be allowed to wear the NATO award because Army rules do not permit soldiers to wear non-British medals − an anomaly that has upset his commanding officer. 'We think he has earned this decoration for gallantry and that it is only right that he should be allowed to wear it,' said Lt-Col James.

But it's the heroic Welsh fusilier who has the last word. 'I did what I was trained to do − the fear didn't hit me until later on.'

No better accolade could exist for British Army training, rightly recognised as the best in the world and capable of turning out characters of true grit who do not wilt under enemy fire.

17
CHARIOTS OF WAR –
PART TWO

With the likes of the Challenger 2 and the Warrior in infantry support, the logistical problem remains of getting the fighting men into and out of battle in a protected environment. The Armoured Personnel Carrier (APC) has been developed in many forms, the most recent being the Saxon, capable of travelling across rough terrains and fording water obstacles up to a depth of 90cm. In addition, the Saxon has excellent battlefield mobility and is extremely versatile. For protection and aggressive defence, the Saxon, best described as a battlefield taxi, carries an L37 GPMG turret in all its variants. These include a Royal Electrical and Mechanical Engineers (REME) recovery vehicle, an armoured ambulance capable of entering a combat zone and defending its crew while they rescue downed personnel trapped by incoming fire (much like the role played by Vikings in the retrieval of the body of the Royal Anglians' Johan Botha on the outskirts of Darvisham), a

command post vehicle, and an internal security version. The latter is used for service in counter-insurgency operations and has a protected Cummins BT 5.1 engine instead of the APC version's Bedford 6-cylinder.

Other enhancements include roof-mounted searchlights, improved armour, a barricade removal device and an anti-wire device. In its internal security role, the Saxon comes in two versions: a troop-carrier with the capacity for ten men or an ambulance capable of carrying two stretcher cases. A strong point in favour of the often hard-driven and abused Saxon is its demand for lower maintenance than that of other APCs or Advanced Infantry Fighting Vehicles, which is down to its design around standard truck parts. The Saxon is essentially a mine-proof lorry and has been used very successfully by the mechanised battalions serving with the UN in Bosnia and in operational duties with British forces in both Iraq and Afghanistan. The Saxon is manufactured by GKN Defence and the British Army took delivery of the first units in the autumn of 1983.

The Fighting Vehicles 430 (FV430) encompasses a family of armoured vehicles that entered service with the British Army in the 1960s and were familiar to anyone who was called to defend Queen and Country in the last years of National Service. Essentially old, these rugged vehicles have enjoyed the benefits of regular maintenance and improvements such as a new power train that have allowed them to stay in service into the 21st century. Of these, the FV432 can be converted to operate over water at a speed of 6kph. Other FV430 variants

remain in service with the infantry as command vehicles, 81 mortar carriers, ambulances and recovery vehicles.

The British Army has recently taken delivery of over 100 up-armoured and upgraded FV430 troop carriers denominated the Bulldog APC. These are now in use with mechanised infantry for armoured mobility around the battlefield, giving protection against small arms and artillery fire while providing excellent strategic and cross-country mobility. The up-armoured FV430 used in counter-insurgency operations provide a similar level of protection as the Warrior and the vehicle is able to carry out many of the same tasks as the Warrior, which serves to relieve pressure on heavily committed combat vehicles in armoured infantry battle groups.

Another task for armoured vehicles is to provide the platform for high-velocity missile systems. The British Army sports a tracked mobile platform in the Stormer, which gives a detachment protection and excellent mobility with eight ready-to-fire missiles and nine stored in reserve inside the vehicle.

The Starstreak High-Velocity Missile system is a low-level, closed air defence (CAD) system with a rapid engagement capacity developed and optimised to counter the ever-present threat from attack helicopters. The highly flexible system is also capable of being fired using the LML lightweight multiple launcher or even from the shoulder. It employs a system of three dart-type projectiles which allows for multiple strikes on a target with devastating effect. Each dart carries an explosive warhead.

The Starstreak system employs a roof-mounted air defence alerting device that provides target detection and prioritisation

in the event of a clustered attack. A panoramic weapon sight is located at the front right of the vehicle.

Armoured reconnaissance is provided by the fleet-footed Scimitar, recently in operation in Afghanistan under the seal of at least one royal approval, and its smaller brother, the Spartan. Scimitar is a fast and agile armoured unit with a primary role of gathering information, bringing it into the category of Armoured Reconnaissance Vehicles. Their operators, known as Recce, are highly trained in the art of gathering battlefield intelligence by stealth, both from their vehicle or on foot, and are tasked with providing such crucial information to battle commanders 24 hours a day regardless of weather conditions. In such operations, the Scimitar, which carries an L21 30mm Rarden cannon for self-defence capable of loosing off 90 rounds a minute when its three-man crew consider the time auspicious, is often called upon to beat a hasty and tactical retreat, which it can do at speeds up to 80kph. As with all UK armoured vehicles, it is also provided with a forced air system, so the crew can lock down in a CBRN environment. For this reason, they are equipped with a boiling vessel (BV) to cook and make hot drinks. As a whimsical reminder of the urgencies of battle, no matter who your vehicle commander is, it also has a hole in the centre of the commander's seat that can be used as a toilet.

The Spartan is a very small armoured personnel carrier but can stretch itself to carry four men in addition to its three-man crew. Its size and capacity therefore fits in with its usefulness in carrying small, specialised groups such as reconnaissance teams,

air defence sections and mortar fire controllers. The Samaritan, Sultan and Sampson also serve as CVR (T) vehicles, with the Samaritan able to take on a field ambulance role, the Sultan as an armoured command vehicle, and the powerful Sampson as an armoured recovery vehicle.

Protected Patrol Vehicles (PPVs) are an essential section of armoured army transport and would be those with which the infantry is in close contact during field operations. They might hear the rattle of the tracks of a Challenger or Warrior going into action but it will be the heavy-duty Land Rover chassis or the articulated Viking bringing supplies and ammunition which will be the more familiar sight through the haze and dust of the battlefield.

The curiously named Snatch 2 was originally designed for use in Northern Ireland, where its mobility and ease of rapid deployment saw it featured in many urban battles as it crashed through blazing roadblocks and provided cover for hard-pressed patrols. The Snatch 2 can be fitted with BOWMAN, the tactical communications system designed to exploit the latest developments in radio and computer technology, even bringing commanders on-the-ground visuals of close-quarter battles as they develop through helmet-mounted video cameras carried into battle as part of the infantry's standard equipment. Due to its vulnerability to IEDs and despite its usefulness as a patrol vehicle in low-risk areas, Snatch 2 is gradually being replaced by the Vector and Mastiff.

Of these, the newest delivery in the range of PPVs is the mighty Mastiff, a heavily armoured 6x6-wheel-drive patrol

vehicle capable of carrying six men in addition to its crew of two. The Mastiff is a derivation of the US Marines' Cougar and is fully mine-protected, capable of ferrying troops around killing grounds with much improved protection. Incorporating the highest levels of survivability, the vehicle build includes such features as a V-shaped steel hull, run-flat tyres, shock-mounted seating, and internal spall liners, made of high-performance polyurethane and rubberised aramid, a type of heat-resistant synthetic fibre. Spall liner panels are mounted internally and are designed to stop small arms projectiles as well as fragments. They have also proved effective in reducing the cone of fragments if the vehicle is penetrated by kinetic energy projectiles or the explosive jet from shaped charges such as the RPG-7.

The blast and ballistic-protective Cougars on which the Mastiff is based have withstood thousands of blast attacks during more than 100,000 days of service in heavy combat conditions. Wheeled patrol vehicles have a less intimidating profile than their tracked counterparts and have been proven to give commanders on the ground more options to deal with whatever threat they are facing. The Mastiff, which is capable of achieving a speed of 90kph, carries BOWMAN radios and electronic counter-measures and can be armed with a choice of 7.62mm GPMG, 50mm cannon, or the formidable 40mm automatic grenade launcher.

Next in the range comes the Vector. Like the Mastiff, the Vector, powered by the Volkswagen 5-cylinder Euro 2 engine, is a fast and lightweight 6x6-wheel-drive patrol vehicle with a

newly armoured body from manufacturers Pinzgauer. Its improved protection and, importantly, increased mobility and capacity compared to Snatch 2 Land Rovers make it very suitable for the rugged terrain and long patrol distances in Afghanistan. It is used as a command vehicle, troop carrier and for both urban and rural patrolling. It has the capacity to mount two GPMGs on its roof, and also has an ambulance variant in order to match the ability of the convoys the vehicle supports.

A smaller and highly mobile weapons platform is provided by the Jackal, which tips the scales at almost the same weight as the Vector at around 6.5 tonnes. The fast-moving, hard-hitting Jackal incorporates a unique air-bag suspension system that allows the vehicle rapid movement across varying terrain, suiting it admirably to operations in the Afghan theatre of war. Its three-man crew rely on a GPMG as crew protection, supplemented by either a heavy machine gun or grenade machine gun as the main weapon system in the fire support role, making the Jackal a firm favourite of commanders for use in reconnaissance, rapid assault, fire support and convoy protection. Almost as if carrying on the tradition of the vehicles of the Long-Range Desert Group of the Second World War, the highly versatile Jackal has the capacity to support itself and its crew over a range of 800km, making it an equally no-competition choice for the 22 Special Air Service and land operations of the Royal Marines' Special Boat Service.

A new addition in the summer of 2009 will be the much awaited Panther Command and Liaison Vehicle, which will eventually replace some of the in-service CVR(T)s, medium

utility trucks such as the Land Rover 110s, Saxons and FV 432 vehicles. First to receive the Panther will be the 1 Mechanised Brigade, followed by troops from 3 UK Division, then 4 Mechanised Brigade. Weighing in at 7 tonnes, the Panther is air transportable and can be under-slung beneath a Chinook helicopter. In its command and liaison role, it is armed with a 7.62mm L7 GPMG remote weapons station, which allows the weapon to be sighted and fired in a closed vehicle environment. Should the theatre warrant it, this can be upgraded to a 12.7mm weapon, either of which is equipped with a day or night sighting system. The armour is protection against small arms fire and Level 3 blast mines.

The Panther is envisaged to be of widespread use for commanders, sergeant majors and liaison officers of armoured, armoured reconnaissance and armoured infantry units, as well as engineer troops, anti-tank, mortar and supporting fire platoons, as well as a rebroadcast unit for battle group nets and regimental signal officers.

The last vehicle worthy of mention is a recent addition to the Army's vehicle pool and has been greeted by the troopers' ultimate accolade as 'a nice bit of kit'. The Viking BVS10 All-Terrain Vehicle has already been put to use in some of the fiercest fighting in the Afghanistan theatre of war, including its role in rescuing fallen soldiers and resupplying three hard-pressed platoons of the Anglians when under fire at Darvisham. The Viking is produced, as its name might imply, by BAe Systems Haaglunds of Sweden.

BV means 'Bandvagen' in Swedish, which means that the

vehicle is driven by rubber tracks. As did the wild forbears of its name, the Viking has an affinity for water and can be deployed via landing craft from ship. As with all medium-weight armour, it is air transportable, either by C-130 or under-slung on a Chinook. There are four variants currently in service: the troop carrier; the command vehicle; the ambulance; and the repair and recovery vehicle. Including bar armour, it has a width of 2.75m and a length between 8.3m and 8.5m depending on its battlefield role. Weighing in at 12.74 tonnes it needs a powerful engine, and has it in the Cummins 5.9 litre 6-cylinder Euro 3 which drives it through a six-gear Allison WT3560 transmission to a top speed of 65kph on land and 5kph through water.

18
AFGHAN EYES

On the morning of 13 March 2005, Haitham al Yemeni, an al-Qaeda explosives expert from Yemen, left his home in a village in north-west Pakistan and drove his car along the track to join the main road into town. Even today, these locations are kept secret although the world knows what happened next. The man didn't hear the suppressed whisper of the aircraft engine above the rattle of his car over the rutted road. Nor did he hear the whoosh of the approaching Hellfire missile that tore him and his vehicle to pieces and scattered the remains over the hard-packed earth.

The MQ-1 Predator that had fired the Hellfire banked in the sky above and turned back towards its operating base where it would land and its recorded tape of the strike be downloaded. The pilot of the aircraft guided it down to its 1,500m-long runway in Uzbekistan and left his console at Langley, Virginia, on the other side of the world.

Haitham al Yemeni would soon be joined by other victims of this silent bringer of death from the skies. The US Central Intelligence Agency had unleashed its secret weapon – a drone aircraft that could observe and kill with stealth – and aerial warfare entered the 21st century.

General Atomics Aeronautical Systems had been awarded a contract to develop the Predator in January 1994, and the initial Advanced Concept Technology Demonstration (ACTD) phase lasted from January 1994 to June 1996. The aircraft itself was a derivative of the GA Gnat 750 UAV, a smaller version developed with CIA funding by Leading Systems Inc. During the demonstration phase, three systems were purchased from GA, comprising 12 aircraft and three ground control stations. From April through May 1995, the Predator ACTD aircraft were flown as a part of the Roving Sands 1995 exercises in the USA. The exercise operations were successful, and this led to the decision to deploy the system to the Balkans later in the summer of 1995. Cost for an early production Predator was about $3.2 million.

The CIA arranged for air force teams trained by the 11th Reconnaissance Squadron at Nellis Air Force Base, Nevada, to fly the agency's Predators. First in Bosnia and then in Kosovo, CIA officers began to see the first practical returns of an unmanned aircraft that could return high and low altitude reconnaissance and that had an obvious future role in delivering laser-guided ordnance or to act as a laser guide for manned aircraft. Against the $70 million price of an F-16 Falcon in 2006, $3.2 million for a drone capable of performing

many of the former aircraft's tasks, excluding those of aerial combat, seemed to offer that sort of financial viability beloved by Congressional bean-counters.

In addition, improvements due to the USAF's satellite communications system now made it possible in theory to fly the drone by remote control from great distances – previously, in the Balkans operation, CIA agents flying the drones secretly out of Albania and Hungary had experienced a two-second time delay between movement of the joystick and a response from the drone's control surfaces. Following modifications, take-off and ascent were controlled by direct signals and improved out-of-sight flight directions were now communicated to the aircraft by a military satellite network linked to the controller.

By the opening of the Afghanistan campaign, the USAF had 40 Predators. Twenty had been previously lost due to control and fuel problems, but the drone was now ready to perform. In 2000, a joint CIA–Pentagon effort was agreed to locate Osama bin Laden in Afghanistan. Dubbed 'Afghan Eyes', it involved a projected 60-day trial run of Predators over the country.

The first experimental flight was held on 7 September 2000. Such was the success and clarity of the video footage obtained that White House Security Chief, Richard A Clarke, hoped that the drones might eventually be used to target bin Laden with cruise missiles or armed aircraft. His enthusiasm for the project was matched by Cofer Black, head of the CIA's Counterterrorist Center (CTC), and Charles Allen in charge of the CIA's intelligence-collection operations. The three men

backed an immediate trial run of reconnaissance flights. Ten out of the ensuing fifteen Predator missions over Afghanistan were rated successful. On at least two flights, a Predator spotted a tall man in white robes at bin Laden's Tarnak Farm compound outside Kandahar; the figure was subsequently deemed to be 'probably bin Laden'.

In Langley, hopes were high that the West's number-one assassination target could be struck down from the skies, but with the advent of autumn, weather conditions had deteriorated sufficiently over the Predator drones' base in Uzbekistan to cause further flights to be cancelled and USAF drone pilots and the 'Osama Watch' force of agents stood down.

It was hoped to resume flights in spring 2001, but debates about the use of an armed Predator delayed a restart. Only on 4 September 2001, after the Bush cabinet approved an al-Qaeda/Taliban plan, did CIA chief Tenet order the agency to resume reconnaissance flights. The Predators were now weapons-capable, but didn't carry missiles because the host country – presumably Uzbekistan – hadn't granted permission. This approval would come after 9/11 and the first Predator capable of armed warfare reached its forward operating base in September 2001.

The first mission was flown over Kabul and Kandahar on 18 September without carrying weapons. Subsequent host nation approval was granted on 7 October and the first armed mission was flown on the same day. On 4 February 2002, an armed Predator attacked a convoy of sport utility vehicles, killing a suspected al-Qaeda leader. The intelligence community

initially expressed doubt that he was Osama bin Laden. On 4 March 2002, a CIA-operated Predator fired a Hellfire missile into a reinforced al-Qaeda machine gun bunker that had pinned down an Army ranger team whose CH-47 Chinook had crashed on the top of Takur Ghar Mountain in Afghanistan. Previous attempts by flights of F-15 and F-16 aircraft were unable to destroy the bunker. This action took place during what has become known as the Battle of Robert's Ridge, a part of Operation Anaconda. This appears to be the first use of such a weapon in a close air-support role.

A smaller drone in operation with the British Army in Helmand is the Desert Hawk, an extremely versatile and small Unmanned Arial Vehicle designed for discrete operations. It is operated normally at company level but is equally well employed above and below that line. It has an extremely good record proven over the last year supporting both 16 Air Assault and 3 Commando Brigades in Afghanistan, where it provides an excellent 'over-the-hill' view for commanders on the ground, capable of relaying back visual information of suspicious ground activity in the case of enemy mine-laying or ambush positions.

A new tactical unmanned aerial vehicle system for the British Army will be Watchkeeper, which is due to come into service in 2010. The aircraft design will include dual-payload configuration, a flexible, all-weather operation with de-icing capability, improved access to sub systems for easier maintenance, and automatic take-off and landing. Fifty-four drones are currently under test with privatised defence researcher Qiniteq and earmarked for 2010 delivery.

19

ARGHANDAB OFFENSIVE

As I approached the final stages of writing this book it became clear that something very significant was occurring in Afghanistan. I heard the news on 13 June 2008 that Taliban fighters had seized control of an area of Kandahar during the evening and had driven a suicide truck filled with explosives through the gates of the city's main prison. The massive explosion shook the city and destroyed the gate and a police post. It was followed by up to 30 motorcyclists whose pillion passengers fired RPGs, machine guns and AK47s at the stunned defenders.

A fierce 20-minute gun battle ensued, with the area around the Sarpoza Prison wreathed in smoke and wracked by small arms fire and explosions. During the ensuing confusion, it was thought more than 1,000 prisoners were able to flee to freedom, including an estimated 400 Taliban. Some prisoners were caught in the vicious crossfire between the attackers and

Afghan police but it was later reported that all the Taliban prisoners had escaped unharmed. At around midnight on the same day, rockets were fired at an ISAF army base in another part of the city.

Over the next few days, there were rumbles of a new Taliban offensive starting in the region of Kandahar, which were more clearly defined on 16 June when Taliban militants seized a string of villages and fruit orchards in the Arghandab district, less than 24km from Kandahar City. From there, Taliban spokesmen threatened to launch attacks against Kandahar itself and 700 Afghan soldiers were flown in to dig in and take up defensive positions around the city's northern suburbs. As they arrived, thousands of Afghan villagers in Arghandab fled their homes – a sure sign they had warning of an impending battle. It is noted by troops patrolling in Afghanistan that a civilian exodus always precedes a battle and a deserted village is a sure sign of a waiting ambush.

By Wednesday, 18 June, the area was alive with Afghan troops patrolling the area between Kandahar and Arghandab in pick-up trucks bristling with mounted machine guns. Also on the scene was a column of Canadian armoured personnel carriers setting up positions along the valley of the Arghandab River. Journalists were prevented from entering the northern district of the city. NATO patrols, which now involved British paratroopers, began to sweep outwards along the western bank of the river and some clashes occurred, claiming the lives of six Taliban fighters and two soldiers of the Afghan Army. Conversely, Taliban sources claimed two ANP vehicles were

destroyed and 16 Afghan security forces killed. The war of claim and counter-claim had begun.

The streets of Kandahar were deserted except for the presence of Afghan police and soldiers and NATO forces manning checkpoints at every intersection. Throughout the day, helicopter gunship traffic increased in the skies over Kandahar and armoured vehicles began to build up in the river valley. Then the word was given to advance on Arghandab.

In the first engagement of the advancing Afghan and ISAF column, 16 Taliban were killed and four wounded in their defence of the fruit orchards around Arghandab. Men fell wounded and dying among the trees bearing the fragrant apricot blossoms and scarlet pomegranate flowers and their blood soaked into the ground. Air strikes were called in to breach fierce resistance in the neighbouring villages of Kohak and Nagahan and, aided by artillery, to counter withdrawals that the canny Taliban fighters had planned before the battle. These were designed to allow counter-attacks ordered by radio to distract the coalition column away from a Taliban entrenchment that was about to be overrun, allowing the survivors to escape through the densely wooded orchards and regroup to fight elsewhere.

The Afghans and ISAF troops were facing an elusive and well-trained enemy. Estimates put the enemy force at around 500 in total, occupying nine villages in the Arghandab district. Advance by the ANA and ISAF forces was made difficult by the Taliban blowing up three river bridges and laying mines on several roads. As the ponderous advance continued, NATO

forces airdropped hundreds of leaflets into Arghandab, warning villagers to stay inside their homes during the impending counter-offensive against the Taliban, but troops on the ground reported that most of the mud-walled dwellings were already empty of their residents, who had fled in fear of the fighting and fear of the Taliban. The common system of house clearing adopted in a combat zone by troops is a grenade followed by a burst of rapid small arms fire. It does not discriminate between an enemy fighter and a householder reluctant to leave his property.

In all, 1,500 families had fled their homes and farms to avoid being caught in the lethal crossfire as Afghan and NATO troops and Taliban clashed along the length of the Arghandab river valley. After heavy fighting, four of the 10 villages under Taliban control had been retaken and the Taliban had taken heavy losses, losing 20 warriors in a NATO air strike on the village of Tabeen and 16 killed in fighting in Khohak.

Meanwhile, civilians were also paying a heavy price in the fighting. In mid-June, the number of civilians killed in fighting between insurgents and security forces throughout Afghanistan in the first half of 2008 stood at 698, 62 per cent more than the 430 killed in the first six months of the previous year and far above the 110 total deaths – including non-combat – of British forces and the Canadian toll of 85. Most of the civilian casualties are caused by insurgents but there are still significant numbers caused by the international military in the country.

The civilian death toll serves as a grim reminder that the population has paid the heaviest price in the battle for power

between the dispossessed Taliban and the NATO-supported Northern Alliance, neither of which plans an administration much to the indigenous population's advantage. Meanwhile, in May 2008, UN Humanitarian Affairs Chief John Holmes announced that insecurity throughout the country was making the work of delivering emergency aid to those hit by the food crisis difficult. Holmes went on to warn that civilian casualties in Afghanistan were at an unacceptable level. 'While it is clear that the insurgents seem to have no regard for civilian life, and that the international military forces are making every effort to minimise civilian casualties and recognise the damage this does and want to deal with it, these problems are still there and we need to deal with them and make sure that the safety of civilians comes first and international humanitarian law is respected by everybody.'

Holmes' fine words were rejected by NATO. Mark Laity, the Alliance spokesman in Kabul, said the numbers quoted by Holmes were 'far higher than we would recognise' but provided no alternative figures. Human Rights Watch estimates the total number of civilians killed in the seven-year war at over 3,000.

Meanwhile, civilians, Afghan security forces and ISAF troops continued to pay the price in the battle of the Arghandab Valley. In June of 2008 alone, 13 UK servicemen and women lost their lives due to enemy action, many of these towards the end of the month in the upsurge of violence that surrounded the Afghan-led counter-offensive in Arghandab.

20

THE BRIDGE
BUILDERS

Any army, both at war and peace, needs constant
maintenance if its equipment and transport is going to
survive the rigours of hard service. At war, it also needs a force
that can lay roads and restore shattered bridges to keep its
infantry and weapons on the move. The Corps of Royal
Engineers, otherwise known as the sappers, has been at the
forefront of army technology since its foundation in the 11th
century, when its forbears accompanied William the
Conqueror and his Norman knights across the Channel in the
invasion of England.

Originally called the Corps of Royal Sappers and Miners, the
former name has stuck with the Royal Engineers throughout
their history. The term originates from the trenches or 'saps'
which engineers were employed to build near enemy positions
in later centuries to allow the placing and detonation of
explosive charges. Early examples of the British sappers' skill

can be seen at various locations in Spain where stand the remains of fortresses occupied by the French during the Peninsular War of the early 19th century. At each site, only half the structures remain and immediately below are the marks of the blackened tunnels dug by British engineers to house the gunpowder that tore the hillsides and the fortresses apart. The same technique was to be used with epic results at Messines Ridge in 1917, the precursor to the horrors of Passchendaele.

From the earliest developments in military aviation, signalling and tank warfare to the very latest bridging systems and map-making techniques, the sappers have operated at the cutting edge of technology and frequently in the most inhospitable conditions. That commitment to ingenuity and the solving of practical problems is as strong today as it has ever been and the sappers continue to fulfil an essential role all over the world.

In their 950-year history, the Royal Engineers have been involved in every major conflict the British Army has fought, as well as carrying out humanitarian roles such as providing clean water and building schools.

The Corps of Royal Engineers has a long heritage that few others can rival − it can claim direct descent from the military engineers that William the Conqueror brought to England. Since then it has lived up to its motto − '*ubique*' ('everywhere') − having had a significant presence at every large-scale battle the British Army has ever fought. It has also introduced new technology to the British Army throughout its history, including diving, telegraphy and the development of the tank.

Aided by today's modern equipment, its engineers clear routes, repair airfields and harbours, and bridge rivers – all at top speed and often under fire – while delaying the enemy's advance with quick and effective obstacles.

A brother corps, the Royal Electrical and Mechanical Engineers, was formed from the Royal Ordnance Corps during the First World War, and has responsibility for the maintenance, servicing and inspection of almost every electrical and mechanical piece of equipment within the British Army, from Challenger 2 main battle tanks and AH64 Apache helicopters to dental tools and cooking utensils, as well as everything in use on the battlefield from rifle to radio, motorbike to missile.

Many other new corps and organisations have been formed from the origins of the Royal Engineers, including the Royal Flying Corps, later the Royal Air Force, and the Royal Corps of Signals formed from the Telegraph and Signal Service, which began life during the Crimean War of 1854–56 when the engineers were given an opportunity to use telegraph equipment. In the 1860s, the Royal Engineers developed a system of flag and lamp signalling for use on military campaigns. By the end the First World War, the Royal Engineers (Signal Service) had so developed and expanded that it was decided that it should become a corps in its own right. The Corps of Royal Signals was formed in 1920.

Organisations that owe their birth to the Royal Engineers include the Ordnance Survey, born in 1747, and one of the first of the Royal Engineers 'specialist' activities. Between the

1820s and1856, soldiers of the Corps of Royal Sappers and Miners assisted officers of the Corps of Royal Engineers in survey duties in the British Isles and elsewhere in the British Empire. Today's Ordnance Survey was developed from the early Royal Engineers survey activities.

Diving as one of the Corps' 'specialist' activities was introduced in 1838 by Colonel (later General) Sir Charles Pasley (1780–1861). In the early days, both Royal Engineers and Royal Sappers and Miners trained as deep-water divers. Shallow-water diving capabilities were developed in the 1950s. The Sappers taught the first Royal Navy divers. All recruits to the Royal Engineers become multi-skilled soldiers, combat engineers and tradesmen. From fighting alongside the Combat Arms to purifying water, making maps and building accommodation, the Royal Engineers play a vital role in the effectiveness of the British Army as well as the Navy and RAF.

As a bonus for sports fans, these able-fingered and nimble-minded men and women who keep the British Army on the move have an additional string to their bow. The Royal Engineers won the FA Cup at the Kensington Oval, London, on 16 March 1875, and were runners-up in 1872, 1874 and 1878.

Nowadays, modern warfare calls for a highly mobile Army, delivered to the battlefront at top speed with obstacles en route overcome with efficiency and speed. Vehicles for river crossings include the M3 Amphibious Rig, which replaced its forerunner, the M2 AR, which was in service for 25 years. The M3 AR can be driven into a river and used as a ferry. When a number are joined together bank to bank, they form a

bridge capable of taking the weight of the Challenger 2 Main Battle Tank.

The M3 has a number of improvements over the M2; it can deploy pontoons on the move in or out of water, it needs no on-site preparation to enter the water and can be controlled from inside the cab when afloat, as well as having automated control functions that have allowed a crew reduction from four to three.

A single two-bay M3 can carry a Class 70 tracked vehicle, where two M2s would have been required for this task with additional buoyancy bags. The Army bean-counters have also assessed its value with their stopwatches – eight M3 units and 24 soldiers can build a 100m bridge in 30 minutes, compared with 12 M2s, 48 soldiers and a construction time of 45 minutes. The M3 is only 1.4m longer and 3.3 tonnes heavier than the M2; it is faster and more manoeuvrable on land and in water with a four-wheel steering capability that gives a turning diameter of 24m.

But rivers aren't the only obstacles met by infantry on the move. Wild, mountainous and desert country, such as that encountered in the Afghanistan theatre, means troops are often faced with ravines and wadis which would mean detours of many kilometres were it not for the introduction of the Titan. Titan is a new armoured engineer vehicle designed to enable troops and vehicles to cross gaps of up to 60m by laying a selection of close support bridges.

Based on the Challenger 2 Main Battle Tank chassis, Titan can carry and lay the current range of In-Service No 10, 11

and 12 Close Support Bridges, providing ground manoeuvre formations with improved operation of the bridges and enabling them to be laid in a greater range of terrain conditions. Improved visibility is achieved by incorporating direct and indirect vision devices with low-light, image-intensifying and thermal-imaging capabilities. The interior and, to some extent, the exterior of the vehicles have been designed around the crew station positions. Titan has the flexibility to support a wide range of operations, including humanitarian missions.

The Royal Engineer BR-90 family of bridges are built from a range of seven modular panels of advanced aluminium alloy fabrication, interchangeable through the various bridge types, to form two interconnecting track-ways with a 4m overall bridge width and a 1m girder depth.

The Close Support Bridge consists of three tank-launched bridges capable of being carried on a Tank Bridgelayer and a Tank Bridge Transporter truck. There are three basic tank-launched bridges (also known as Close Support or Assault Bridges): the No 10, No 11 and No 12. The General Support Bridge system utilises the Automated Bridge Launching Equipment (ABLE) that is capable of launching bridges up to 44m in length. The ABLE vehicle is positioned with its rear pointing to the gap to be crossed and a lightweight launch rail extended across the gap. The bridge is then assembled and winched across the gap supported by the rail, with sections added until the gap is crossed. Once the bridge has crossed the gap, the ABLE launch rail is recovered.

A standard ABLE system set consists of an ABLE vehicle and 2 x TBT carrying a 32m bridge set. A 32m bridge can be built by 10 men in about 25 minutes.

There are two basic spanning systems: the long-span system allows for lengthening a 32m span to 44m using ABLE; and the two-span system allows 2 x 32m bridge sets to be constructed by ABLE and secured in the middle by piers or floating pontoons, crossing a gap of up to 60m.

To protect infantry and vehicles on the battlefield, defence against enemy armour can be deployed rapidly by the Shielder Anti-tank System, which gives commanders the facility to create efficient anti-tank barriers as rapidly deployed protection against enemy armour. The system consists of modular mine dispensers which can be fired to either side or to the rear, mounted on a flat-bed version of the Stormer Armoured Personnel Carrier. As a humanitarian aid sadly lacking in most other mine manufacture, the anti-tank mines deployed by the Shielder have a programmable life, at the end of which they self-destruct.

Shielder will only lay anti-tank mines – the British Army does not use anti-personnel mines. These mines are carried in canisters, each of which hold six mines with up to 40 canisters, and are carried on a launcher rack. These are on the rear of the Stormer flatbed and discharge the anti-tank mines either side as the vehicle moves across the terrain. A dispenser control unit provides fire signals, testing and arming of the self-destruct mechanism.

Vehicle recovery on the battlefield is a dangerous operation.

The Challenger Armoured Repair and Recovery Vehicle, known as CRARRV, is a highly evolved armoured vehicle designed to recover and repair damaged tanks in the field of battle. The vehicle has both a main and auxiliary winch, and an Atlas hydraulically operated crane capable of lifting a complete Challenger 2 power pack. The front bulldozer blade can be used as an earth anchor, as a stabiliser for the crane, or to clear obstacles and dig fire positions. Based on Challenger components, the CRARRV carries a crew of three plus two Royal Electrical and Mechanical Engineers (REME) fitters in a separate compartment.

A lightly armoured, highly mobile, general support engineer vehicle optimised for battlefield preparation in the indirect fire zone is the Terrier, which is set to replace the existing Combat Engineer Tractor (CET) from 2008, providing mobility support consisting of obstacle and route clearance, counter-mobility of the enemy by the digging of anti-tank ditches and placing other obstacles, and providing cover and survival aids by the rapid digging of trenches and Armoured Fighting Vehicle slots, or berms. Terrier is claimed to be faster, more mobile and with more effective armour and mine protection than the CET. The vehicle is operated by a crew of two or may be operated remotely in particularly hazardous environments. The vehicle can also tow a trailer carrying fascines (a bundle of rough brushwood for track laying), track-ways and the Python minefield breaching system, clear scattered mines, remove or enhance obstacles, and establish routes while keeping pace with other armoured vehicles such as the

Challenger 2 Main Battle Tank and the Warrior Infantry Fighting Vehicle. It is fitted with day- and night-vision systems and is air-portable.

The Titan's bigger and weightier counterpart at arms is the mighty Trojan, an armoured engineer vehicle designed to open routes through complex battlefield obstacles and to clear a path through minefields. Standard equipment includes a winch and a knuckle-arm excavator shovel. Along with Titan it gives a common heavy armour fleet based on the Challenger 2 Main Battle Tank chassis. A Pearson Engineering Full-Width Mine Plough can be mounted at the front to clear mines and a Pearson Engineering Pathfinder lane-marking system can also be fitted. It can also carry fascines to drop into ditches and can tow a trailer-mounted Python rocket-propelled mine-clearing system. Improved visibility is achieved by incorporating direct and indirect vision devices with low-light, image-intensifying and thermal-imaging capabilities. The interior and, to some extent, the exterior of the vehicles have been designed around the crew station positions. Trojan has the flexibility to support a wide range of operations.

The RE's final card in the armoured defence suite is the Python, a highly effective minefield breaching system which has been successfully tested with the British Army. It replaces the ageing Giant Viper, which dates back to the 1950s, and has the ability to clear a much longer 'safe lane' than its predecessor. It is also faster into action and far more accurate. It can clear a path 230m long and 7m wide through which vehicles can pass safely. The system works by firing a single

rocket from a newly designed launcher mounted on a trailer which has been towed to the edge of the mined area. Attached to the rocket is a coiled 230m long hose packed with 1.5 tons of powerful explosive. After the hose lands on the ground, it detonates and destroys or clears over 90 per cent of mines along its entire length, leaving a vigilant following troop to cross with enhanced safety.

21

HIGH-SPEED
KILLERS

Whether high-explosive shells, surface-to-air missiles, or self-propelled guns, the soldier on the ground relies on heavy armament to come to his assistance when the going gets rough and, when pinned down by superior forces, the going can be very tough indeed.

Threats from high-performance, low-flying aircraft do not currently exist against ISAF forces in Afghanistan since the Taliban do not possess an air force. Nonetheless, the highly intelligent Starstreak High Velocity Missile (HVM) is designed to counter a variety of threats, including those from 'pop-up' strikes by helicopters. It would seem, with the money from the escalating drug industry, that it could be simply just a matter of time before ISAF troops in Afghanistan could find themselves facing determined air attacks, possibly launched from neighbouring – but not in the least neighbourly – Iran.

The Starstreak is a low-level Close Air Defence (CAD)

system with a rapid engagement capacity developed and optimised to counter the attack helicopter threat. This highly flexible system is capable of being fired from the shoulder, from a lightweight multiple launcher or from the Stormer armoured vehicle, which is equipped with an eight-round launcher and can carry another twelve missiles inside the vehicle.

The missile, which travels at more than three times the speed of sound, employs a system of three dart-type projectiles which can make multiple hits on the target. Each of these darts has an explosive warhead. All shoulder-launch missiles have proved to be extremely lethal to enemy forces holding positions in bunkers or caves, especially the latter of the Tora Bora and Zhawar Kili mountain ranges, which coalition forces in 2001 suspected of being the hiding place of Osama bin Laden.

Less sophisticated but equally capable of packing a volatile punch is the AS90 Self-Propelled Gun that equips six field regiments of the Royal Horse Artillery and the Royal Artillery. Fitted with a standard barrel, the AS90 can fire the NATO L15 unassisted 155mm projectile weighing 43.6kg to a distance of 24.7km. With a long 52-calibre barrel, the gun can reach out to 30km using standard ammunition, and 60–80km with extended range (ERA) ammunition. The AS90 is equipped with an autonomous navigation and gun-laying system (AGLS) based on the vehicle's inertial navigation system, the dynamic reference unit (DRU). All main turret functions are controlled by the turret control computer (TCC).

The smaller L118 105mm Light Gun is used by the Parachute and Commando Field Artillery Regiments. The

versatile weapon can be towed by a medium-weight vehicle, such as a Pinzgauer TUM/HD or Hagglund BV206 all-terrain vehicle, or carried around the battlefield under-slung from a Puma or Chinook helicopter. All Royal Artillery L118 Light Guns are fitted with an automatic pointing system, which enables the gun to be unlimbered and in action in 30 seconds. The APS is based on an inertial navigation system, operated via a touch screen, and replaces the traditional dial sight. New Light Gun ammunition is in development, with an increasingly lethal round and an extended range.

Also in the Royal Artillery's armoury is the state-of-the-art Guided Multiple Launch Rocket System (GMLRS), nicknamed, because of its range and accuracy, the '70 Kilometre Sniper'. The Sniper can deliver a 200lb high-explosive warhead with pinpoint accuracy at twice the range of other artillery systems in operation with the British Army.

The Royal Artillery's newest long-range precision land attack rocket is currently in use on operations in southern Afghanistan following a recent series of successful trials. Deployed in several locations throughout Helmand Province, the global GPS-guided rockets contain the latest advanced computer technology, giving them unsurpassed accuracy. The system takes far fewer rockets to defeat targets, while also reducing the risk of collateral damage. The weapon system is manned by a small crew of three gunners and is mounted on a tracked armoured launcher, which is highly robust and easy to manoeuvre. The launcher easily copes with the harsh environment and challenging terrain found in southern

Afghanistan and has been used to target enemy bunkers in southern Helmand. GMLRS is ideally suited to destroying this type of enemy position and a single missile can be used, whereas in the past conventional artillery may have required multiple rounds.

In addition, constantly watching the skies over Afghanistan is the Rapier Field Standard C, a technologically advanced Short-Range Air-Defence System (SHORAD) in service with the Royal Artillery. It is a 24-hour, all-weather guided weapon system with a primary role of providing limited area Air Defence (AD) cover against fixed-wing aircraft, helicopters, Unmanned Air Vehicles (UAV) and cruise missiles. It has the capability of engaging two targets at once. Rapier FSC is compact, mobile and air-portable, making it suitable for worldwide operations. It is used in a combined system with the Blindfire 2000 tracking radar and the Dagger surveillance radar. Eight missiles can be carried ready to fire, each with a high-explosive warhead and missiles (designated MK2B) and fitted with a proximity fuse. The missile's propulsion system is a two-stage enhanced solid-propellant rocket motor capable of around Mach 2.5. The guidance is automatic infra-red and radar command to line of sight.

While air cover and support may be called in from coalition aircraft using fast air bomb delivery on Taliban targets, or even weapon-equipped drone aircraft, close air support is provided by helicopter in the form of the AH-64 Apache. The Apache is designed to hunt and kill tanks and has significantly improved the Army's operational capability. Apache can operate in all

weathers, day or night, and detect, classify and prioritise up to 256 potential targets in a matter of seconds. It carries a mix of weapons including rockets, Hellfire missiles and a 30mm chain gun. The aircraft is equipped with a Day TV system, thermal-imaging sight and Direct View Optics. It also possesses a state-of-the-art, fully integrated Defensive Aid Suite. It is the only attack mode helicopter in service with British forces in Afghanistan and is described as a modern, tandem-seat, armoured and damage-resistant combat helicopter.

Its original design features call for it to continue flying for 30 minutes after being hit by 12.7mm bullets coming from anywhere in the lower hemisphere plus 20 degrees; it must also survive 23mm hits in many parts. It has a target acquisition and designation sight (TADS) and pilot night-vision sensors (PNVS) mounted in the nose and carries a low-airspeed sensor above the main rotor hub. Avionics are stored in lateral containers. A chin-mounted chain gun is fed from an ammunition bay housed in the centre-fuselage.

The Apache has air-to-ground capability thanks to four weapon pylons on stub-wings – six when air-to-air capability is installed. The AH-64 is also eminently transportable; two AH-64s will fit in a C-141, six in a C-5 and three in a C-17A. The main transmission, manufactured by Litton Precision Gear Division, can operate for one hour without oil and the tail rotor drive, by Aircraft Gear Corporation, has grease-lubricated gearboxes with Bendix driveshafts and couplings that can operate for one hour after ballistic damage. The main rotor shaft runs within an airframe-mounted sleeve, relieving

transmission of flight loads and allowing removal of the transmission without disturbing the rotor.

While the intrepid pilots of the ponderous Chinooks perform miracles in logistics supply and troop transport, the British Army's primary battlefield utility helicopter is the fast and agile Lynx. Such is the advance of technical development in attack aircraft that today even the CH-47 Chinook, at its top speed of 170 knots, is faster than the attack helicopters of the 1960s. The Lynx is even faster, at 330kph, and proves to be a deadly tank killer when armed with eight TOW anti-tank missiles. In addition to its three-man crew, including a door gunner to man its two 7.62mm GPMGs, it can carry ten troops over an operational range radius of 100km with a two-hour 'loiter' capacity. Two versions are currently in service with the Army – the AH7 with skids, and the wheeled AH9. Lynx helicopters can also carry missile counter-measures and a stabilised roof sight.

A smaller relation of the Lynx is the Gazelle, whose primary role with the British Army is observation and reconnaissance. Similar in appearance to its US cousin – the MH-6 Little Bird of US Special Forces fame – the Gazelle is a vital component of anti-tank helicopter operations and is also used in a wide variety of supporting roles, such as as an air observation post (AOP) to direct artillery fire, as an airborne forward air controller (ABFAC) to direct ground-attack aircraft, for casualty evacuation, liaison, command and control, and as a communications relay. It is equipped with a Ferranti AF 532 stabilised, magnifying observation aid.

The latest development in fixed wing aircraft is the Defender 4000, an upgrade of the earlier BN2T Defender aircraft. The new Defender meets the need of the Army Air Corps to operate a lightweight aircraft from short airstrips in all weather conditions, by day and night. Its increased payload, low noise signature and economical operating costs are proving to be ideally suited to urban surveillance and counter-terrorism operations. Design improvements include an extended fuselage, larger wing for greater internal fuel capacity and enhanced cockpit and cabin visibility.

The Defender 4000 is designed to carry the most sophisticated navigation and sensor equipment such as a thermal-imaging camera and 360° search radar as optional extras. The standard aircraft incorporates advanced avionics, an electronic flight instrument system (EFIS) and a full range of communications equipment. It is powered by twin Rolls-Royce (Allison) turbine engines, which are flat-rated at 400HP and are also fitted as standard. A new nose structure has been developed specifically to accommodate a high-performance, 360° rotating antenna. The nose section can also be modified to accommodate a three-axis FLIR ball and 120° sector scan surface search and weather radar.

22

BOATS AND KILLER GAS

By tradition, British naval ships have carried detachments of the Royal Navy's amphibious infantry, the Royal Marines. While it is not the purpose of this book to discuss Britain's élite Special Forces Group, no mention of the Royal Marines would be complete without reference to the Royal Navy's Special Boat Service (SBS), the lesser-known sister unit of the British Army's 22 Special Air Service (SAS) Regiment. Based in Poole, Dorset, the SBS is a special forces unit which specialises in special operations at sea, along coastlines and on river networks and shouldn't be confused with the equally élite Fleet Protection Group Royal Marines based at HM Naval Base Clyde, Helensburgh, Argyll and Bute, previously known as Commachio Group. The SBS also has a team on standby for maritime counter-terrorism (MCT) operations.

While the unit specialises in water-borne activities, they are also highly skilled on dry land. Recent operations have taken

place in the mountains of land-locked Afghanistan and deep in the deserts of Iraq. Previously known as the Special Boat Squadron and exclusively drawn from the Royal Marines, the SBS is now open to members of other regiments and services from throughout the UK military.

In Phase 1 and 2 training, the British Army recruit will have learned how to cross streams and rivers using the air trapped in the Bergen as a flotation device, but there still remains water-borne assault manoeuvres using a variety of craft. The Mk 5 assault boat is usually paddled for a silent or night-time approach, and its all-aluminium frame can be carried by four men or dragged overland by two. A versatile, general-purpose craft designed to carry up to 20 troops or 1,043kg of stores, it also makes a useful ferry craft when fitted with an outboard motor. It is fitted with built-in grab rails, buoyancy tanks and protective keels, which act as stabilisers in the water. Assault boats may be stacked six deep for storage or transport.

In addition, the British Army can field the Combat Support Boat (CSB), a powerful, versatile craft whose major role is to support both bridging and amphibious operations. Water-jet propulsion allows high thrust at shallow draught. It can also be used as a general-purpose working boat in support of diving operations, ship-to-shore re-supply and inland water patrols. The boat is carried on a purpose-built launching and recovery trailer. The Combat Support Boat, while versatile enough to be employed on clandestine missions, is more regularly used by the Royal Engineers.

Another craft in service with the Royal Engineers as well as

all Special Forces groups is the Rigid Raider. Rigid Raiders are fast patrol craft with glass-reinforced plastic (GRP) hulls, used for patrolling coastal and inland waterways. The craft are equipped with single or twin 140hp outboard motors and come in two versions: the Mk 1, which can carry a coxswain plus eight troops, or 1,000kg of stores and has a maximum unladen speed of 50 knots against 30 knots when laden; and the Mk 2, with a coxswain plus 10 troops and 650kg of stores, or 20 troops and a maximum speed of 30 knots when laden.

The Ramped Landing Craft Logistic (RCL), which last saw service in the Falklands War, is used for amphibious operations and is designed to deliver men and material on to beaches and long ago replaced its counterparts, the DUKWs and LCVPs or 'Higgins Boats' of the Second World War beachhead fame. The RCL craft are crewed by the Royal Logistics Corps (RLC). Two RCLs – the Andalsnes and Akyab – are based in Cyprus.

While water-borne assaults have figured in the annals of war for centuries, chemical warfare is by comparison a new concept that first made its mark in history in the First World War, before which time its use, unlike the storming of beaches, was considered uncivilised. Necessity, unfortunately, once again proved to be the mother of invention and the development and use of poison gas was necessitated by the requirement of wartime armies to find new ways of overcoming the stalemate of unexpected trench warfare. Although it is popularly believed that the German Army was the first to use gas, it was, in fact, initially deployed by the French.

In the first month of the war, August 1914, the French Army

fired tear-gas grenades containing xylyl bromide against the Germans. The German Army seized on the idea and responded with its own invention capable of delivering the gas, or 'Weisskreuz' – 'White Cross', as they called it. They developed the 'T-shell' (named after its inventor Hans Tappen), an artillery shell containing a warhead of explosive and a second compartment containing the liquid gas.

But volatile tear gas was not the only chemical agent to be suffered by troops on both sides of the battle lines. The gases ranged from disabling chemicals, such as tear gas and the severe mustard gas, to lethal agents like phosgene and chlorine. This chemical warfare was a major component of the first global war and first total war of the 20th century.

The killing capacity of gas was limited – only 4 per cent of combat deaths were due to gas – although the proportion of non-fatal casualties was high, and gas remained one of the soldiers' greatest fears. Because it was possible to develop effective if primitive counter-measures against gas attacks, it was unlike most other weapons of the period. In the later stages of the war, as the use of gas increased, its overall effectiveness diminished. Thus the legend of the Evil Hun and his ungentlemanly killer gas that was fed to our great grandparents by the Government propaganda machines of Asquith and Lloyd George was untrue. Nevertheless, the German Army was the first to give serious study to the development of chemical weapons and the first to use them on a large scale.

Nowadays, the threats are much more severe with nerve

gases capable of killing all life forms over vast areas but leaving buildings and material intact, a huge bonus in reconstruction costs for the conquering heroes. Added to these are biological agents that make up a list of all the deadliest plagues and diseases known to man and the radioactive threat of small nuclear devices and shells detonated on the battlefield. The British Army's answer to all this is the cumbersome CBRN protective battle suit.

CBRN is an acronym referring to chemical, biological, radiological and nuclear. It is in common use worldwide, generally referring to protective measures taken against CBRN weapons or hazards. As opposed to HAZMAT incidents which are accidental, CBRN incidents are deliberate, malicious acts with the intention to kill or sicken and disrupt society. CBRN tasks are primarily concerned with conducting military operations within various hazardous environments or the elimination or mitigation of those environments. These environments can be generated via the use of weapons, or they can be the result of accidental contamination of the environment. The alarm is triggered by a portable Integrated Biological Detection System. IBDS is installed in a container which can be mounted on a vehicle (standard 4 ton) or ground dumped and can be transported by either fixed-wing aircraft or helicopters and provides the commander in the field with early warning of a chemical or biological warfare attack.

The IBDS is often transported by the amphibious Fuchs, which is manufactured by the German company Thyssen-Henschel as the Transporter Panzer 1. Fuchs is an amphibious,

six-wheeled, armoured vehicle, used in chemical reconnaissance. An important part of the UK's Nuclear, Biological and Chemical Defence Regiment, it was first purchased by the British Army during the Gulf War. Fuchs has a maximum road speed of 105kph, a water speed of 10kph, and is operated by two crew members. The Integrated Biological Detection System (IBDS) carried by the vehicle has recently replaced the Prototype Biological Detection System (PBDS) in service with the UK Joint NBC Regiment. This modern system provides an enhanced and automated NBC detection system. Major IBDS elements include a detection suite, including equipment for atmospheric sampling, a meteorological station and GPS, NBC filtration and environmental control for use in all climates, and chemical agent detection. The unit functions with an independent power supply and carries cameras for 360° surveillance.

The Light Role Specialist Monitoring Team provides support to expeditionary operations, providing early warning, surveying and evidence-gathering and offer advice to the commander on NBC ops and protection. The Light Role Team (LRT) capability is currently produced by assorted Urgent Operational Requirements (UOR). The LRT System, when operational, will include a fully integrated, Bowmanised specialist CBRN capability. The LRT will be based upon the Pinzgauer 6x6 Command and Cargo variants, with the specific equipment being developed in response to forthcoming invitations to tender (ITT) to specialised manufacturers.

23

HEIRS TO
CHAOS

In the event of a British withdrawal from Afghanistan, those who will have to take up the yoke of protecting the country from both enemies within and without will be the troops of the Afghanistan National Army. While withdrawal from the bloody battlefields of the country is constantly debated, with the UK seeking an approving and unlikely nod from Washington, informed opinion puts its money on UK troop deployments to the Afghanistan theatre lasting well into the next decade. Meanwhile, the responsibility for training those Afghan nationals drawn to military service by a lack of employment wrought by eternal war is divided among the coalition forces with varying levels of success.

The Afghan National Army has existed since the late 19th century, the time of Russia and Britain's 'Great Game', when it was formed by Ameer Abdur Rahman Khan. Prior to that formation, the Army of National Defence had existed as a

mixture of tribesmen and militia who would be called upon, or take it upon themselves, to support the Ameer. After Britain was persuaded to allow Afghanistan to decide its own foreign policy, the Army was modernised during the reign of King Zahir Shan in the 1930s. It enjoyed Soviet patronage once again in the decades between 1960 and 1990, being equipped and trained by Gorbachev's Moscow at a distance after the Russian withdrawal. This situation, however, lasted only until the dissipation of the Army as a cohesive fighting force scant years later.

During the Russian invasion of the country in support of the Marxist People's Democratic Party of Afghanistan, the ANA was primarily loyal to the Government and fought alongside Russian troops against the *mujahedin* rebels. But as the conflict grew, many began to desert to the rebels, who had the sympathy of the majority of the Afghan people. Those who remained in the Soviet-trained Army found themselves in an unenviable position when the Army of the occupation was withdrawn by Gorbachev in February of 1989 and, with the subsequent fall of the Russians' puppet communist Government in Kabul, the ANA ceased to exist. As had been the tradition for hundreds of years before, the warlords reclaimed their old territories and policed them with their own militias. The Afghanistan National Army had become lost in the mist of history.

During the last years of Russian occupation, the ANA had been divided into 11 infantry divisions and three armoured divisions. Under Russian tutelage, it had expanded to contain

two mountain infantry regiments, a commando brigade and three commando regiments. Just prior to the Russian withdrawal, these divisions were at quarter strength with roughly 2,500 men in total; that strength also included several élite units, such as the 24th Airborne Battalion, and the 37th, 38th and 444th Commando brigades. The fate of the Airborne Brigade had been patchy – it had rebelled in 1980 and suffered severe retaliation at the hands of the Soviets. The commando units, trained by Spetsnaz instructors, were politically loyal but suffered heavy casualties in contacts with the wily *mujahedin* and, as a result, were reorganised into co-dependent battalions. But after the Russians left on 15 February 1989, things changed dramatically. The ANA's eventual new master was the Taliban and their Islamic Emirate of Afghanistan, which sorely lacked administrative efficiency.

The Taliban regime, which gained its foothold in 1996, removed the militia forces and attempted to control the country by the assertion of Islamic Sharia law. Wisely, however, they retained their own small group of army troops and commanders, some of whom were trained by Pakistani military and intelligence agents and the ever-present CIA in camps set up for that purpose on the border. Meanwhile, many elements of the former Army that had fought alongside the Russians were either hunted down by the vengeful new Government or sensibly saw themselves absorbed into the militias of the *mujahedin* warlords who were in fierce opposition to the Taliban.

The Taliban's 'Army', for want of a better word, consisted of

elements of assorted armed groups with varying degrees of loyalty, commitment, skill and organisation; much in the style of the old Saxon *fyrds*. But in 2001, these ill-prepared rag, tag and bobtail groups were to experience organised warfare meted out on an unprecedented scale. It wasn't until late 2001, when the Taliban were in retreat, that the urgency of the existence of a new, well-equipped and reformed national Army to rise from the ashes of war became apparent to the victorious US and NATO coalition.

On his election to the presidency of Afghanistan, Hamid Karzai set a goal of an army of at least 70,000 men by 2009, although many Western military experts believed that figure to be insufficient to meet national needs of defence against a resurgent Taliban or the constant threat of bin Laden's al-Qaeda and put the figure at more than three times that amount. Initially, recruitment suffered from the fear of reprisals against the families of the soldiers and a misconception among young Afghans of what they could expect as recruits of a potentially American trained and equipped Army. The discovery that it would not consist of an aeroplane trip for training at Fort Bragg with US rates of pay and eventual US citizenship plus lessons in literacy did much to dampen enthusiasm but, nonetheless, first training commenced in May 2002 and, by January 2003, just over 1,700 troops – five *kandaks* or battalions – had completed the 10-week training course. By June 2003, the number had risen to 4,000. Soldiers in the new Army initially received US$30 a month during training and US$50 a month on completion of boot camp. Pay

for trained soldiers has since risen to US$120 a month and US$90 during the training phase.

The language used during early training was Pashtun, Tajik and some Arabic due to the diversity of ethnic groups. However, there were many trials facing the coalition instructors. Desertion, especially, was at an unprecedented high, especially when the new recruits had received their personal weapons – usually reconditioned AK47s – and other military equipment. There is also no doubt that some of the equipment supplied was sub-standard.

By the summer of 2003, the desertion rate in the ANA was estimated at 10 per cent and figures for March 2004 showed desertion stood at 300. Many of the new recruits were under 18 years of age and illiterate. Many spoke only Pashtu, the national language, which accounts for 42 per cent of spoken language in Afghanistan and 15.42 per cent in neighbouring Pakistan, and found drill difficult since this was hampered by interpreters who spoke only Dari – a form of Afghan Persian.

Nonetheless, growth continued and Army and police strength in early 2008 stood at 100,000 on paper. Despite problems, the ANA has recorded several tangible and important achievements with the result that, overall, it is generally regarded as the most effective of all Afghanistan security forces in contrast, for example, to the morale-deficient police force. Perhaps the latter circumstance offers no surprise considering that Taliban raids increasingly target the police and early recruits faced the prospect of being gunned down in revenge attacks.

In July 2003, 1,000 ANA troops were deployed in the US-

led coalition operation Warrior Sweep in the Zormat and Ayubkhel valleys of southern Paktia Province. The operation was in response to intelligence that Taliban insurgents were moving into the area. It marked the first major combat for the unblooded ANA and was successfully completed in September. But plans still call for the indigenous forces to grow to around 150,000 from the current level of 100,000 to have any hope of autonomous control of the country. While some experts express concern at the problems of sustaining such a large number of troops and police in a long-term scenario, there is no doubt that such a large force will need to be in place before there can be any discussion on coalition withdrawal.

The USA planned to spend US$3.4 billion in 2007 on the establishment of efficient Army and police units. According to Steven Ross, a research consultant for the Post-Conflict Reconstruction Project at Washington's Center for Strategic and International Studies, 'The beefing up of security forces in Afghanistan was highly under-invested in the first years following 2001 and almost everyone sees the money now coming in as a positive.'

Six years on from its formation, it remains difficult to assess the fighting capabilities of the ANA. American military advisers believe it may take as much as a decade before Afghan units are capable of autonomous command and of carrying out independent operations. There is no doubt that there are still many challenges left to be overcome, not the least being the resurgence of the Taliban forces exhibited in the 2008 early summer breakout at Arghandab and Kandahar.

Another bone of contention is, as in every Army in the world, conditions of accommodation and equipment. As stated earlier, the standard personal weapon is the AK47, in this case of Chinese manufacture exempt from US laws on Chinese purchase since the weaponry is supplied by other coalition members, which is plagued by reports of unreliability in combat conditions, probably a case of getting what one pays for. Despite the decent wage by Afghan standards – a new recruit is now paid US$90 – desertion by early 2008 had risen to 30 per cent.

New uniforms and equipment for the ANA recruits is provided by the USA with assistance from other coalition members. Romania, for example, recently supplied 1,000 Chinese-manufactured AK47s for range training. Heavy weapons to date include 82mm mortars, recoilless rifles and Russian-built PKM machine guns. Some of these weapons were recovered from Taliban caches throughout the country.

Basic training is undergone at Kabul Military Training Centre (KMTC) in Pol-e-Charki, near the site of the infamous Afghan prison, with financial and logistical support provided by coalition forces. The first training procedures at KMTC were provided by the French, with the USA in an alternating role. In May 2003, the USA took over full responsibility for troop training, with the UK training NCOs, and the French with responsibility for officers. Nonetheless, the task of building an effective volunteer Army, even of the size originally planned, will be exceedingly difficult. The main reason is socio-cultural; Afghan men are the heads of their

family unit and prefer to remain in close contact with their wives and children. This presents the major problem in attempting to form centralised military structures. Pay rises could partially address this issue but the sustainability of such a measure is doubtful. Less than 50 per cent of trained ANA troops recently chose to re-enlist after completing their initial three-year tour of duty.

But at this point in time, the main weakness of the fledgling Afghanistan National Army appears to be its reliance on coalition instructors embedded with the Afghan units. In the formative six years of the ANA, not one battalion has moved on from the embedded training programme, even though the original plan expected a transformation to full independency after two years. One of the heaviest dependencies of the modern ANA, especially given the escalation of the war over the past two years, is on coalition close air support. There does not appear to be any move on the part of the ANA to develop its own close air support skills, which are currently provided by an embedded training team. The current training programme of the ANA is naturally based on that of their US field instructors. Combat tactics therefore rely on the US practice of using infantry to force the enemy to reveal itself and then destroy the threat with decisive air strikes. There is little evidence that ANA units would be able to control the battlefield without such air support, or that they are learning the necessary skills.

Although the country's air force was established in 1925 and reached its peak under the Soviet-backed Government of the

1980s, it was virtually extinguished in the civil war that followed and is only now struggling back into existence. A new hangar at Kabul Airport houses the fledgling air force operations unit. The military has recently taken delivery of 26 new or refurbished aircraft, including Czech-made helicopter gunships and, with US money, the Government has also acquired transport helicopters and Ukrainian military planes to be added to the 20 or so helicopters the Army already has. But training in effective collaboration between aircraft and ground controllers still has to be established and comprises a long training process.

The result is that the ability of the ANA and the Afghan Ministry of Defence to plan and conduct complex operations without coalition support will not be tested until the Afghans are left to their own devices, and may well precipitate an all-out bloody civil war. Rather like a finger holding down a detonator pressure switch, equal pressure must be applied as soon as the first finger is removed or the result is oblivion. International sponsoring of the ANA means that it seldom operates in the small units that would be most effective in engaging insurgent troops without the fallback of air support. Currently, such engagements are undertaken by coalition special forces, which means that the skills of clandestine warfare are not being passed on to the Afghan troops. Such counter-insurgency skills will not be readily acquired in the field following a coalition withdrawal, and this also is true of logistic capabilities.

Another problem is created by tribal loyalties within

Afghanistan. When researching material for this book, no one I spoke to in the UK MoD nor the US Pentagon would discuss data relating to ethnic groupings within the ANA, yet my research elsewhere shows that more than 70 per cent of battalion commanders are Tajiks, the Persian-speaking and predominantly Sunni Muslim community that represents only around 34 per cent of the Afghan population, as opposed to the Pashtuns, who form around 45 per cent. Before the Soviet invasion, when many of the Pashtun population fled to neighbouring countries, the Pashtuns of Afghanistan had represented 81 per cent. Clearly, keeping an ethnic balance within the ANA is as difficult as it is important.

Socio-behavioural experts in the military are well aware that the Afghan soldier who deserts each October to bring in the harvest has little unit loyalty and the fear is that given a civil war in the country, without an ethnic balance being struck in the Army, any trained and armed majority group would dominate. Perhaps the Persian-speaking Tajiks are too close to their Iranian roots for someone in Arlington.

Of ANA progress throughout the country, the 1st Battalion ANA is garrisoned in Kabul and is specifically assigned to the presidential palace guard, responsible for the security of Hamid Kharzai, especially following the assassination of vice-president Abdul Qadir in July 2002. The 2nd Battalion passed out in August 2002, closely followed by the 3rd in October of that year. The 4th Battalion, under instruction from the French 27th Brigade d'Infanterie de Montagne, began its training in September 2002 and passed out, 400 strong, in mid-

November. Training of the 5th Battalion was under alternate US/French instruction and responsibility for the 6th reverted to the Americans.

Meanwhile, the British were doing their bit and passed out 104 non-commissioned officers from the Military Training Centre in Kabul. In the first shift of emphasis on training personnel, future classes were to be conducted by the Afghans themselves but there the home-grown collusion in training ended. A House of Commons Foreign Affairs committee reported that only 10,000 members of the ANA, against the target of 12,000, had been trained up to June 2004. It also found that the ANA's establishment was below coalition targets, was not ethnically representative of the population and suffered a high rate of desertion.

Whatever the hopes of a speedy withdrawal of British troops from Afghanistan, American military officials make it clear that any move to reduce the level of Western troops would be disastrous until the ANA and other Afghan security forces were able to function independently. The US-led invasion of Afghanistan took place with one purpose – the fall of the Taliban and the capture of Osama bin Laden. The success of the first goal is questionable, the second a non-starter. Afghanistan has become the coalition's Vietnam and looks like being with the West for many years to come.

24
BLOODY RETREAT TO GANDAMAK

Probably the greatest enduring battle involving British troops occurred in 1842 during the Great Game, which was played out by Britain and Russia in Afghanistan in the 19th century and brought about one of the most horrendous massacres of British troops and civilians, greater than that that would take place 37 years later at Isandlwana in Zululand, when 1,200 men of the 24th Foot along with elements of the Royal Artillery and Natal Native Infantry under Lieutenant Colonel Durnford were slaughtered by the *impis* of Cetshwayo.

The tragedy that would become known as the Retreat to Gandamak took place in January of the harsh Afghan winter of 1842, when 4,500 British troops and Indian cavalry armed with lances, muskets and bayonets and escorting 12,000 wives, children and civilian servants from the garrison of Kabul were harassed and placed under constant day and night attacks by more than 30,000 Afghani Ghilzai tribesmen as they withdrew

north-east under the imagined protection of a purported agreement from the ruling Beluchis of safe passage to India. The besieging tribesmen were armed with swords and the long-barrelled *jezail*, the ornately decorated smooth-bore musket now replaced by the Kalashnikov and the RPG.

The British colonies in India in the early 19th century were controlled by the East India Company, whose wealthy investors included many top-ranking British politicians. A long-feared threat was the potential invasion of India by Russia by way of the 'buffer' state created by Afghanistan. As such, British military presence was obligatory in the wild and mountainous country bordering the Punjab and prompted an ill-advised attempt by Lord Auckland, at that time British Governor General in India, to invade the country in 1839, launching what would become known as the First Afghan War.

The invasion was triggered by the entry of the essentially Hindu East India Company Army crossing the Indus River into the territory ruled by Ameer Ghuznee Dost Mohammed Khan to take Kabul. As ever, an invading force has the purpose of dethroning a ruler and filling the resulting vacuum of power with a puppet of its master's choosing. In the case of Afghanistan, the British East India Company had chosen Shah Shuja, who had been previously deposed by Mohammed Khan, of whom it felt it could comfortably pull the strings. The British official in charge of the 'expedition' was Sir William McNaughten, Auckland's envoy, accompanied by his staff of political officers.

In March 1839, the British forces crossed the Bolan Pass and began their march to Kabul. They advanced through rough

terrain, crossed deserts and towering mountain passes but made good progress and took Kandahar on 25 April 1839. Through an act of treachery by a traitor to the ruling Ameer Dost Mohammed Khan, they also captured the impregnable fortress of Ghazni on 22 July in a surprise attack, suffering only 17 casualties. An Afghan betrayed his sovereign and the British troops managed to blow one fortified gate and marched into the city in a euphoric mood. The failing morale of the British and Indian troops rose swiftly on discovering that Ghanzi was well supplied, a fact that would ease the hardships of the continued advance on Kabul. Dost Mohammed fled and sought refuge in the wilds of the Hindu Kush. Shoja Shah was proclaimed emir and Kabul fell on 6 August 1839 without a fight. Dost Mohammed surrendered to MacNaughten on 4 November 1840.

The Indian force, now joined by soldiers of the British 44th Foot – which would, incidentally, later become the Essex Regiment and is now the Royal Anglian Regiment, who would have their own bloodbath in Afghanistan nearly 170 years later – entered Kabul with the puppet Shah Shuja in tow on 7 August 1839. The journey had not been easy, not even eased by the capture of Kandahar and the rout of Ghuznee Dost Mohammed. The Bengali troops had been reluctant to leave Hindustan, fearing a loss of caste in entering their fearsome neighbour. They had been plagued by heat, disease and lack of supplies on the route to Kandahar, as well as suffering constant attacks by the wild hill tribes along their route through the mountain passes.

Once on garrison duty in Kabul, the Bengali Army began to demonstrate a marked lack of morale which culminated in a refusal by its cavalry to follow its British officers into battle against the recovered Ghuznee Dost Mohammed, who had now gathered tribesmen around him and was bent on retrieving his throne. Less than two decades later, the discontent of the Bengali Army with its foreign generals and onerous duties on behalf of British imperialism was to result in the Great Mutiny of 1857.

Within a year, the garrison was in trouble. Trapped in Kabul by the harsh winter and with its supply trains from India constantly attacked and harried by the Ghilzai tribesmen in the Khyber Pass, the regime of Ameer Shah Shuja found the area of Northern Baluchistan and especially its reaches around the Helmand River − the same areas served by hard-pressed British troops today − virtually ungovernable. In addition, the Kabul garrison found itself facing the inhospitable mountainous terrain, the extremes of weather, and an intractable and warlike population that seemed genetically disposed towards inter-tribal warfare; all this was exacerbated by the contemporary Victorian system of appointing officers from the titled and landed classes who had little experience of war or tactical decision-making; a failing that led to such bloodbaths as the Light Brigade's disastrous charge against the Russian guns at Balaclava in the Crimea 14 years later.

Meanwhile, unwilling to bear another fierce Afghanistan winter in the mountains, the deposed Dost Mohammed eased the situation only slightly by dispersing his army of Baluchi

warriors and surrendering to McNaughten. He was escorted into exile in India by a division of British and Indian troops under the command of Commander-in-Chief Sir Willoughby Cotton, thus reducing garrison strength to a dangerous level.

McNaughten and Shah Shuja, perhaps prompted by Dost Mohammed's fear of winters, moved down to the gentler climes of Jalalabad, leaving the Kabul garrison in the hands of untrained officers and the ever-present political officials bent on preserving the interests of their colonial masters across the border in India.

On their arrival at Kabul a year earlier, the British and Indian troops had taken possession of Balla Hissar, a fortified palace outside the city. Now, as peace settled over the garrison with an unease characteristically ignored by pretentious Victorians in occupation, the garrison was ordered to withdraw from the palace and to build accommodation in the form of permanent cantonments 2.5km outside the city. Weakening the garrison further, an entire brigade was withdrawn.

The remaining troops and garrison civilians further domesticated their surroundings by bringing out their wives and children to join them and generally settling into a routine regularly followed by British garrisons across the border in marginally less volatile India. The occupying forces enjoyed themselves, arranging cricket matches, horse races and hunting parties. In the evenings, amateur dramatics were staged, where officers and their wives played Shakespeare's *A Midsummer Night's Dream*. It was considered a special honour to be invited to Lady Florentina Sale's evening companies, at which salmon

and stew with Madeira, port wine and champagne were served. They even built themselves a racecourse.

To further confuse matters, orders from London removed Willoughby Cotton, who had been content to remain in India, leaving McNaughten as Governor in Kabul, and replaced him with the irascible General William Elphinstone, an elderly invalid known for his inability to delegate command in the field, who had been further described by a colleague, General William Nott, as 'the most incompetent soldier ever to become general'. The stage was being set for the worst massacre of British troops and civilians ever seen on the field of battle.

On 2 November 1842, Akbar Khan, the son of exiled Dost Mohammed Khan, proclaimed a general revolt against the British occupiers, and the citizens of Kabul were quick to take up the call. Garrison troops in Kabul were down to 4,500, of which 690 were Europeans. While Elphinstone and McNaughten blustered, Afghans stormed the house of Sir Alexander Burnes, a high-ranking political officer, and murdered him and his staff. The ineffective Elphinstone railed at the attack but failed to show strength in his command and more attacks followed.

In Kabul itself, the poorly defended supply fort was stormed and supplies lost. A distraught McNaughten, appalled at Elphinstone's lack of command, attempted to negotiate an unhindered retreat to India for the British troops and the 12,000 British and Indian civilians trapped in Kabul and the cantonments. The Afghani diplomats, now firmly in control of the city, agreed to meet McNaughten to discuss terms but no

sooner had the British delegation arrived at the meeting place, they were hauled from their mounts and slaughtered by the warriors of Akbar Khan. The detachment of British troops detailed to protect the delegation had not shown up and McNaughten's body was dragged through the streets of Kabul.

It became apparent that the frail and inept Elphinstone had lost control of his troops and his authority was badly damaged. He sought no reprisal for McNaughten's murder and capitulated to the Afghans' terms for safe passage out of Kabul. Several officers and their families were to remain behind as hostages. The withdrawing troops would leave behind their gunpowder reserves, their newer muskets and most of their cannon. For this, the British and Indian garrison were promised a safe retreat and troops and civilians – among them women, children and the elderly – began to move out on 6 January 1842.

The aim was to reach Jalalabad, which lay 144km away through the snowy mountain passes. The sick and those too old or frail to make the journey were left behind to the mercy of the Akbar Khan's Afghans, who promised their safety but, as the last British soldier left Kabul, the tents were set on fire and they were massacred.

The retreating column's first main obstacle lay 25km outside Kabul – the towering Khord Kabul Pass – but instead of sending a group to hold the pass to ensure safe passage for his column, the broken Elphinstone and his demoralised officers called a halt just 10km from Kabul and were immediately attacked. Throughout the long night of fighting for their lives in freezing

temperatures, many troops and civilians, especially the smaller children and the elderly, succumbed to hypothermia.

The next day, the march continued through the wild Hindu Kush. By now, attacks upon the column, despite the promises of safe passage from Akbar Khan, were continuous, with Elphinstone's aide, the boorish and surly Brigadier Shelton, rallying the 44th Foot into counter-attacks against the encroaching tribesmen as a battling rearguard. As evening fell, the column was approached by Akbar Khan himself, who ordered Elphinstone to halt the column and parlay. Elphinstone, who by now had ceased even to give his contradictory orders which were largely ignored by his subordinates, offered no resistance and the column halted for another freezing night without cover. During the parlay, Akbar Khan insisted that no further harm would come to the column, provided that a large sum of money exchanged hands and more officers and their families submitted to being taken as hostages. The hostages, according to Akbar Khan, were to ensure that the British left Kandahar and Jalalabad and that the Jalalabad commander, Brigadier Sale – one of the few efficient officers serving in Afghanistan – returned to India. The brigadier's wife, Lady Sale, was travelling with Elphinstone's column.

The next morning found a seriously debilitated force approaching the 8km-long Khord Kabul Pass. As the baggage train carrying the sick and wounded entered between the towering walls, it was ambushed by hordes of Ghilzai tribesmen firing their own *jezail* muskets and those surrendered by the British in Kabul. Some 3,000 civilians and soldiers lay dead and

dying from the continuous fusillade of musket fire and a band of 100 soldiers, perhaps more resolute than their dying companions, attempted a breakout back towards Kabul but were cut down to a man before they left the pass.

It was later reported by one of the column's few survivors, Assistant Surgeon William Brydon, that throughout the slaughter and the whistle and ricochet of musket balls General Elphinstone had ceased to give any orders and sat silently on his horse gazing at the chaos about him with 'unseeing eyes'. The frail general had obviously lost his marbles at this point and would survive only by giving himself as hostage to Akbar Khan to die in captivity three months later.

The next day, having survived the slaughter, Lady Sale and other officer wives reluctantly agreed to be taken hostage by the Ghilzais. General Elphinstone and his deputy, Brigadier Shelton, who had led the 44th Foot to protect the rear of the column, abandoned all pretence at dignity and allowed Akbar Khan to take them to join the hostages. There is no doubt that the Afghan leader saw the capture of the general and his second in command as a powerful negotiation tool in his efforts to force the British to withdraw from the country, but it's also certain that both officers were aware that if they had remained with the doomed column they would have died within days.

Nonetheless, their abandonment of their troops, who remained under the leadership of Brigadier Anquetil, remains as a uniquely degrading act in military history. While the feeble and frail Elphinstone was doomed to die in captivity, Shelton would

be rescued along with other British and Indian hostages when a British revenge force freed them from captivity in the town of Bameean a month after Elphinstone's death from pleurisy.

Now deserted by the two most senior of its officers, the column under Anquetil continued its staggering trek towards the safety of the Jalalabad garrison. On 12 January, it reached the crest of the Jugdulluck range and there found its passage blocked by barriers of thorn bushes dragged into place by the Ghilzais, who were determined that no foreign soldiers or civilians would continue a step beyond the pass. The pitifully few troops remaining, mostly made up of survivors from the 44th Foot, charged the barrier and just 40 out of the column of 16,500 souls that had left Kabul a week before managed to fight their way through.

The next day saw the survivors reach Fatehabad, near the village of Gandamak, where the remnants of the force found themselves surrounded by Ghilzai tribesmen who offered them a chance to lay down their arms and were famously answered by a sergeant identified by a survivor as Sergeant Friel of the 44th Foot, 'Not bloody likely!' Out of food and with only a few rounds of ammunition left between them, the men of the 44th Foot prepared for their last stand. All but 14 were killed in the ensuing mêlée and only five would survive, terribly wounded, to reach Jalalabad.

The most notable survivor was Assistant Surgeon William Brydon, who reached the Jalalabad garrison fort on 13 January when troops defending the walls against scattered skirmishes by the Ghilzais saw a lone man and his mount making slow and

painful progress towards the garrison gates. A part of Brydon's skull had been sheared away by a sword stroke in that last desperate stand at Fatehabad where the gallant Sergeant Friel had spat his defiance at the Ghilzai before falling to their swords. As Brydon was gently lowered from his mount by willing hands, a trooper asked him what had become of the Army?

Brydon's supposed reply has become the stuff of legend: 'I *am* the Army,' he is reported to have replied, before slipping into unconsciousness. He was followed into the fort over the next few days by four other survivors, although he has been widely accepted to have been the sole survivor of the march. Brydon recovered to avoid death 15 years later when he narrowly escaped from the British residency at Lucknow in India after being shot in the leg when the residency was stormed by rebels of the Indian Army in the Great Mutiny of 1857. He survived to retire from active service and die peacefully in Scotland on 18 March 1873.

But the trouble plaguing the British East India Company in Afghanistan did not end with the slamming of the gates of the fort at Jalalabad behind Brydon and the few pitiful survivors of Elphinstone's Kabul garrison. Encouraged by a victory over British forces that would not be seen again until the fall of Singapore 100 years later, Akbar Khan led his wild Ghilzai and Baluchi tribesmen in an assault and siege on Jalalabad.

The Jalalabad garrison was commanded by Brigadier Sir Robert Sale, whose wife, Lady Florentia, was now a hostage of Akbar Khan, having agreed to go into what must have been a marginally more comfortable and safer captivity along with

General Elphinstone and Brigadier Shelton on the retreat to Gandamak. Her Indian maids and Sepoy bodyguards, having no hostage or ransom value, were massacred as soon as the hostages reached Khan's camp.

Sale had occupied Jalalabad in November of 1841, and had found the defences in a ruinous state. Troops under Sale included the 13th Foot, the 35th Bengal Native Infantry, Number 1 Squadron of Skinner's Horse, a squadron of Shah Shuja's sappers under Captain Broadfoot, and some artillery.

Broadfoot's sappers got to work repairing the garrison walls. The repairs were completed none too soon, for the Ghilzais of Akbar Khan were soon surrounding the fort and pouring fire into the perimeter from the surrounding hills. The British in Afghanistan, it seemed, had still not realised the wisdom in building on high ground. Constant sorties were made against the tribesmen with varying success. One, led by Colonel William H Dennie at the head of his 35th Bengal Native Infantry, led to a fierce encounter with the besiegers in which Dennie's infantry suffered many casualties before driving off or killing most of the Agfhan marksmen and capturing a number of weapons. Meanwhile, news was reaching the garrison of the dismal state of affairs in Kabul along with Elphinstone's frantic orders to march to relieve the capital.

It must have been a grim decision for General Sale to remain at Jalalabad, knowing his own wife, British troops and many of their families were within the besieged Kabul garrison. However, his decision was vindicated when, on 12 January 1842, news arrived that the garrison had abandoned

Kabul and was travelling through the mountains of the Hindu Kush towards Jalalabad in a negotiated retreat into India.

A day later, the severely wounded William Brydon arrived at Jalalabad to tell of the massacre of the 16,500-strong column and the taking of Lady Sale, Elphinstone and many of his officers as hostages against the surrender of Jalalabad. One may wonder at General Sale's emotions at the news but he once again refused to surrender his garrison in the best British tradition and ordered his troops to man the ramparts and be prepared to sell their lives dearly.

However, his resolve wavered some days later with the news that a hoped-for relief force under General Wilde was unable to negotiate the Khyber Pass until the spring thaw. This was followed by a message from the East India Company's puppet Ameer, Shah Shuja, still inexplicably on the throne in Kabul, to hand Jalalabad over to the Afghan governor and withdraw to India.

A council of war was held with the senior officers of the garrison, with Sale and his chief-of-staff, Major Macgregor, strongly for abandoning the town and withdrawing to India. However, the proposal was strongly opposed by Broadfoot, Captain Oldfield of the artillery, and Captain Havelock, who all warned of the treachery of Akbar Khan and advised General Sale and his chief-of-staff to look no further than the Kabul massacre to become aware of the fate that would await a retreating Army. It says a lot for General Sale's philosophy of command that democracy won the day and the garrison settled down to weather the siege until the spring.

On 12 February, new demands arrived from Shah Shuja that the garrison should be abandoned and were rejected by the defenders, heartened by a message from General Pollock, the new commander of the relieving Army, that he would advance to break the siege as soon as the opportunity presented itself with the spring thaw, less than a month away.

A matter of puzzlement for observers of the Jalalabad siege must be how messengers, let alone the wounded and exhausted Brydon and the other few survivors from the Kabul massacre, managed to pass through the siege lines. In that, the observer probably imagines the tightly drawn lines of medieval sieges, yet it is true that even then it was possible for individuals to avoid road patrols guarding routes into the fortress or besieged castle. Certainly in Jalalabad, the besieging Afghans saw it necessary to prevent only food and ammunition from reaching the defenders and would have been quite happy for Shuja's envoys to pass on their message. Brydon and his fellow survivors may also well have been seen as harbingers of doom to the garrison, arriving with their tale of death and the fall of the Kabul garrison.

Under Broadfoot, the efforts of the sappers to rebuild the defences had continued apace, despite an earthquake that destroyed much of the new earthworks. While these were being rebuilt, morale was raised when a sortie led by Colonel Dennie captured 500 sheep carelessly left to graze in the shadow of the fortress walls, adding substantially to the garrison's food supplies but, by April, provisions were again running low and disturbing news reached the garrison after it

had observed much rejoicing and firing of weapons in the besiegers' camp as if in celebration of a great victory.

The news was not long in coming that General Pollock and his relieving force had been engaged and defeated in a mighty battle in the Khyber Pass. With no way of knowing whether the tale was true, the garrison descended into despair with the only way of breaking the siege now appearing to be by force from the garrison itself.

Brigadier Sale and Major Macgregor set about preparing their plan for a brigade attack on the enemy. This would entail a major sortie but the odds were not good – 1,500 British and Indian troops would be going up against an enemy of between 4,000 and 5,000 battle-hardened Afghan tribesmen. At dawn on 7 April 1842, Sale launched his attack.

At their Brigadier's signal, three heavily armed columns streamed from the fortress gates and advanced towards Akbar Khan's warriors, camped three miles away on the banks of the Kabul River. Halfway to the Afghan camp lay a ruined fort, occupied by some of Akbar Khan's tribesmen. Knowing that bypassing the position left the danger of an attack from the rear, Colonel Dennie rallied his 35th Bengal Native Infantry into an attack on the fort and soon breached its defences. Once inside, however, fierce hand-to-hand fighting developed into a bloody clash of bayonet against sword and many Indian troops suffered from the horrendous cuts and thrusts of the occupying Ghilzai, with Dennie himself falling wounded. Finally, the opposition was overcome and the bloodied 35th fell back to join the other two columns commanded by

Havelock and Monteith of the 13th Foot and pushed on to the Kabul River camp.

The Afghan camp was in total confusion as British artillery came up in support of the advancing columns and bombarded the enemy positions, allowing the three columns to storm the camp with sword and bayonet, capture Khan's artillery pieces, and put the enemy to rout. After a bloody 27 hours of battle, the Jalalabad garrison had lifted the siege and Monteith's 13th Foot led the 35th Bengal Native Infantry and the Havelock's artillery with its captured pieces into Jalalabad in triumph.

On 13 April, Pollock's relief force arrived – later to become known as the Army of Retribution when it stormed and burned Kabul to ashes – and was played into Jalalabad to the strains of the band of the 13th Foot playing the Scottish air 'Oh But You've Been a Lang Time Acoming'. The British and Indian garrison of Jalalabad had suffered 64 casualties throughout the siege and in the final sortie, including Colonel Dennie of the 35th BNI, who died of wounds received in taking the Afghan position in the advance on the forces of Akbar Khan at the Kabul River camp. Afghan casualties were never recorded.

The successful defence of Jalalabad by the brigade under Brigadier Sale – whose wife, incidentally, was released soon after by the Afghans and, a year later, went on to publish her contemporary account of the retreat from Kabul, *A Journal of the Disasters in Afghanistan: A Firsthand Account by One of the Few Survivors*, which has been the basis of much of the research in the writing of this chapter – was a tremendous boost to the

morale of the British in India after the disasters of Kabul and Gandamak. Indeed, such was the impetus of the victory of Sale's force at Jalalabad that General Pollock's Army of Retribution lost no time in inflicting an old-fashioned revenge on the Afghans in Kabul and the region by putting many to the sword and burning towns and villages as it went. 'Don't mess with the British Empire' seemed to be the message that the unfortunate Afghans had ignored at their peril – a far cry from the circumstances of today.

Queen Victoria was so pleased with the defence put up by the 13th Foot – it was the custom in those days to ignore the efforts of the colonial regiments such as the 35th Bengal Native Infantry and Skinner's Horse who were considered to be doing only what was expected of them – and ordered that the regiment should henceforth become 'Light Infantry', carry the title of 'Prince Albert's Own', and wear a badge depicting the defence of Jalalabad. It was also rumoured that every garrison the 13th passed on its march back through India, on its way to embark for transport to Britain, fired a ten-gun salute.

AFTERWORD

In the months that have occupied me in writing this history of the bloodiest battles that have taken place in Afghanistan since Britain joined other NATO forces in operations to drive out the Taliban and restore peace to that beautiful yet besieged country, I have had constantly to update casualty lists of those servicemen and women who have died cruel deaths from roadside bombs, grenades and bullets. It has been a bitter and humbling experience.

In my research, I have also taken time to read the hundreds of reports filed daily by journalists, war correspondents and students of the war and I have taken the liberty of including some of the gist of their scholarship in my copy. I offer them my gratitude for recording so many of the facts, figures and technical data that I have plundered in my research.

In describing combat I have, as far as possible, gone to the horse's mouth and spoken to those who were there when the

bullets and grenades started to fly. What has always been evident in their words is that war is never glamorous and the perceived image of the fighting man laughing into the faces of his enemies is pure fiction. Combat is a face full of mud experienced when a Bergen climbs up the wearer's back in the prone position; it is the fear of waiting for the rip and tear of a 7.62 round finding its way around body armour and into flesh; it is the stinging reek of cordite and the heat of ejected rounds; it is the barrel of the GPMG that glows red from sustained fire and takes precious water to cool down; it is the cry of a wounded comrade and the sight of a torn and dead body. The term T4 – terminal death – has the lasting finality of a face never to be seen again.

British soldiers are underpaid, of that there is no doubt – £1,000 a month may be below the norm in peacetime, but it is woefully inadequate when the recipient is expected to put his or her life on the line 24/7. More inadequate still is the payout of compensation to those whose livelihood carries the risk of traumatic amputation on a daily basis.

The examples of paltry compensation are many. Private Kevin Challis of the Princess of Wales Royal Regiment was 23 years old when he received gunshot wounds to the arm and back while on service in Iraq. He was left unable to work and received just £1,100 in compensation. Lance Corporal Mark Keegan of the same regiment received a not much better payout when he was wounded in the groin by a grenade blast when storming a trench in Iraq – he was paid £2,144. Private Steve Baldwin of the 1st Battalion Staffordshires lost an arm in

the same conflict and suffers from post-traumatic stress disorder – compensation £10,000. Eighteen-year-old Private Jaimie Cooper of the Royal Green Jackets lost the use of a leg when struck by shrapnel bombs. His army career all but over, he was offered £157,000.

A roadside incendiary bomb attack in Afghanistan cost L/Cpl Martyn Compton of the Household Cavalry the loss of his ears and nose and horrific scarring from burns. The 24-year-old is disfigured for life and has been offered a paltry £98,000. The maximum award granted by the MoD was £285,000 paid to Lance Corporal Ben Parkinson of the Parachute Regiment for the traumatic amputation of both legs, severe brain damage and speech loss in combat in Afghanistan.

Consider all these against the £202,000 payout to an MoD employee who injured his back picking up a printer, or the RAF typist who received £484,000 in MoD compensation for repetitive strain injury, and the case is clear. The woman was working as a data input clerk for the RAF when she developed an injury in her right hand. It was later diagnosed as de Quervain's tenosynovitis – a repetitive strain-type injury in which the tendons at the base of the thumb become inflamed. The award was made after the typist claimed the injury left her unable to work and caused her to become depressed.

This dwarfs the sums offered to serving members of the armed forces who could expect a one-off payment of just £16,500 for the same injury. It is almost double the £285,000 a soldier can expect if he loses two limbs while fighting for his country.

The official tariff of maximum compensation for injuries

lists £28,750 for someone blinded in one eye; £57,500 for the loss of a leg and just £8,250 for injuries associated with surviving a gunshot wound. Serving military personnel operate under what are called Queen's Regulations. Under these rules they give up certain rights normally available to British employees. In contrast, MoD personnel are employed under civilian working laws which make suing for compensation easier. But why should the MoD, which insists it takes the welfare of its personnel, especially those serving on operations, 'very seriously', avoid the issue as in the case of Sergeant Trevor Walker, who lost a leg while serving in Bosnia? His limb was shattered by a shell from a Serbian tank as he was building a road with the Royal Engineers in May 1995.

Despite 13 operations, the leg had to be amputated above the knee the following year and Sgt Walker applied for £150,000 compensation. But the MoD refused to pay because it had decided – without telling troops – that the compensation rules would not apply to soldiers injured while serving in the former Yugoslavia. If Sergeant Walker, from Gillingham, Kent, had been serving in Northern Ireland, which was at peace, it would have paid out under the Criminal Injuries Compensation Overseas Scheme. His lawyers appealed to the High Court, claiming that the Government had behaved unfairly by changing the rules without telling troops, but lost the case and, at the time of writing, no compensation had been paid.

Yet, apart from the very strong complaints about pay, accommodation and compensation, most of the young

servicemen and servicewomen I spoke to in research are happy with their lot. In the British Army, they have found a family. We can only thank our personal gods that such a family exists to allow us to sleep safely in our beds and to see a future for our society's children.

As I wrote these final words in July 2008, an announcement by Defence Secretary Des Browne promised that compensation payments for severely wounded troops would be doubled, with the maximum amount to be paid now rising to £570,000. Smaller rises will apply to those who have sustained less serious injuries. Other long-overdue benefits that will now come into force include post-service degree courses, better medical care with sustained NHS status, and improved housing. One might ask what took them so long?

APPENDICES

I

THE BRITISH FALLEN

The following list does not take into account the courageous men and women of other NATO contingents and of the Afghanistan security forces who have also given their lives on the battlefields of Afghanistan. Although not named here, the memory of their brave sacrifice should not be forgotten by those of us fortunate enough never to have been called upon to bear arms in defence of our nation and its children.

As at 29 June 2008, a total of 110 British forces personnel or MoD civilians have died while serving in Afghanistan since the start of operations in October 2001. Of these, 83 were killed as a result of hostile action; 27 are known to have died either as a result of illness, non-combat injuries or accidents, or have not yet officially been assigned a cause of death pending the outcome of an investigation. The balance of these figures may change as inquests are concluded.

Lance Corporal James Johnson, B Company, 5th Battalion the Royal Regiment of Scotland, was killed while part of a vehicle checkpoint patrol operating in the Lashkar Gar area on Saturday, 28 June 2008.

Warrant Officer 2nd Class Dan Shirley of 13 Air Assault Support Regiment, Royal Logistics Corps, was killed while on a Logistic Patrol from Sangin to Camp Bastion when the vehicle he was travelling in rolled over, on Friday, 27 June 2008.

Warrant Officer 2nd Class Michael Williams of 2nd Battalion the Parachute Regiment (2 PARA) and **Private Joe Whittaker** from 4th Battalion the Parachute Regiment were killed in Helmand Province, Afghanistan, on Tuesday, 24 June 2008.

Corporal Sarah Bryant (Intelligence Corps), **Corporal Sean Robert** (Royal Signals), **Lance Corporal Richard Larkin** and **Trooper Paul Stout** of 21 SAS died on 17 June 2008, when their vehicle, which was on an intelligence-gathering mission, hit a mine near Lashkar Gah. Corporal Bryant was the first British servicewoman to die in Afghanistan.

Private Jeff Doherty and **Lance Corporal James Bateman**, both of C Company 2nd Battalion the Parachute Regiment, were killed by enemy fire on 12 June 2006 while on foot patrol in the Upper Gereshk Valley.

APPENDICES

Private Nathan Cuthbertson, **Private Daniel Gamble** and **Private Charles Murray** of 2nd Battalion the Parachute Regiment (2 PARA) were killed when their patrol suffered a suicide explosive device on Sunday, 8 June 2008 in Helmand Province, Afghanistan.

Marine Dale Gostick was killed near Sangin, Helmand Province, on 25 May 2008.

James Thompson was killed in the Musa Qaleh area of Afghanistan on 19 May 2008.

Trooper Ratu Sakeasi Babakobau of the Household Cavalry Regiment was killed in Helmand, Afghanistan, on 2 May 2008.

Trooper Robert Pearson of the Queen's Royal Lancers Regiment was killed in Afghanistan on 21 April 2008.

Senior Aircraftman Graham Livingstone of the Royal Air Force Regiment and **Senior Aircraftman Gary Thompson** of the Royal Auxiliary Air Force Regiment died when the vehicle they were travelling in was caught in an explosion in Kandahar Province on Sunday, 13 April 2008.

Lieutenant John Thornton and **Marine David Marsh**, both of 40 Commando Royal Marines, died when the vehicle they were travelling in was caught in an explosion in the vicinity of Kajaki, Helmand Province, on Sunday, 30 March 2008.

Corporal Damian Mulvihill from 40 Commando Royal Marines was killed in an explosion while taking part in an outreach patrol to disrupt enemy forces north of Sangin in Helmand Province on Wednesday, 20 February 2008.

Corporal Damian Stephen Lawrence was killed during a joint UK–Afghan National Army night patrol in Kajaki in Helmand Province, southern Afghanistan, on Sunday, 17 February 2008.

Corporal Darryl Gardiner (REME) was killed near the town of Musa Qaleh in Helmand Province, southern Afghanistan, on Sunday, 20 January 2008.

Sergeant Lee Johnson of 2nd Battalion the Yorkshire Regiment (Green Howards) was killed in southern Afghanistan on Saturday, 8 December 2007.

Trooper Jack Sadler of the Honourable Artillery Company was killed in an explosion in southern Afghanistan on 4 December 2007.

Captain John McDermid of the Royal Highland Fusiliers, 2nd Battalion the Royal Regiment of Scotland, was killed in southern Afghanistan on Wednesday, 14 November 2007.

Lance Corporal Jake Alderton of 36 Engineer Regiment died in southern Afghanistan on Friday, 9 November 2007.

The vehicle he was travelling in left the road and rolled off a bridge.

Major Alexis Roberts, serving with 1st Battalion the Royal Gurkha Rifles (but usually an Officer of 2nd Battalion RGR), died as a result of an improvised explosive device in southern Afghanistan on Thursday, 4 October 2007.

Colour Sergeant Phillip Newman, 4th Battalion the Mercian Regiment, and **Private Brian Tunnicliffe**, 2nd Battalion the Mercian Regiment (Worcesters and Foresters), died in a tragic accident in southern Afghanistan on Thursday, 20 September 2007.

Corporal Ivano Violino from 36 Engineer Regiment died in Helmand Province, southern Afghanistan, on Monday, 17 September 2007.

Sergeant Craig Brelsford and **Private Johan Botha**, both from 2nd Battalion the Mercian Regiment (Worcesters and Foresters), were killed in Helmand Province on Saturday, 8 September 2007.

Private Damian Wright and **Private Ben Ford**, both from the 2nd Battalion the Mercian Regiment (Worcesters and Foresters), were killed in Helmand Province, southern Afghanistan, on the morning of Wednesday, 5 September 2007.

Senior Aircraftman Christopher Bridge from C flight, 51 Squadron Royal Air Force Regiment, was killed in Kandahar Province, southern Afghanistan, on the morning of 30 August 2007.

Private Aaron James McClure, **Private Robert Graham Foster** and **Private John Thrumble** of 1st Battalion the Royal Anglian Regiment were killed after air support was called in during a firefight with the Taliban and a bomb tragically struck the soldiers' position, north-west of Kajaki, in northern Helmand Province on Thursday, 23 August 2007.

Captain David Hicks of 1st Battalion the Royal Anglian Regiment was killed during an attack on his patrol base north-east of Sangin in Helmand Province on Saturday, 11 August 2007.

Private Tony Rawson of 1st Battalion the Royal Anglian Regiment was killed in southern Afghanistan on Friday, 10 August 2007.

Lance Corporal Michael Jones (Royal Marines) was killed in action during operations in southern Afghanistan on Sunday, 29 July 2007.

Sergeant Barry Keen of 14 Signal Regiment was killed by a mortar attack in southern Afghanistan on Friday, 27 July 2007.

APPENDICES

Guardsman David Atherton from the 1st Battalion Grenadier Guards was killed in southern Afghanistan on Thursday, 26 July 2007.

Lance Corporal Alex Hawkins, aged 22, of 1st Battalion the Royal Anglian Regiment, was killed in southern Afghanistan on Wednesday, 25 July 2007.

Guardsman Daryl Hickey from the 1st Battalion Grenadier Guards was killed in southern Afghanistan on Thursday, 12 July 2007. Guardsman Hickey was part of a fire team providing covering fire as others in his platoon assaulted a Taliban position.

Sergeant Dave Wilkinson, from 19 Regiment Royal Artillery, died following an explosion during a routine joint patrol with the Afghan National Army in Gereshk, Helmand Province, on Sunday, 1 July 2007.

Captain Sean Dolan of the 1st Battalion, the Worcestershire and Sherwood Foresters Regiment, died as a result of a mortar round in Helmand Province, Afghanistan, on Saturday, 30 June 2000.

Drummer Thomas Wright, 21, from 1st Battalion the Worcestershire and Sherwood Foresters Regiment, was killed on Sunday, 24 June 2007, when the vehicle he was travelling in was caught in an explosion near Lashkar Gah, Helmand Province.

Guardsman Neil 'Tony' Downes was killed on Saturday, 9 June 2007, when his vehicle was hit by an explosion on a patrol with the Afghan National Army close to the town of Sangin in Helmand Province, Afghanistan.

Lance Corporal Paul 'Sandy' Sandford, from 1st Battalion the Worcestershire and Sherwood Foresters, was killed while taking part in an offensive patrol with his company aimed at disrupting Taliban forces in the Upper Gereshk Valley area of Helmand Province on Wednesday, 6 June 2007.

Corporal Mike Gilyeat, from the Royal Military Police, died on Wednesday, 30 May 2007, when the American Chinook helicopter he was travelling in crashed in the Kajaki area of northern Helmand.

Corporal Darren Bonner of the 1st Battalion the Royal Anglian Regiment died on Monday 28 May 2007, in Helmand Province, Afghanistan, as a result of an incident involving an explosive device.

Guardsman Daniel Probyn from 1st Battalion the Grenadier Guards died on Saturday, 26 May 2007 following an overnight operation in Garmsir, southern Afghanistan.

Lance Corporal George Russell Davey was killed on Sunday, 20 May 2007 as a result of injuries sustained in a tragic accident at the British base in Sangin, Afghanistan.

APPENDICES

Guardsman Simon Davison, 1st Battalion Grenadier Guards, was killed by small arms fire in the town of Garmsir on Thursday, 3 May 2007.

Private Chris Gray was killed in action while fighting the Taliban in Helmand Province, Afghanistan, on Friday, 13 April 2007.

Warrant Officer Class 2 Michael Smith from 29 Commando Regiment Royal Artillery died from injuries sustained when a grenade was fired at the UK base in Sangin, Helmand Province, on Thursday, 8 March 2007.

Marine Benjamin Reddy of 42 Commando Royal Marines was killed when his unit came under fire in the Kajaki area of Helmand Province on Tuesday, 6 March 2007.

Lance Bombardier Ross Clark and **Lance Bombardier Liam McLaughlin**, both of 29 Commando Regiment Royal Artillery, were killed during a rocket attack in the Sangin area of Helmand Province on Saturday, 3 March 2007.

Marine Scott Summers of 42 Commando Royal Marines died as a result of injuries sustained in a road traffic accident earlier that month in Afghanistan on Wednesday, 21 February 2007.

Royal Marine Jonathan Holland from 45 Commando was killed by an anti-personnel mine during a routine patrol in the Sangin District of Helmand Province on 21 February 2007.

Lance Corporal Mathew Ford, from 45 Commando Royal Marines, was killed in Afghanistan on Monday, 15 January 2007.

Royal Marine Thomas Curry died on Saturday, 13 January 2007 when elements of 42 Commando Royal Marines were engaged in a deliberate offensive operation near Kajaki, in northern Helmand, Afghanistan.

Lance Bombardier James Dwyer was killed when the vehicle he was driving struck an anti-tank mine while on a patrol in southern Helmand on Wednesday, 27 December 2006.

Marine Richard J Watson was killed on Tuesday, 12 December 2006, in Now Zad, in the north of Helmand, Afghanistan.

Marine Jonathan Wigley died as a result of wounds sustained during an operation on the outskirts of the village of Garmsir, southern Helmand, on Tuesday, 5 December 2006.

Marine Gary Wright died as a result of injuries sustained when a suicide-borne improvised explosive device detonated next to the vehicle in which he was patrolling in Lashkar Gah, Helmand Province, Afghanistan on 19 October 2006.

APPENDICES

Lance Corporal Paul Muirhead, who was very seriously injured during an attack by insurgents in northern Helmand Province on Friday, 1 September 2006, died from his injuries on Wednesday, 6 September 2006.

Lance Corporal Luke McCulloch of 1 Royal Irish Regiment died as a result of a contact with insurgent forces in northern Helmand Province on Wednesday, 6 September 2006.

Corporal Mark William Wright was killed when a routine patrol encountered an unmarked minefield in the region of Kajaki, Helmand Province, on Wednesday, 6 September 2006.

Private Craig O'Donnell was killed after the military convoy he was travelling in was attacked by a suspected suicide bomber in Kabul on Monday, 4 September 2006.

Fourteen personnel were killed following the crash of a Nimrod MR2 aircraft on Saturday, 2 September 2006. They were:

Flight Lieutenant Steven Johnson, aged 38, from Collingham, Notts

Flight Lieutenant Leigh Anthony Mitchelmore, aged 28, from Bournemouth

Flight Lieutenant Gareth Rodney Nicholas, aged 40, from Redruth, Cornwall

Flight Lieutenant Allan James Squires, aged 39, from Clatterbridge

Flight Lieutenant Steven Swarbrick, aged 28, from Liverpool

Flight Sergeant Gary Wayne Andrews, aged 48, from Tankerton in Kent

Flight Sergeant Stephen Beattie, aged 42, from Dundee

Flight Sergeant Gerard Martin Bell, aged 48, from Ely, Cambridgeshire

Flight Sergeant Adrian Davies, aged 49, from Amersham, Bucks

Sergeant Benjamin James Knight, aged 25, from Bridgwater

Sergeant John Joseph Langton, aged 29, from Liverpool

Sergeant Gary Paul Quilliam, aged 42, from Manchester

Corporal Oliver Simon Dicketts, the Parachute Regiment

Marine Joseph David Windall, aged 22, Royal Marines

Ranger Anare Draiva of 1 Royal Irish Regiment, died during a contact in Helmand Province at 1600 local time on Friday, 1 September 2006.

Lance Corporal Jonathan Peter Hetherington died following an attack on the Platoon House in Musa Qal'eh, northern Helmand Province, in the early hours of 27 August 2006.

Corporal Bryan James Budd was killed as a result of injuries sustained during a firefight with Taliban forces in Sangin, Helmand Province, southern Afghanistan on Sunday, 20 August 2006.

APPENDICES

Lance Corporal Sean Tansey from the Life Guards was killed in an accident at a UK military base in northern Helmand Province on the afternoon of Saturday, 12 August 2006.

Private Leigh Reeves was killed in a road traffic accident at Camp Souter in Kabul on Wednesday, 9 August 2006.

Private Andrew Barrie Cutts was killed during operations against insurgent positions in Helmand Province on Sunday, 6 August 2006.

Captain Alex Eida, **Second Lieutenant Ralph Johnson** and **Lance Corporal Ross Nicholls** were killed following an incident involving insurgent forces in northern Helmand Province on the morning of Tuesday, 1 August 2006.

Private Damien Jackson of 3rd Battalion the Parachute Regiment was killed in an incident involving insurgent forces on Wednesday, 5 July 2006.

Corporal Peter Thorpe and **Lance Corporal Jabron Hashmi**, from the 3rd Para Battlegroup, were killed following an incident in Sangin, Helmand Province, southern Afghanistan on 1 July 2006.

Captain David Patten and **Sergeant Paul Bartlett** were killed on the morning of 27 June 2006 in Helmand Province.

Captain Jim Philippson of 7 Parachute Regiment Royal Horse Artillery died in Helmand Province, southern Afghanistan, on the evening of Sunday, 11 June 2006, when the mobile patrol in which he was travelling was engaged in a firefight against suspected Taliban forces.

Lance Corporal Peter Edward Craddock of 1st Battalion the Royal Gloucestershire, Berkshire and Wiltshire Regiment died as a result of a road traffic accident in Lashkar Gah, southern Afghanistan on Monday, 27 March 2006.

Corporal Mark Cridge of 7 Signal Regiment died in Camp Bastion, Afghanistan, on 22 March 2006.

Lance Corporal Steven Sherwood of the 1st Battalion, the Royal Gloucestershire, Berkshire and Wiltshire Light Infantry was killed on 29 October 2005, as a result of hostile action in Mazar-e-Sharif, Afghanistan. Five other members of Sherwood's patrol were injured when they came under fire.

Private Jonathan Kitulagoda was killed, and four soldiers injured, by an apparent suicide bomb attack in Afghanistan on Wednesday, 28 January 2004. Private Kitulagoda was aged 23 and came from Clifton in Bedfordshire and was a student in Plymouth. A member of the Rifle Volunteers, a Territorial Army battalion, he was serving in Kabul with the International Security Assistance Force.

APPENDICES

Sergeant Robert Busuttil and **Corporal John Gregory** of the Royal Logistic Corps, both aged 30, died from gunshot wounds at the British base at Kabul International Airport, on 17 August 2002.

Private Darren John George from the Royal Anglian Regiment died on Tuesday, 9 April 2002 following an incident during a security patrol in Kabul.

THE INFANTRY REGIMENTAL LISTINGS
UK INFANTRY BATTALIONS (FROM LATE 2007)

The Guards Division

1st Bn Grenadier Guards	1 GREN GDS
1st Bn Coldstream Guards	1 COLDM GDS
1st Bn Scots Guards	1 SG
1st Bn Irish Guards	1 IG
1st Bn Welsh Guards	1 WG
Territorial Army Battalion	
The London Regiment	LONDONS

There are generally three battalions from the Guards Division on public duties in London at any one time. When a regiment is stationed in London on public duties it is given an extra company to ensure the additional manpower required for ceremonial events is available.

The Scottish Division

The Royal Regiment of Scotland
Regular Battalions

The Royal Scots Borderers, 1st Bn the Royal Regiment of Scotland	1 SCOTS
The Royal Highland Fusiliers, 2nd Bn the Royal Regiment of Scotland	2 SCOTS
The Black Watch, 3rd Bn the Royal Regiment of Scotland	3 SCOTS

The Highlanders, 4th Bn the Royal Regiment of Scotland	4 SCOTS
The Argyll and Sutherland Highlanders, 5th Bn The Royal Regiment of Scotland	5 SCOTS

Territorial Army Battalions

52nd Lowland, 6th Bn the Royal Regiment of Scotland	6 SCOTS
51st Highland, 7th Bn the Royal Regiment of Scotland	7 SCOTS

The Queen's Division

The Princess of Wales's Royal Regiment
(Queen's and Royal Hampshires)

Regular Battalions

1st Bn the Princess of Wales's Royal Regiment (Queen's and Royal Hampshires)	1 PWRR
2nd Bn the Princess of Wales's Royal Regiment (Queen's and Royal Hampshires)	2 PWRR

Territorial Army Battalion

3rd Bn the Princess of Wales's Royal Regiment (Queen's and Royal Hampshires)	3PWRR

The Royal Regiment of Fusiliers

Regular Battalions

1st Bn the Royal Regiment of Fusiliers	1 RRF
2nd Bn the Royal Regiment of Fusiliers	2 RRF

Territorial Army Battalion

5th Bn the Royal Regiment of Fusiliers	5 RRF

APPENDICES

The Royal Anglian Regiment

Regular Battalions

1st Bn the Royal Anglian Regiment	1 R ANGLIAN
2nd Bn the Royal Anglian Regiment	2 R ANGLIAN

Territorial Army Battalion

3rd Bn the Royal Anglian Regiment	3 R ANGLIAN

The King's Division

The Duke of Lancaster's Regiment
(King's, Lancashire and Border)

Regular Battalions

1st Bn the Duke of Lancaster's Regiment   1 LANCS
(King's, Lancashire and Border)

2nd Bn the Duke of Lancaster's Regiment 2 LANCS
(King's, Lancashire and Border)

Territorial Army Battalion

4th Bn the Duke of Lancaster's Regiment   4 LANCS
(King's, Lancashire and Border)

The Yorkshire Regiment

Regular Battalions

1st Bn the Yorkshire Regiment   1 YORKS
(Prince Of Wales's Own)

2nd Bn the Yorkshire Regiment   2 YORKS
(Green Howards)

3rd Bn the Yorkshire Regiment   3 YORKS
(Duke of Wellington's)

Territorial Army Battalion

4th Bn the Yorkshire Regiment   4 YORKS

The Prince of Wales's Division
The Mercian Regiment (from August 2007)
Regular Battalions
1st Bn the Mercian Regiment (Cheshire)   1 MERCIAN
2nd Bn the Mercian Regiment (Worcesters   2 MERCIAN
and Foresters)
3rd Bn the Mercian Regiment (Staffords)   3 MERCIAN
Territorial Army Battalion
4th Bn the Mercian Regiment   4 MERCIAN

The Royal Welsh
Regular Battalions
1st Bn the Royal Welsh (the Royal   1 R WELSH
Welsh Fusiliers)
2nd Bn the Royal Welsh (the Royal   2 R WELSH
Regiment of Wales)
Territorial Army Battalion
3rd Bn the Royal Welsh   3 R WELSH

The Light Division
The Rifles
Regular Battalions
1st Bn the Rifles   1 RIFLES
2nd Bn the Rifles   2 RIFLES
3rd Bn the Rifles   3 RIFLES
4th Bn the Rifles   4 RIFLES

5th Bn the Rifles	5 RIFLES
Territorial Army Battalions	
6th Bn the Rifles	6 RIFLES
7th Bn the Rifles	7 RIFLES

The Royal Irish Regiment

Regular Battalion	
1st Bn the Royal Irish Regiment	1 R IRISH
Territorial Army Battalion	
The Royal Irish Rangers	RANGERS

The Parachute Regiment

Regular Battalions	
1st Bn the Parachute Regiment	1 PARA
2nd Bn the Parachute Regiment	2 PARA
3rd Bn the Parachute Regiment	3 PARA
Territorial Army Battalion	
4th Bn the Parachute Regiment	4 PARA

Note: 1 PARA have formed the core element of the new Special Forces Support Group and as such have been removed from the formal Infantry structure

The Brigade of Gurkhas

1st Bn the Royal Gurkha Rifles	1 RGR
2nd Bn the Royal Gurkha Rifles	2 RGR

APPENDICES

III

A SURVIVOR'S TALE

An account from memory of the report of Assistant Surgeon William Brydon (44th Foot) to Brigadier Sale, Officer Commanding the Jalalabad garrison on 13 January 1842, as recalled in the diary of Captain Julius Brockman, January 1842, Jalalabad, Afghanistan. (In order not to detract from Captain Brockman's contemporary account, the original punctuation has been left unaltered.)

Yesterday it had been impossible to write the horrible news of the day, and my soul is now filled with anguish at the melancholy catastrophe which has overtaken the Cabool Force —— all are lost —— the force is annihilated to a man. —— Yesterday, about 1 P.M., Brydon, an Assistant Surgeon, of the Shah's Service, reached this place, (on a horse scarcely able to move another yard) wounded and bruised from head to foot with stones, and he, alone, has arrived to tell the fearful tale.

Captain Julius Brockman, Jellalabad, 1842

An account from memory of the March of the Troops
It was given out to the Troops, on the 5th Instant, that the arrangements had been completed for our retreat to Hindustan. Such of the sick and wounded as were unable to march were left under the medical charge of Doctors Berwick and Campbell, and Lieut. Evans of HM 44th in Command.

247

Capt. Drummond; Capt. Walsh; Lieut. J. Conolly; Lt. Webb, Warburton and Airey were placed as Hostages, in the hands of Mohamed Zaman Khan. The sick were lodged in Taimur Shah's fort; the hostages with the new King.

We marched from Cantonments about 9 am on the 6th of January; The 5th NI formed the Advance guard with a hundred Sappers and the Guns of the Mountain Train, under Brigadier Anquetil, next came the main body, under Brigadier Shelton, followed by the Baggage, to the rear of which came the 6th Regiment SSF. Lastly the Rear Guard, composed of the 5th Light cavalry and the 54th NI with two H:A: Guns and the remainder of the Sappers all the Guns excepting those of the HA: and the MT: were left in the Cantonments, together with a large quantity of magazine Stores.

The Rear Guard had no sooner marched out of the Cantonments (which they did not effect until dusk) than they were fired on from the Ramparts; Lieut. Hardyman 5th L.C. was Killed at this time, and the place set on fire. A great quantity of property, Public and private, was carried off between the Cantonments and Seea Sung hill, at which place the two Guns with the Rear Guard were abandoned The Rear Guard arrived at its ground across the Loghar river about midnight Though this march was not more than 5 miles, a great number of women and children perished in the snow, which was about 6. Inches deep.

We marched, on the Morning of the 7th (Advance Guard the 54th NI. Rear guard the 44th Foot and Mountain Train) to Boot-Khak, a distance of about 5. Miles. The whole Road from Cabool, at this time, being one dense mass of people In the march,

as in the former, the loss of property was immense and towards the end of it there was some sharp fighting in which Lieut. Shaw, of the 54th NI. Had his thigh fractured by a shot The guns of the Mountain train were carried off by the Enemy, and either two or three of those of the Horse Artillery were spiked and abandoned.

On the following Morning, the 8th, we moved through the Khoorde Cabool Pass (our troops did not attempt to crown the heights) with considerable loss of life and property the heights were in possession of the Enemy who poured down an incessant fire upon our Column Lieut. Sturt, of the Engineers, was Killed by a shot in the groin, and Captain Anderson's eldest child was missing when we arrived, at our ground, at Khoord Cabool Captain Troup was also wounded.

The next day, the 9th all the Baggage which remained to us was loaded and off the ground by about 9.o'clock, when it was recalled and orders given for a halt which, owing to the intense cold at this elevated spot, proved exceedingly destructive of the Sepoy's and Camp followers at this place the married officers, with their wives and families, and also the wounded officers, were delivered over to Mohamed Akbar for safe convoy to Jalalabad, much difficulty being expected on the road for the Troops.

On the Morning of the 10th we resumed our March over the Huft Kotal towards Tezeen So terrible had been the effects of the cold and exposure upon the Native Troops that they were unable to resist the attacks of the Enemy, who pressed on our flanks and Rear and upon arriving at the Valley of the Tezeen, towards Evening, a mere handful remained of the Native Regiments which had left Cabool

We halted a few hours at Tezeen and found that five officers of the 5th NI.; one of the 37th NI.; one of the 54th, and four Doctors were Killed or missing and three European women, and one or two soldiers of the 44th were carried off by the Enemy; after a rest of a few hours, and when it was quite dark, our diminished party again moved on leaving the last of the Horse Artillery Guns on the ground: the Cavalry being the advanced Guard. We marched all night and arrived in the Morning at Kutta Sung...... having sustained some loss from the Enemy, who fired upon us from the heights during the whole time We remained about an hour at Kutta Sung, where, from the nature of the ground, it was not deemed advisable to halt;

We again pushed on towards Jigdalak, where we arrived about noon; still hard pressed by the enemy from the hills; Lieut. Fortyre of HM.: 44th was killed close to our ground; shortly after arriving at which, General Elphinstone; Brigadier Shelton; and Captain Johnson, went over to Akbar Khan as Hostages for the March of Troops from Jalalabad; Here we halted the next day, but were greatly annoyed by the constant fire of the Enemy who had possession of all the surrounding hills many officers and men were wounded, and captain Skinner, of the Commissariat, Killed by this fire; About an hour after dark an order was given to march, owing (I believe) to a note being received from General Elphinstone telling us to push on at all hazards, as treachery was suspected: owing to this unexpected move on our part, we found the abattis, and other impediments which had been thrown across the Jigdalak Pass, undefended by the Enemy, who, nevertheless, pressed upon our rear, and cut up great numbers

The confusion now was terrible all discipline was at an end, and the shouts of "Halt," and "Keep back the cavalry" were incessant The only Cavalry were the officers who were mounted and a few Sohars (the Cavalry were at Jigdalak, but I do not remember them afterwards) Just after getting clear of the Pass, I, with great difficulty, made my way to the front, where I found a large body of men and officers, who, finding it perfectly hopeless to remain with men in such a state, had gone ahead to form a kind of advanced Guard But, as we moved steadily on, whilst the main body was halting every second, by the time that day dawned we had lost all traces of those in our Rear.

Our Party became broken up as we proceeded, till, on arriving at Fatehabad, it consisted of captains Bellew, Hopkins, and Collyer; Lt. Bird, Steer & Gray; Doctor Harper; Sergeant Friel, and about five Europeans Captain Bellew & Lieut. Bird were cut down near Fatehabad, and also Lieut. Gray and the Europeans Captains Hopkins & Collyer and Dr. Harper, being well mounted, soon left Lieut. Steer and myself far behind About three miles from Jalalabad, Lieut. Steer told me he would hide till night, and left the road to do so I pushed on alone and, with great difficulty reached this place about 1 P.M. on the 13th ——

APPENDICES

IV

AFGHAN NATIONAL ARMY
– ORDER OF BATTLE

The strength of the ANA currently stands at approximately 60,000 out of a goal of 80,000. In February 2008, the organisational goals for the ANA were updated. The purpose of the new plan is to complete the fielding of the following units by September 2009:

80,000 troops

Five corps HQ

15 brigade HQ including:

  13 light infantry brigade HQs

  One armoured brigade HQ

  One commando brigade HQ

  One support brigade HQ

78 battalions including approximately:

  40 infantry battalions

  Six commando battalions

  Two armoured/mechanised battalions

  15 combat support battalions

  15 combat service support battalions

Given Afghanistan's limited resources, the plan is designed to create a sustainable force that Afghanistan can maintain over the years. New ANA units continue to be trained and deployed. All five corps HQs are operational.

Since early 2008, 201st Corps has redeployed its brigades.

1st, 2nd and 3rd Brigades each now have their own areas of responsibility (AORs) in eastern Afghanistan. By spring 2008, 201st and 203rd Corps were due to receive two new brigades. It is likely each corps would receive one new brigade, resulting in each being composed of four brigades.

205th Corps has expanded to four brigades with one brigade each in the provinces of Helmand, Kandahar, Uruzgan and Zabol.

207th Corps has started training a second brigade that will be based in Farah Province. It will be operational by spring of 2009.

No further expansion of 209th Corps is expected.

Brigade Deployment

12 of 15 combat brigade HQs are deployed:

There are 11 light infantry brigades; 2 more light infantry brigades were scheduled to deploy by spring 2008.

There is 1 armoured brigade, 3rd Brigade/201st Corps, based in Jalalabad, now being trained and deployed as infantry due to a lack of the required heavy equipment. It is unclear when this situation will change. The status of the commando brigade HQ is unknown.

Battalion Deployment

52 of 78 battalions are deployed, comprised of 36 infantry battalions, 4 of 6 commando battalions (the last 2 were expected to deploy by September 2008), 2 heavy battalions have been trained and deployed as infantry due to the lack

of heavy equipment. In addition, each of 15 brigades is to have a combat support battalion. These battalions, however, are still in a very early stage of development. Ultimately, they will include an armoured reconnaissance company, an engineer company and an artillery battery. Artillery capability is being implemented first and this activity is only just beginning. Several brigades are in the processes of training an artillery section (3 guns). It is likely be September 2009 before all combat support battalions are formed, equipped, trained and deployed.

6 infantry and 2 combat service support battalions have yet to deploy. These will complete the 2 remaining infantry brigades that are scheduled for spring 2008.

Equipment

A major effort is under way to convert the ANA from Russian-designed small arms (AK47 assault rifles, RPK PKM machine guns) to US-designed small arms (M16/M4 rifles, M249, M240B machine guns). The first to convert were the commando battalions and 1st Brigade of 205th Corps. However, there is still a drastic shortfall in equipment.

The ANA is standardising on D30 122mm guns as its primary artillery pieces. The ANA is starting to receive up-armoured Humvees.

Afghan National Air Corps (ANAC)

A new eight-year plan for the development of the ANAC has been announced. Over the next four years, development will

focus on air transport capability, first on MEDIVAC using helicopters flying from Kabul and Kandahar, followed by operational transport capability using C27 cargo planes. Close air support and intelligence, surveillance and reconnaissance (ISR) capability will follow, becoming operational by 2015. Until the later capability is in place, there can be no discussions regarding the withdrawal of coalition forces, which currently supply embedded instruction teams to call in coalition air support. Training in directing close air support and the training of combat pilots, the lack of which carries the inherent danger of blue-on-blue 'friendly fire' episodes, is considered an urgent priority.

Afghan National Police (ANP)

The strength of the ANP currently stands at 76,000 with a goal of 82,000. There are significant training and equipment shortfalls.

Afghan National Civil Order Police (ANCOP)

The ANP began developing the ANCOP in 2006. With selective recruiting and a 16-week training programme, the ANCOP is a high-end SWAT unit. The ANCOP was originally envisioned to be forces distributed around the country, but it has been re-tasked and is now being extensively used to support the 'Focused District Development' training programme for the Afghan Uniform Police. There are currently 10 ANCOP battalions.

Afghan Uniform Police (AUP)

By far, the most important development in the ANP has been the implementation of a major new training plan. This

plan consists of additional training resources and two new training programmes.

Improvement in resources came from the temporary deployment of 2,300 Marine trainers and an additional 200 trainers from other NATO countries. In the long run, however, training resources are still about 50 per cent under requirement. The new training programmes consists of the 'Individual Training' programme and the 'Focused District Development' programme:

• Individual Training: 15 training centres have been set up throughout Afghanistan to provide new recruits with eight weeks of basic training.
• Focused District Training programme: this programme is targeted at the 40,000 AUP that are already in the field but have not been adequately trained. In this programme, eight districts at a time are selected, the most critical districts first. The AUP are removed from their districts and sent for eight weeks of collective training. While they are gone, they are replaced by an ANCOP unit. The programme started in January 2008. The plan is to complete the training of the 52 most critical districts in 2008 and all 414 districts and urban precincts in Afghanistan by the end of 2011.

Summary

Overall, significant progress has been made. Development in 2007–08 is occurring at a much faster pace than in 2002–06. ANSF is now leading fights, winning battles and becoming a

respected institution. It is hoped that the ANSF will be able to take over security for Afghanistan around 2011, allowing ISAF to start reducing its forces. There is still a long way to go.

APPENDICES

BIBLIOGRAPHY

Among the Wild Tribes of the Afghan Frontier, TL Pennell (1909)

Animal's People, Indra Sinha (2007)

The Auxiliary Territorial Service, JM Cowper (1949)

Battlefield Afghanistan, Mike Ryan (2007)

Corsets to Camouflage – Women and War, Kate Adie (2004)

The Destruction of Lord Raglan, Christopher Hibbet (1961)

The Diary of Captain Julius Brockman Backhouse (January 1842)

The Dictionary of National Biography, Vol. XVII, Stephen, Leslie (1889)

Encyclopaedia of Famous Military Firearms, Major Frederick Myatt MC (1979)

Encyclopaedia of Modern British Army Regiments

Global Terrorism Analysis, Waliullah Rahmani (the Jamestown Foundation 2006)

The Great Game, Oxford University Press, Peter Hopkirk (1990)

Jane's Defence Weekly, PD Griffin (2006)

A Journal of the Disasters in Afghanistan: A Firsthand Account by One of the Few

The Oxford Dictionary of National Biography, Oxford University Press (2004)

The Oxford History of the British Army, David Chandler, IFW Beckett (2003)

Reminiscences of Forty-Three Years in India, Sir George Lawrence (1874)

Service with the Army, Helen Gwynne-Vaughan (1942)

The Story of the Women's Transport Service (1908-1984), Hugh

Popham (1984)

Survivors, Lady Florentia Sale (1843)

Women in Uniform, D Collet Wadge (1946)

William Brydon (1811–1873), Claire E. J. Herrick (2004)

Websites

www.army.mod.uk

www.wikipedia.com

www.defence-estates.mod.uk

www.pathfinder.armyjobs.mod.uk

www.modreunited.com

www.rncom.mod.uk

www.familyrecords.gov.uk

Videos

Ross Kemp in Afghanistan, Tiger Aspect (2007), Sky TV

Other Sources

BFBS Gurkha Radio, Shorncliffe, Hampshire, UK (Frequency 1278)

The Lancers PH, Staines Road, Hounslow